"An enriching East-West guide to the voice as a spiritual practice … rooted in a range of essential vocal practices, the 'Note from Heaven' deepens self-inquiry, and awakens your heart's ears through a joyous process of creative intention, self-discipline and expression."
Chloe Goodchild, author, singer, voice pioneer, founder of thenakedvoice.com

"I have read Githa's fantastic book and my copy is full of red and blue underlines! The book has started so many exciting thoughts in my head. You have done in practice what I intuitively got close to and believed in when I made the film *As in Heaven*.
Kay Pollak, director of the Academy Award-nominated film *As in Heaven*

"More and more people are discovering that one of the most potent forms of therapy lies hidden in their voice. Our voice is able to build a bridge between mind and body. It can activate, relax, open the mind for new dimensions and expose buried emotions. Githa Ben-David is one of the pioneers in this area. The method she has developed, regressive cell-singing, is based on her wealth of experience. This book will contribute to even more people discovering the undreamt of possibilities lying within our natural voice."
Audun Myskja, general medical practictioner, professor, specialist in music used as therapy

"What a wonderful eye and heart-opening book! *TheNote from Heaven* is for anyone who is wounded in body and soul. The miracles lie right in front of us, we just need to bend down and pick them up."
Hella Joof, award-winning actress and director

"*The Note from Heaven* is nothing less than a treasure trove of knowledge. It is a masterpiece and a pedagogic work of art."
Helle Hewau, psychologist, spiritual mentor, sound healer

THE NOTE FROM HEAVEN

BY GITHA BEN-DAVID

HOW TO SING YOURSELF
TO HIGHER CONSCIOUSNESS

WATKINS

Sharing Wisdom Since
1893

This edition published in the UK and USA 2016 by
Watkins, an imprint of Watkins Media Limited
19 Cecil Court, London WC2N 4EZ
enquiries@watkinspublishing.co.uk

Design and typography copyright © Watkins Media Limited 2016
Text copyright © Githa Ben-David 2013, 2016
Illustrations copyright © Githa Ben-David 2013, 2016

Githa Ben-David has asserted her right under the Copyright, Designs
and Patents Act 1988 to be identified as the author of this work.

Translated from Danish by Jane Helbo and Susan Andersen
The Note from Heaven I – How to Sing Your Self (*Tonen fra himlen*); *The Note from Heaven II – How to Sing Your Self Free* (*Syng dig Fri*, Universal Gratefulness)

1 3 5 7 9 10 8 6 4 2

Designed by Gail Jones

Printed and bound in Finland

A CIP record for this book is available from the British Library

ISBN: 978-1-78028-935-9

www.watkinspublishing.com

Publisher's note: The information in this book is not intended as a substitute for
professional medical advice and treatment. If you are pregnant or are suffering
from any medical conditions or health problems, it is recommended that you
consult a medical professional before following any of the advice or practice
suggested in this book. Watkins Media Limited, or any other persons who have
been involved in working on this publication, cannot accept responsibility for any
injuries or damage incurred as a result of following the information, exercises or
therapeutic techniques contained in this book.

MY HEARTFELT THANKS TO ...

First and foremost, Mangala Tiwari, my teacher
of classical Indian singing, who led me to my path.

Lars Muhl, my beloved husband, who supports me
with love in all I do.

My two singing sons for their open minds, purity
and support.

Jane Helbo, Susan Andersen and James Hodgson
for translation and editing.

Michael Mann and all at Watkins.

Graham Bishop, Doctor Karl and the White Brotherhood
for their invaluable support.

All you who are open to the power of inspiration.

OVERTURE

A bush and a tree. They stand there in the middle of the field, marking my turning point.

The walk has taken me through snow-covered fields in December's hazy darkness. It's about 5pm. Imagine this never-ending white landscape, which seems to merge into the sky, is merely a small section of an endless Mongolian steppe …

In the distance the hum of traffic can be heard. It doesn't help to cover my ears. The sound vibrates imperceptibly through my body. The silence of nature is indescribably healing, and right now, my whole being yearns for it.

So, here we are, the bush, the tree, and I – tranquilly drawing breath. The trees humbly spread out their arms to receive whatever comes from above. It strikes me that the serene silence expressed in this humility makes up for the absence of a Mongolian steppe. The trees seem unaffected by the cars passing by on the distant horizon. Even if threatened by a chainsaw, they would firmly stand their ground, unshakable in their faith. The branches unfold the best they can. If there is too much western wind, they bend. If a neighbouring branch gets in the way, they twine around it.

Obstacles make us bend and look for another way. No matter how complicated, the way forward is towards the light.

The snow drifts gently down onto my head. I welcome these magic crystals with reverence and feel blessed. There are many different types of vegetation in the patchwork of fields. On closer inspection it is clear that each one has its own distinctive character – trees, bushes, all equally beautiful in their existence.

I too raise my arms to the heavens and, for a moment, experience eternity within myself.

Why do we have to make ourselves so all important?

In times of hardship, life will block your path. At some point, you bend, find the way forward – or perhaps break down. It all depends on what you are up against, and who you are. Fate, combined with the fact that you did what you could.

So simple and beautiful. The thought appears naked in this greyish, opaque darkness.

CONTENTS

The Note from Heaven Book II – Sing Your Self Free

The Note
from Heaven
Book I

How to Sing
Your Self

In memory of Mangala Tiwari (1955–2010)

INTRODUCTION

My first encounter with India and Indian singing, in December 1986, led me into something that I am only now beginning to understand. This inexplicable something made my career as a classical/rhythmic saxophone player seem pale and uninteresting by comparison. I felt drawn to singing, to creativity for its own sake, and my efforts to achieve public success worked against that.

In 1999, I started writing a book about this 'something', because I felt that writing would enable me to reach out wholeheartedly to my surroundings with my music. At first, the process felt more like a duty than something I really wanted to do, so I tried to get it over with as quickly as possible. However, that was not to be. It took no fewer than three rewritings and a substantial editing down before *The Note from Heaven* was born.

Writing the book caused remarkable changes in my spiritual life. There was a pleasant tingling in my scalp, and with every page I wrote I learned more and more from all the information and ideas that simply fell into my lap.

The Note from Heaven is based mainly on my own personal experience. It was only after completing the book that I compared its contents to material from other relevant books.

In 1986 my singing teacher in India, Mangala Tiwari, said to me: 'Go home, and sing "Aaar" on your root note for one hour every day.' In fact, this single instruction is really everything you need to know. Anyone who perceives the value of this instruction and follows it will be whirled into a process of spiritual development. However, I have shared my experiences and developed them further, so this book is longer than the above mentioned sentence.

Working with the Note from Heaven has set me on fire and put a wind behind me. I am never alone, as long as I listen to that wind and spread out my wings, doing whatever I possibly can to stay on track.

The Note from Heaven is pure inspiration and love. My heart quivers daily with gratitude. Gratitude for gratitude. Love, love, love.

The Note from Heaven gives the singer a vibrating experience of oneness, a sound to which each of us brings our own qualities – a healing sea, full of light.

The sound of the Note from Heaven has a healing effect. The first time I healed someone through my voice was when a woman with a headache regained hearing in her totally deaf left ear. I didn't even know she was deaf in that ear. I have healed people several times since then. The first time I tried to heal tinnitus, it worked. I got very excited, thinking that now I could heal anyone with tinnitus. But that's not how energy works. This kind of thinking is the voice of the ego popping up and will cause the healing power of the Note from Heaven to vanish.

The 'I' is a flute. It is nothing in itself, but the wind can make it sound like heaven. Our duty as flutes is to keep our selves open and humble.

'Go and sweep the chamber of your heart.
Prepare it for dwelling in the abode of the Beloved one.
As you go, He will come.
In you, emptied of yourself, He will unfold His beauty.'
Mahmud Shabistari: Rose Garden of Mystery (13th century)

The tangible effects that have come from working with the Note from Heaven include the ability to see colour and images in my mind's eye, a tingling, mainly in the hands and on the top of my head when healing or doing other work in an inspired state, and a heightening of my intuition.

If you experience these kinds of effects, don't attribute more significance to them than they deserve. They are the manifestation of a natural spiritual development. It is important to let this growth process happen gradually, naturally, without letting the ego get carried away by thinking, 'Oh, now I see colours, so I'm spiritual.' All human beings are spiritual. Just treat them as positive signs on your path.

What is the 'Note from Heaven'?

The Note from Heaven is the tonal expression of a divine state that we all have within us and we can all contact.

The Note from Heaven is not, in itself, the goal. Its function is to free the voice, and through that to expand consciousness. It balances the body's energy system, in preparation for conscious work with meditation and healing and for expressing yourself directly from the heart through song. It develops your intuition, your ability to sense and trust that what feels good deep inside is truly valid.

When you experience the Note from Heaven, the note seems to sing you, rather than you singing it. Therefore my method is addressed to all readers who have an interest in spirituality.

Since song is an expression of how we breathe, and breathing is influenced by our state of mind and body, it is hard to provide a self-help method that everyone can use. Traditional singing teachers might even claim that it is impossible.

But I am going to try anyway, because the listening process required to find the Note from Heaven is such an invaluable aid to self-discovery.

The experience of being able to find the way to a divine state *by yourself* is the overriding goal.

In this way the degree of healing that occurs when the voice opens up is dependent upon the degree to which the performer has been capable of inwardly listening to himself or herself. A student who follows my instructions in a teacher/student situation, for example, will most likely experience the Note from Heaven, but at the same time will not quite be convinced that it belongs to him or her. Our fear of perceiving our own divine nature will give rise to all kinds of excuses to justify not doing this or that thing ourselves. This fear makes us dependent on our surroundings and gives us a false sense of security, since we cannot completely control them. Therefore, the purpose of Book I and the practice download is to inspire you to sing your self. It is this self that is the source of true learning. **The practice session for this book can be downloaded for free at www.thenotefromheaven.com (or www. gilalai.com on the English page.)**

I recommend that you read the first part of Book I and, for approximately one month, practise opening up to the Note from Heaven by singing a single note, the root note. This is really important, because such intense absorption in the sound is the only way to really understand and experience the point of this book.

How much time will I need to spend?

If you are a beginner, you will need to practise for about an hour each day for a month to establish good contact with your support (the laughter muscles in the stomach area) and to learn to find your way into the state of the Note from Heaven by singing the root note. Remember, the idea is to concentrate on one note only. Find a place where you will not be disturbed, so that you can listen intently to yourself. Once you have established the experience of finding the Note from Heaven in your body, you will be able to return to it at any time. This also works for people who believe that they are tone deaf.

Then it will take approximately one year of daily practice to extend your connection to the Note from Heaven to the rest of the notes in the register, as well as to learn to sing the note language at a slow speed.

PART I

ESTABLISHING CONTACT WITH THE NOTE FROM HEAVEN

DISCIPLINE, HEARING AND FEAR OF FAILURE

Discipline

Devoting one hour a day to singing requires a great deal of discipline. Following through with regular practice, regardless of your mood or unexpected events in daily life, is a beneficial process in itself that gives great joy and self-respect. For it is through this persistence that you curb your ego and become uncompromisingly faithful to your innermost desires. When you give up on something you had seriously decided to do, you, on some deep level, disregard your higher self and let yourself be controlled by your ego. The result is that you end up with a flat feeling, and that kind of experience drains self-confidence.

Most of us have ingrained ways of viewing ourselves that tell us what we are good at and what we are not good at. They are part of our self-image. Strict discipline is necessary to break such patterns. Years of repeating thoughts and statements like, for example, 'I can't sing', leave their mark in the form of habitual thinking. It is the ego that is responsible for these habits – it pops up full of angst and seduces us into arresting all personal growth. When we conquer the ego, the road ahead is free: our potential is infinite.

Your ego is the doubtful inner voice saying, 'No, that can't be true.'

Discipline is your weapon. Follow through with your decision at all costs, despite negative feelings such as boredom, fear, doubt, frustration and low self-worth which you may face at times.

The importance of hearing

Most of us are born with everything in place – like tiny, fully developed angels. Our hearing has functioned since we were four-month-old embryos. As babies we rely on our surroundings to stimulate our senses. The fact that some people's hearing has not been correctly stimulated does not mean that the original sense, for example, the ability to listen to oneself, has been lost. Like Sleeping Beauty, it is merely hidden behind the thorn bushes in a deep sleep. In order to take the decision to penetrate the thorn bushes and liberate this Sleeping Beauty, we first need to recognize that she exists.

Once we fully understand that we are divine in our essence and therefore have the potential to sing from a divine place in ourselves, the ego's fears quickly dissolve. It is impossible to gain such an insight by reading even the wisest of theories in a book. It has to be experienced as a physical state, as a part of oneself.

When you first access the Note from Heaven, it is like a spiritual appetizer; the body is granted a spiritual experience through the ears.

The fact that the sound of your own voice might disturb you at first, because it doesn't sound as you expect it to, is a positive sign, a confirmation that your listening function is active.

Since the voice can express only what the ears can hear, it is important not to focus on your singing performance, but instead attach greater importance to sensing what kind of sound your ears would like to hear.

When the soul has its way, the ears want to hear something that feels good in the body. However, if the ego pops up it can make us aspire to sound like a singing idol instead of our ultimate self. In that case, push the ego aside. We are looking for the authentic nightingale, not the artificial one.

When you start listening to what feels good for you, your whole sensory system develops. Everything that we can sense, but not express in words, is made up of vibrations of differing frequencies, just as sound is. Science has long pointed out that all matter is actually composed of vibrations with differing degrees of density. We, too, are vibrating masses. Therefore, people develop intuition when they begin listening closely to themselves. We improve our sensitivity to vibrations as we develop the ability to listen.

Fear of failure and performance anxiety

When fear of failure arises during a practice session, all you can do is face it and fight it. It is not necessarily an easy battle, but recognizing the fear is already a big step. As mentioned before, an ego on the loose will naturally want to prevent us from experiencing ourselves as divine.

By looking the fear straight in the eye and continuing to sing, you will eventually succeed. Concentrating on the knowledge that you are essentially divine will cause the fear to evaporate. The following exercise is another, more tangible approach to curing the fear of failure.

Physically, fear manifests itself as a tightening of the throat and/or solar plexus. It is possible to restore free breathing by concentrating your thoughts on the solar plexus, for example, and then imagining that you are moving the tension from that area up to the middle of your forehead (an energy centre known as the 'third eye'). The blocked emotional energies, expressed as tension, can most easily be moved with the help of one's breathing.

Remedy for tightness in the solar plexus or the throat

- Close your eyes and breathe through your nose. Make a nasal sound like someone deeply asleep, but not snoring, as you breathe in and out.
- On the in breath, draw the energy in your body upwards along the spine.
- By surfing on the flow of energy created by the in breath, you can move the tensions from the solar plexus or throat up to the forehead.

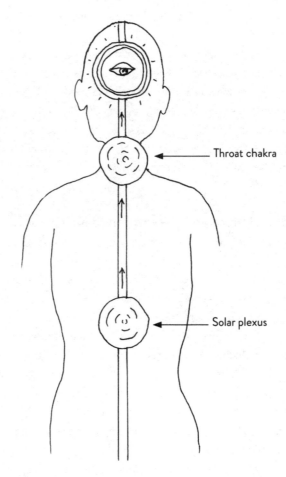

Use your in breath to unblock energy in the throat or solar plexus by moving it up to the forehead (the third eye).

- On the out breath, pull the energy downwards along the spine. Surf on this flow of energy in order to move it back down to the solar plexus or throat.
- Imagine the field of tension as a transparent, round, white disc that you can move up the front of your body using the flow of your breath.
- Move the disc up to your forehead (the third eye) by using a couple of breaths.
- Following this, meditate by concentrating on the middle of the forehead until you are breathing freely through the solar plexus. Carry on doing this for 5–8 minutes.
- If this exercise brings on a headache, try moving the disc to the top of the head (the crown chakra) instead.

Fear of failure is natural and can be regarded as a gift that we humans would have difficulty living without. We are able to become conscious of our divinity only when we acknowledge its opposite – namely, our fear of failure. Those who seem to have been given everything in life tend to be lost on a deeper level: they take their paradise for granted because they do not have anything to measure it against.

Our quality of life is linked to the degree of gratitude we feel for all that we have been given. It is our awareness of life's contrasts that makes us feel gratitude.

The way we were loved as children produces a learned pattern of behaviour. Very few of us have experienced unconditional love. Most people have been conditioned to believe that they need to pursue achievement in order to deserve the reward of love. This learned perception of love also reflects inwards in the way in which we treat ourselves.

Therefore, when we feel fear of failure it is, in reality, the fear of not being able to live up to loving ourselves. 'Should' or 'ought to' are dangerous words, as they carry the expectations others have laid upon us.

We don't need to perform at all.

It is a state that we are seeking – a state in which we are able to love ourselves by literally massaging our vibrating body mass when we tune into it using sound.

ENERGY CENTRES

When you begin to work meditatively with your sound, you will eventually find that the sound induces a humming energy in your body. The reason for this is that deep and thorough breathing releases tension, both on a physical and an energetic level. The largest magnetic fields in the body are situated along the spine. There are seven major fields (chakras) and these are connected by three currents of energy that run the length of – and through the middle of – the spine. In Sanskrit terminology the feminine, inward-flowing energy current to the left of the spine is called the *ida*. The masculine, outward-flowing energy current to the right of the spine is called the *pingala*. The *sushumna* is the spiritual canal, where the feminine and the masculine energies join at the centre of the spine.

A deep breath can feel like an internal massage up and down the spine. With the Note from Heaven, you feel as if you yourself become a channel of energy – a connection between the energy centres is created and at the same time the energy collects at the *sushumna*. For that reason, it can feel as if the spine is an open pipe resonating as the wind blows through it via the breath.

Life's influences on us are expressed in our voice. This is because the body's muscles store the compensations and repressions with which we have protected ourselves. In this way, a pattern of tension has been created that affects, among other things, how we breathe.

A massage can relieve muscle pain, but it will not automatically remove the pattern created by deeply buried traumas. Tensions function similarly to bad habits if you have lived with them for many years. Wherever there are tensions it will be difficult for the energy to flow freely, resulting in a constant loss of energy.

Therefore, by listening for your natural voice, you are also seeking a tension-free state. This occurs quite subconsciously as you focus totally on the sensation of the quality of the sound experienced in your body. Our ears are the key to re-experiencing ourselves as whole. Thus, vocal expression is not an isolated phenomenon, but rather an integral part of a greater unity of energy. A totality whose essence it reflects.

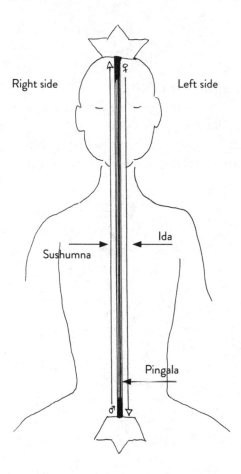

The three currents of energy running in and along the spine are known as the sushumna, ida and pingala. Note that the ida and pingala are reversed in left-handed people.

Since I will be referring to the body's seven primary energy centres throughout the book, the following is a simple explanation of their functions, especially in relation to singing. These centres have different names in different languages (notably in Japanese, Chinese, Sanskrit and English). I have chosen to use the names that I personally feel impart the greatest depth of meaning. In Sanskrit, an energy centre is called a 'chakra' meaning 'wheel'. Right away, this word gives a deeper meaning than 'centre', because each chakra rotates.

Root chakra (*muladhara*)

The root chakra is located near the coccyx (tailbone). *Kundalini* is a pure life force that lies coiled in the root chakra. In the event of a total purification of all the chakras (i.e. an unblocking of the energy flow between the chakras), this force can rise up within the body and bring

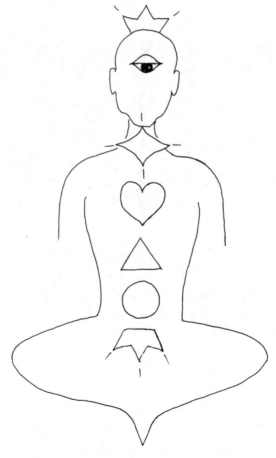

The seven main chakras are located along the centre of the body.

about an experience of cosmic consciousness. Such an experience can lead to illumination, also called 'enlightenment'.

The root chakra is our connection to the earth. If this centre is poorly connected to the others, while the connection between the higher chakras in the throat and head are open, you will need to ground yourself. After all, it is not really all that satisfying to be very spiritual and floating high if you cannot choose when you will come down to earth again.

If you climb a tree with weak roots, you risk the whole tree falling down. That is why the root chakra is the first stone on the path to enlightenment and to a healthy voice.

In humans, the basic note is a rather deep note, symbolizing contact with the root chakra. The deeper the sound is – the more coarse the vibration – the further down in the body it oscillates. Therefore, the foundation for a healthy voice depends on contact with the deep tonal register.

The root chakra represents, among other things, the instincts. The associated sense is smell. The sublimated form is secretion or elimination, and the colour is red. Earth is the element that belongs to it.

Sacral chakra (hara) ◯

The sacral chakra is located a hand's breadth below the navel. Fertility, sexuality, vitality, balance, motivation, and appetite are associated with this chakra. The degree of strength and power in the voice is dependent on contact to the hara.

Tight pants, belts and other things that constrict the waist diminish the connection to the sacral chakra. In this way, people cut themselves off from their own power. Therefore, women who aspire to a narrow waist and a flat stomach risk confirming their stereotype as the 'weaker sex'.

Every time we inhale deeply, an undulation in the sacral chakra stimulates and massages our inner organs. The same thing happens when, for example, we feel pleasure, have a hearty laugh, sob, or sing devotedly. This activates and releases the energy in the sacral area to flow freely again and interact with the surrounding chakras. The associated element is water; the sense is taste; the sublimated form is energizing of various types (note: water conducts electricity). The colour is orange.

Solar plexus chakra (*manipura*) △

The solar plexus is located in the soft triangle situated where the ribs separate under the chest. Among other things, emotions relating to the ego are associated with this chakra.

This is the most complicated chakra with regard to singing. Linked to the autonomic nervous system, the fear of failure can manifest itself as a tension that locks the solar plexus in a tight grip.

Similarly, most people feel discomfort in the solar plexus area when they are psychologically out of balance. This is because the autonomic nervous system reduces their contact to the chakras below the chest – a survival mechanism that cuts off the energy supply to the digestive system.

In a life-threatening situation, where you need to make the right response in order to avoid death, this is an excellent mechanism. However, if you are on stage and become overwhelmed by fear, a tense solar plexus will prevent you from breathing freely with the result that you get short of breath, and can, therefore, only express yourself through a weak and shaky voice.

From my own experience, a tense solar plexus reflects a frightened ego. Uncontrollable emotional reactions like self-pity, fear, jealousy and desperation compress the energetic field of the solar plexus. The result is paralyzation leading to loss of grounding and clear thinking.

In fact, our mind can become overwhelmed by delusions that appear completely real and true. That is how the snowball starts rolling, getting bigger and bigger until we consciously step in and stop it.

Awareness of what our physical reactions indicate can prevent such delusions. During a demanding singing situation a tensed solar plexus can be overcome merely by recognizing that it is the symptom of our fear of failure, and nothing more. In any case, the fear diminishes when the singer becomes overwhelmed by the higher state of the music and surrenders to the Note from Heaven.

To release a traumatized solar plexus, by which I mean that the muscles have been tense for years, requires physical stimulation combined with singing. Here a deep emotional release can relax the muscles, when you sing your self free.

Personally, I am not an advocate of reliving traumatic experiences. There is a risk that painful re-experiencing can result in the ego and the emotions overpowering consciousness. With its cool overview and objective outlook, it is consciousness that gives us the best chance of breaking free from the trauma. Therefore, it seems obvious to me that healing of trauma needs to take place on an impersonal level. The Note from Heaven is a tremendous tool for that purpose.

The solar plexus is associated with the element fire. Movement (from one place to another) is the sublimated form; the sense is sight; and the colour is yellow.

Heart chakra (*anahata*)

The centre of the heart chakra is located in the middle of the breastbone. If you look at the picture of the menorah, the seven-armed Jewish candlestick (also found on the altar in Christian churches), then you will find the heart chakra, the fourth chakra, right in the middle. The menorah image also shows how the other six chakras are paired with each other (for example, the solar plexus chakra with the throat chakra).

The heart is the path. Through loving care and devotion to our fellow human beings we can forget ourselves. All problems disappear. They are simply not present when we sincerely do things for others that make them feel good. This 'forgetting of the ego' creates a temporary space for the soul to commune.

The same is true when we sing. When you sing from the heart, something magical happens. All the muscle tensions disappear and the body functions as if it had forgotten all the injuries life has ever inflicted upon it.

It is indeed magical that you can sing yourself into a state where everything feels whole, where time disappears, and where you hardly remember anything afterwards.

Even more magical is the unmistakeable sound of someone singing from the heart. A sense of sacredness descends over the listeners and the singer. You can feel your hair stand on end. Something higher than us is present. The performing singer has conveyed something that cannot be

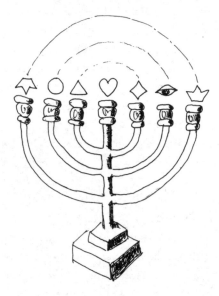

The Jewish seven-armed candelabrum known as the menorah is an excellent illustration of the seven chakras' communal and paired relationships.

interpreted as a personal achievement, but more as a spiritual experience that fills us with a deep gratitude for being alive.

The experience of release that comes when we sing from the heart demonstrates that we are so much more than just our body. Miracles are a possibility at any given moment.

In the 'Key images' section (see page 31), I will describe a method designed to help you to sing from the heart.

The heart chakra is associated with the element air. The sublimated form is care and creativity; the sense is feeling; and the colour is green, or sometimes light pink with a green border.

Throat chakra (*vishuddha*) ◇

The throat is the bridge between the body and the head. In terms of energy, it is a key point as it connects the four lower chakras with the two higher chakras in the head.

The energy centres in the head rule, respectively, the higher consciousness and the soul (the mental aura), which represent our potential for spiritual powers. Since we all have a soul and a higher consciousness, we all possess the ability to connect to them, if our organism allows it. When your throat chakra is more or less closed, it can be difficult to access your spiritual powers. This is not because you are not spiritual (we all are), it is because the energy cannot flow freely from the body up to the head.

There are people who speak in a slightly grating voice. This grating wears the vocal cords and therefore the speaker's voice quickly tires. I have noticed that people develop a business-like, objective timbre to their voice with this kind of abuse.

For example, a doctor might need to convince a patient that he or she has things under control. So, subconsciously, the doctor begins to adopt a slightly grating tone. As well as conveying authority to the patient, this change in tone also subconsciously bolsters the speaker's own self-confidence. Physically, the soft palate behind the hard palate is lowered. It actually feels as if you are closing off the connection to the head by making the palate flat and loose.

In terms of energy, this reaction stems from our human need to have solid ground under our feet in order to feel safe. With a connection to the spiritual centres in the head, the soul is able to take over from the ego. The resulting sensation of an abyss underneath us can be so intense that we get frightened if we do not know how to manage this connection. That is why many people close off in the throat chakra by using the voice 'inappropriately'. This phenomenon is elaborated on pages 40.

Another form of closing off in the throat can occur when an emotional reaction is repressed. A lump in the throat or tears held back can cause our facial muscles to stiffen into a mask as we struggle to maintain a controlled façade. Crying is a way to clear the throat and solar plexus chakras. The pent-up energy that the muscle contractions have been holding on to is released. If the tears from a traumatic situation are not released or compensated for in another way, then a chronic closure of the throat and solar plexus can ensue. That is why some people suffer, for example, from a feeling of strangulation.

The experience of fear fully taking over during a performance – whether it be in speaking, singing, or another mode of expression – can result in a third form of closure in the throat.

You become 'speechless' – the shoulders slide up towards the ears while the solar plexus in the diaphragm contracts like a fist. Subconsciously, you turn your hands and arms inwards.

The body stiffens from fear. As previously mentioned, by becoming aware of the purely physical manifestations of fear you can help yourself to view your situation with some detachment, and thus resolve to pull yourself together.

There is a very good reason for doing this. Just a single experience of helplessness in front of an audience can create a trauma. Repeated experiences of this sort of trauma can result, for example, in tone deafness, stammering and difficulty in breathing.

As mentioned before, strengthening your connection to the heart chakra can temporarily dissolve such traumas stored in the body. Since the heart is the centre of the whole chakra sequence, and the solar plexus and throat chakras are connected on either side like the two closest planets, it seems obvious that an energy charge in the heart must have a contagious effect.

The throat chakra represents the element ether. The sublimated form is communication; the sense is hearing; and the colour is sky blue. The throat chakra is associated with communication, active contact to intuition, the arms (action), and to a state where desires are fulfilled.

The third eye (ajna)

The third eye is located between the eyebrows. The centre of the chakra is the uppermost point of a triangle, of which the eyes are the other two points. We touch this spot spontaneously when we need reassurance or to concentrate. For example, consider how when we are worried we cradle our forehead in our hands, or when we are crying we hide our face in our hands, with our fingertips resting on our forehead. Then there is the thinker, who, with fingertips placed on the third eye, intensifies his concentration. An agitated child is comforted by gently stroking the forehead.

When meditating with closed eyes, it is possible to see a spot, a light, which at a certain level appears to the inner sight as a violet or blue-coloured eye.

Higher consciousness resides in this the sixth chakra. Connection to it calms us by giving us a matter-of-fact view of our situation without the interference of emotional energies.

If you imagine the body as a circle, then the higher consciousness would be located in the centre.

Higher consciousness is the fulcrum on which we achieve balance. The same is true of the sound of our voice because the centre for the free-flowing sound of the Note from Heaven is located in the third eye. The circle's circumference corresponds to the power source in the sacral chakra and the encircled space corresponds to the body's resonance. If we return to the seven-armed candlestick, then you will see that the sacral chakra and the third eye are paired with each other. When singing the Note from Heaven, the location of the note and the power become one. The circle dissolves and is replaced by a sense of being purely present in the here and now, a state in which we disappear.

The same phenomenon can be seen in Zen Buddhist archery. The archer seeks to merge with the aim, and when he disappears as a person the arrow, as if by magic, always hits the bull's eye. This phenomenon also occurs in other sports. Take the example of golf, where a 'hole in one' is a similarly mystical experience.

The third eye represents inner sound. The colour is violet or indigo blue. (With the two higher chakras in the head, no element or sublimated form is associated with them, since we are moving beyond the physical plane.)

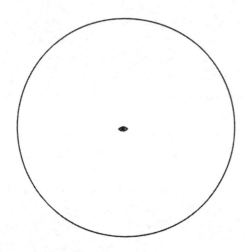

The centre and body of the Note from Heaven are placed, respectively, at the psychological and physical balance points – the third eye and the sacral chakra.

Crown chakra (*sahasrara*)

The crown chakra is located at the top of the head, in the soft spot of the fontanelle. This chakra is the soul's entrance to the body. Here we have a breathing hole, which we literally use in dreams, meditation, when we get inspired, and when we 'disappear' in other ways – for example, when singing the Note from Heaven. This opening is also used for healing purposes. It is through the crown chakra's breathing hole and the hands, respectively, that you receive and transfer light energy. The healing energy feels like small, fine vibrations. Sometimes during and after singing you can feel a faint quivering on your scalp or chest, and your hands get warm and occasionally quiver as well.

When we sing the Note from Heaven, our body opens up and becomes a channel for a higher power, just like it does for a healer. Therefore, singing the Note from Heaven is comparable to healing.

The higher the note we sing, the higher up in the body the sound resonates. This is how a gradual ascension in the notes you sing will bring you to a point where the sounds are mainly in the head – the point that in classical terminology for a male voice is called falsetto.

Before singing high notes, however, you need to develop the ability to sing low notes with the total support of your stomach muscles. A high note is created when the vocal cords are stretched like a rubber band: the more tense the vocal cords, the easier it is to injure our voices and ourselves. This is like practising mountain-climbing techniques in a low place before actually tackling a steep mountain. When you have mastered the techniques, you can climb without too much risk.

In the worst of all possible cases, the psychological effect of pure contact with the crown chakra, before having purified the lower ones, is madness. This madness comes entirely from an inability to control one's state of mind. An enlightened person can draw on the infinite knowledge they gain precisely because they can control their state of mind.

My experience is that the high notes you sing yourself stimulate the crown chakra from within. The voice has a useful cut-off mechanism that ensures it becomes hoarse if you try to force it up too high without giving it a grounding in the form of body support. This can act as a safeguard against the risk of madness.

As we have seen from the menorah image, the crown chakra is connected to the root chakra. Both these centres are sources of energy, the framework for our life, Mother Earth and Father Sky. A definition of the 'I' – a form to relate to.

The crown chakra represents inner light; the colour is white or violet.

BEFORE YOU START

Environment

If singing is still something new for you, try to find a place where you can practise alone.

If that is impossible, you can sing your way through any concerns you may have about other people's opinions. Singing the root note repeatedly makes the people around you quite quickly lose interest. When others perceive the singing as a form of meditation, it can help you to become immersed in your self and tame the ego's thoughts about what other people might be thinking.

Finally, it is possible to sing in the car or out in the countryside. There you can benefit greatly by developing awareness of your breathing, your support (the use of stomach muscles), sensing the location of the note in the third eye, and awareness of the soft palate. (See page 38.)

Understand, though, that it is essential to develop your ability to listen within. This must be done in a quiet and closed room.

A room with good acoustics gives self-confidence. Good acoustics can be found in large or sparsely furnished rooms, in front of a window or in the bathroom. Factory buildings and echoing churches can be beautiful to sing in. However, they are not revealing enough for the work of listening. The acoustics swallow the little thorn bushes that we need to weed out. If your only option is a room where the acoustics are not so good, you can intensify your listening concentration by cupping your hands behind or in front of your ears.

It is a good idea to develop some small rituals associated with your daily practice. These might include choosing a good fragrance, a bouquet of flowers or a picture of someone you love dearly, lighting a candle, tidying the room before you begin, drinking a warm cup of tea, or pouring yourself a glass of water to have at hand. (However, do not drink milk, as it causes mucus in the throat.)

Such preparations signal that you are now taking care of yourself and your senses, which makes a good start to the practice session more likely. Our senses are entry points to the past. Just think how evocative a smell, taste or melody can be. A flower, for example, can conjure up innocence through its appearance and fragrance.

Warming up the body

Stimulating our muscles influences our energy centres and eases muscle tension. In general, warming up the body is beneficial for singing, because it opens the flow of energy between the chakras. A balancing occurs, we get warm and our mind and body open up, allowing for freer expression while singing.

Some exercises create an overall flow of energy in the body and will strengthen posture and consequently the position of the spine, which, when surrendering to the Note from Heaven, will reach up like a flower towards the sunlight.

It is essential to keep the spine supple, since the body's three main sources of energy, the *ida, pingala* and *sushumna* (see page 14), run along it. One way to achieve this is through prayer. People naturally bend down while praying and kneel on the ground in a position similar to the foetal position. In religions where the practitioner bends down to pray several times a day, this movement creates a flow in the spine that, combined with the increased grounding from the kneeling position, strengthens the energy flow through the chakras. In this way, an appropriate position and movement support the mind's submission to the divine powers. Another possibility is to concentrate your exercises on specific energy centres in the body.

If you have tensions in the diaphragm, for example, it would be obvious to work with breathing exercises combined with movement, contracting and releasing the muscles involved.

If the stomach muscles are slack they need to be strengthened because, no matter how good our intentions, the strength and dynamic of the tone we produce will be governed by the muscles of the diaphragm. Building up these muscles will strengthen the energy in the sacral and root chakras, as well as grounding us.

Tense shoulders and arms and a painful neck will affect our ability to open up while singing. In this case, the principal offender could be the tongue, since its muscle tissue stretches from the back of the throat and all the way down to the chest and the collarbones.

The jaw can refuse to open up enough to say a genuine 'Aaar' with a relaxed open mouth. This can be due to an instinctive fear of revealing our teeth and tongue. In order to keep the lips protectively over the teeth, the body compensates with tension in the jaws.

There is a selection of physical exercises described on pages 82–92. Try to do the exercises with ease and in a meditative state rather than with achievement in mind. All you need to do is to choose the exercises that are right for you and your needs.

Singing posture

Sitting cross-legged is a good position for singing because it creates contact between the ground and the root chakra. This position will continually stimulate the root chakra and hold you to the ground like an anchor. If you prefer to sit on a chair, you can sit on the edge for a similar effect. For both positions, it is recommended that you sit on a slanting pad, as shown in the illustration. Sit without a back support, if possible. If you sit on a chair, then plant your feet solidly on the ground, with them pointing forward, a shoulders' width apart.

You can relieve any discomfort caused by sitting cross-legged or without back support by using pillows, blankets etc. for support. This is especially important, since pain can prevent you from listening inwards.

Later, when you are immersed in the singing, it is easy to forget the body. Often you do not, for example, even notice that your legs have gone to sleep.

Make sure there is enough room to spread your arms out, so you won't need to worry about hitting furniture or walls.

Keep your eyes closed as much as possible while singing, as this will sharpen your listening skills.

Use a wedge-shaped cushion while sitting cross-legged.

In addition to sitting on a wedge-shaped cushion, you can avoid pain in the legs and back by supporting the knees with pillows.

BREATHING

As mentioned earlier, our breath reflects our physical and psychological state. The act of concentrating on your breathing function can, in itself, feel so unfamiliar that you become nervous, and so tension gathers in the solar plexus, restricting the breathing. Therefore, breathing is a delicate matter. If breathing 'with the stomach' feels unnatural, you should practise to breathe correctly in your daily life before going on to singing.

Practising deep and natural breathing is most easily achieved by observing your breath. This means that, at first, your breathing practice is more a matter of concentrating on the breath than on controlling your muscles. Becoming conscious of the way you breathe is in itself the first form of progress.

Our lungs function rather like bagpipes. When filled with air, they inflate like balloons. Metaphorically speaking, that means we suck air into our inbuilt balloons when breathing in. We squeeze the air out of the balloons when breathing out by pressing on the thickest part of the balloons with the 'laughter muscles', which lie a hand's width down from the navel.

For those who are unfamiliar with deep breathing, the physical exercises 12, 13, 14, and especially 15, on pages 86–88 are recommended.

Physical effect of an extended exhalation

When singing the Note from Heaven, your exhalation becomes three or four times longer than normal. A long exhalation actively made from the stomach clears and balances the nervous system and alkalizes the body, which means that acids and toxins are breathed out. Stuck energy is released from the cells, which then begin to breathe freely again.

In Barbara Wren's book *Cellular Awakening: How Your Body Holds and Creates Light*, she describes how the cells' ability to absorb light photons and to detoxify is dependent on our ability to listen to ourselves and respond to what we notice. Chronic illnesses/stress are interconnected with the dehydration of body cells, which when feeling threatened, make their cell walls thicker in order to protect themselves. This restricts absorption of light photons/energy and over the years

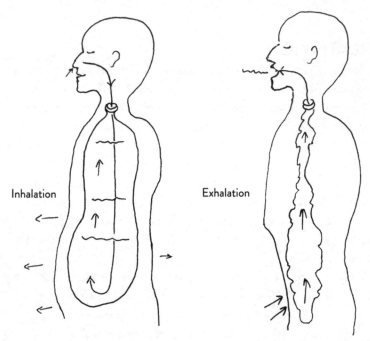

Inhalation

Exhalation

Symbolic illustration of inhalation and exhalation in which the lungs are likened to balloons.

can lead to illness. The key to stopping this kind of chronic state of emergency lies in the large intestine.

When a person connects to the Note from Heaven, the cells are revivified, which can feel like a tingling in the body. The large intestine is activated, so that the sound is literally expressed from the bottom of the torso via active belly breathing. The singer can become quite moved by re-experiencing old emotions that now are liberated and once again see the light of day. A detoxification at the physical level takes place, which can produce temporary side effects if the transformation has been deep. These can be alleviated through diet, intestinal cleanses, enemas, liver cleanses, vitamin supplements – all of which support the purification process.

Dr Mark Sircus, author of the book *Sodium Bicarbonate*, states: 'The bottom line is that we can create miracles in medicine simply by adjusting the flow of a person's breath ... a natural way to instantly reduce stress hormones, calm emotions, boost oxygen levels, let go of stress [and] detox .... in addition to increasing cell voltage and improving pH.'

Key images

Instinctive exclamations like 'Ah', 'Uuuh', 'Oooh' and 'Aaar' are genuine sound reactions – spontaneous expressions of feeling without interference from the judging intellect.

'Aaar' is normally expressed when the body finds something very pleasurable. The vibration of this syllable is universal.

To really feel the 'Aaar' and encourage a genuine reaction that gives a true expression from the heart, we can consciously guide our thoughts to a place where our body and mind overflow with joy. I call this place a key image.

An experience of a sunrise, a favourite flower and its fragrance, a joyful experience, a dream, the fulfilment of a wish, someone you love with all your heart ... The image needs to animate something pure and authentic in you. The kind of image is not important. The only thing that matters is that it should fill you with pure joy.

Experiment with various images in your practice. The ones that work can be used again and again.

Breathing exercise with key images

- You have now chosen to concentrate on a specific key image. Place the visualization of the image in the third eye and keep it there for a while.
- Express your wish to allow yourself to overflow with joy by saying 'Aaar'. At first, this can feel awkward and artificial. Treat it as a joke and let your body respond as it wishes. Laughing and smiling is a good sign, because then joy is within reach. The deeply felt 'Aaar' can cause half-smothered giggles, red faces and outbursts of laughter, especially when sitting in a group. It means a positive atmosphere is already developing.
- Keep concentrating on the image and move it down to the sacral chakra, a hand's breadth below the navel.
- Inhale through the nose and feel how the air is causing your stomach and flanks to extend.

- Stop for a moment and fix your awareness on the joy generated by your key image as it nourishes the air in your stomach.
- Share this joyful feeling with the world through an 'Aaar', and note how the stomach muscles are pressed inwards, pushing the air upwards.
- On the out breath you can imagine that the air current, and the joy it carries, flows out through the mouth. In this way, you are passing the joy on to the world.
- This cycle of breathing can be used until joy takes hold in your body. When the voice, and with that the body, have opened up and the state of joy can be maintained, then you can stop the exercise and open up even more through a total surrender to joy.
- Play track 2 on the practice download (tanpura and guide song) if you want singing support. Play track 21 (tanpura only) if you can find the root note yourself, which in this case is note A.
- Make the joyful 'Aaar' tone ring, and concentrate on keeping in contact with the key image rather than evaluating your sound.
- As your joyful sound gradually takes hold, you can begin to experiment with how to make the sound feel even better in your body. The main thing is to gradually open, open and open even more with each breath.

If you have difficulty controlling the current of air with your stomach muscles – for example, if the current acts in the opposite way to that described in the exercise – then keep your concentration on the key image and forget completely about the way in which you are breathing. Place your image in the heart chakra (in the centre of the breast bone) and surrender to it totally while singing 'Aaar'.

Surrendering to joy generally induces correct breathing, because the stomach muscles are brought into use. Take, for example, laughter. Who can laugh heartily without using the diaphragm?

Students who have difficulty surrendering to the full breath with joy are usually either fearful or intellectually focused on the technical details of breathing.

If you have a similar tendency you will have to transcend this barrier by jumping over an abyss. Close your eyes and jump unconditionally. You will experience that the jump itself is the rescue. Surrender is faith. We lose our need to be self-controlling when we surrender. We need to believe that something else will take over.

When the ego releases its control, the soul, the divine aspect, takes over. There is nothing to lose and everything to gain.

AWARENESS OF TONE

In language communication our words account for just 10 per cent of expression. The tone of our voice is an important element of the remaining 90 per cent.

Relating to sound is difficult, because it occurs in the present moment and disappears immediately after being expressed. When you remember a sound, you remember the feeling it produced in your body. Every reproduction of a sound will be a new sound, because the moment will be a different one.

The sound behind the words is a major cause of emotional frustration. We remember the way the words were spoken by recalling their sound in our body. They may, for example, have been said in a hurtful manner. Tone can create incredible emotional confusion, since it provokes feelings that are impossible for the intellect to grasp.

In this way tone conveys the subconscious, that which everyone can clearly feel, but only a few can consciously explain. The closest we come to an explanation could be, for example, 'She spoke to me in a derogatory way.' However, who knows how I myself sound, without being aware of it?

Just like a melody loses its true meaning when a single phrase is removed, the same thing happens when we relate our experiences to others. The experiences are no longer completely authentic. They become distorted. By developing the ability to listen deeply, we increase our awareness of the tonal vibrations that we and others send out and perceive.

We expand our consciousness in this way, because something we were not aware of before is now picked up by our consciousness.

Listening to the tone of a voice, or of another source of sound, and consciously noticing whether what we are hearing feels good, will protect us from frustrating feelings in the body.

Objectivity allows us to recognize, for example, that 'She is speaking in a derogatory tone' and by recognizing this, we can see that it is her problem. Her tone is not sucked into our subconscious by agitated emotions that get our thoughts whirling in an attempt to figure out what just happened. The experience has become impersonal, because our consciousness rather than our emotions is governing our ego. The ego will not, therefore, go on red alert. At most, it will gently nudge the event to one side.

The root note

The main purpose of classical Indian singing is to become one with your self, with your divine essence.

A good singer is 'god gifted'.

In order to be a divine instrument, the body needs to be used in a way that allows for optimal sound. When it functions like an open pipe, it achieves just that.

We decide, therefore, to open our body up to one note. With the help of this one note, it is possible to create a sound hole, which can later be expanded to also include the other notes in the full register. Sticking to one note in the beginning is of the utmost importance.

For women, the basic note is located around the note A below the piano's keyhole.

For men, the area of the note is less definable, because there is a big difference in where they feel most comfortable. For some men (basses) it is the same as for women with the sound A. They just sing it in a deeper pitch (an octave below). That is why the root note on the practice dowload is A. Most women and some men will feel comfortable with that note.

It is an interesting detail that the note A was also once the starting point in western musical notation. The alphabet was transferred to the notes. In the northern countries, we have partly forgotten this, because there was a writing mistake when the note system was introduced: a monk

When establishing the root note, remember:

Start with the note that feels most relaxed and pleasant when you sing 'Aaar'.

It should be possible to sing deeper than the note you choose as your root note. (You should be able to sing 'Pạ', which corresponds to a fifth below the root note.)

You can sing the note for extended periods of time without your voice getting tired or sore.

Use the note that sounds most full and beautiful on 'Aaar'.

Use the note that feels best in your body.

wrote the letter b rather indistinctly and it was interpreted as an h. That is why Danes still operate with a note system that is: A, H, C, D, E, F, and G. This is contrary to the rest of the world, where the H is named B.

If the root note on the practice download does not feel good for your voice, you can create your own root note. This can be done either by experimenting with the help of a sound-source like a piano, or by finding a singing teacher or vocal sound healer who understands the principles in this book.

If your root note is close to A, it is possible to regulate the sound of the practice download up or down by using a standard recording computer program.

Another option is to get yourself a shruti box, an Indian organ or a tanpura. Female tanpuras tune around A, male tanpuras tune around C or E. Note though, that you need to be able to tune the tanpura, and that the strings can break if tuned too high. The quality of tanpuras varies a lot, so, if possible, let a trained musician check whether the tanpura can hold its tuning (for example A if it is an A tanpura), that it has correct strings, and that the strings will play overtones when you add threads to the meeting point with the bridge. Do not use the salesmen in tourist areas of India; ask a musician where to buy good instruments.

Alternatively, accompany yourself with a musical instrument (piano or guitar, for example). It is easy for a beginner to learn, since you only need to play very few notes, namely the root note and the fifth (seven halftones up from the root note).

You can make it more musical either by including the third and playing a whole chord or just by doubling the fifth and the root note.

'Aaar'

We have been saying the sound 'Aaar' since we were babies. The vowel is round and not flat like in 'Aaah', where the soft palate is lowered. Classical Indian singing is based on a combined training of the two halves of the brain; partly by training the consciousness in the mutual, vibrational connection between the notes, which is done by working with the note names, and partly by training the subconscious by working with the sound 'Aaar'.

Besides being the spoken vowel that opens the mouth the most, 'Aaar' is also the easiest vowel to sing deeply. The body opens to 'Aaar'. You can experience this directly, by experimenting with different vowels.

In certain yoga systems, 'Aaar' represents the sound of the heart. Esoteric philosophy and psychology speak of the physical body as having different energy bodies. The subtlest energy level is called the causal body and the sound connected to it is 'Aaar'.

Rudolf Steiner's eurythmics involves a system of body positions and associated sounds. 'Aaar' is coded together with a position very similar to the one I learned to initiate healing sessions with. You stand or sit with your arms open and the palms lifted up in the air. In healing, this is done in order to become a channel for a higher energy to flow through. It is useful to do exactly the same thing when singing.

It is a human instinct to put up your hands when surrendering Peoples from the East dance with their arms and hands lifted upwards. This gives the dancing an ecstatic element, since the body seems to surrender to a higher power. In Scandinavia, we dance more with our hands in slightly clenched fists, which we box with, while the rest of the body stamps in time to the rhythm. That kind of movement gives grounding.

Some people are unaccustomed to surrendering, with their hands reaching up. If you find this gesture odd, ask yourself what may be trying to hold your arms back when the final surrender to the Note from Heaven takes place. Raised arms make it easier to let go, as this is the body's way of saying 'yes'. An additional benefit of this movement is that the lungs get more space in the rib cage.

Especially at the start of this process, you should be aware of the singing guidelines listed in the box [overleaf]. These four points will gradually be encoded into your nervous system. The sound itself will reveal to trained ears when something is wrong. For example, you can hear immediately when the support is not functioning (see point 3).

Surrendering to the Note from Heaven leads to a distinct feeling of being a channel for something higher than yourself. Physically, the act of surrender is encouraged by a gesture of submission: the throat is bared, as the neck tilts slightly back and the open hands are lifted up towards the heavens.

1. The mouth needs to be completely open, preferably too much rather than too little. When the face muscles have been suitably stretched, you will be able to find the open-mouthed position that is most natural for you.

2. The tongue lies relaxed at the bottom of the mouth with the tip touching the lower teeth.

3. When you are tuned into your key image, take a moment to make sure that your breathing is correct.

4. If you usually breathe in reverse order, which is called paradoxical breathing, it is a good idea to observe your breathing throughout the day. Repeatedly remind yourself of when the stomach needs to be going in, and when it should be going out. Combine this with one or more of the breathing exercises that you feel at ease with.

The soft palate

There is a spot in the soft part at the back of the roof of your mouth that is instinctively raised when you are overwhelmed by your feelings. This can occur when you laugh or feel moved, cry or are about to cry and when you yawn. I mention these three examples, because their common denominator is the sound 'Aaar', which is a component of the sound we make when we laugh, cry and yawn.

Picture yourself in these three situations and sense how the space in your mouth expands. The soft palate is raised and the resonating space in the oral cavity increases. Note how you can get tears in your eyes, whether from joy, yawning or grief, merely by raising the soft palate.

There are healers who consciously raise the soft palate, and with the help of this gesture get in touch with their healing powers.

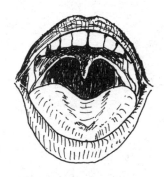

Position of the tongue when singing 'Aaar'. The tongue lies relaxed at the bottom of the mouth with the tip touching the lower teeth.

In several sessions with Daniella Segal, a healer in Israel, I noticed that I yawned noisily at the end of the healing. It always happened when I was overwhelmed by a sense of deep gratitude to the divine powers. I felt embarrassed about the yawning, since I felt anything but tired. Daniella explained that it was a normal reaction: we yawn simply to make room for an overpowering feeling.

Similarly, think about why it is we gawp or say 'Uuuh' when someone frightens us. In these cases, the soft palate is also raised – the body tries to help us by accommodating the feeling and simultaneously giving us the means of releasing a sound.

As the space in the oral cavity expands when the soft palate is raised, the pressure increases on the space connecting the nose with the throat – the nasal cavity.

The nasal cavity leads up to the frontal sinus, the seat of the pituitary and pineal glands and the third eye/higher consciousness of the energy system. The body is so ingeniously put together that it stimulates contact to the centre of higher consciousness to help us accommodate overwhelming feelings.

We always instinctively breathe deeply before raising the soft palate when we are in the grip of any sort of deeply felt and uncontrollable outburst. Try to breathe very lightly high up in the throat and yawn at the same time. It is impossible.

Note that a deep breath accompanies every real yawn. The same thing applies to a hearty laugh or cry: there needs to be wind to fill the sail. On the other hand, when we work against the body's reflexes, the soft

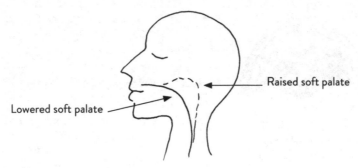

The raised soft palate puts us in contact with the 'higher self' (the soul).

palate is held down and breathing is inhibited. You will, for example, get a lump in your throat if you try to refrain from laughing, crying, or yawning by subconsciously keeping the soft palate down. If the soft palate is raised, nothing can hold back the real reaction.

Therefore, one of the cornerstones of the Note from Heaven is a raised soft palate, which again is connected to efficient breathing, another cornerstone that supports the roof of the singing temple.

If it is easy for you to sing an open-sounding, round 'Aaar' and your voice doesn't tire when you talk for a long time, then take no further notice of this section. Your soft palate is in good shape.

The grating voice that closes up the throat chakra, discussed on page 21, is caused by a slack soft palate. There are people whose soft palate is lowered most of the day. This results in the muscle getting so loose that the voice can no longer sound beautiful in the head, because the loose soft palate blocks the way. Try to say 'Aaah' and then 'Aaar'. Which vowel sounds more free and spacious?

The soft palate is automatically raised when you sing a spacious 'Aaar'. If you have difficulty in saying 'Aaar' and have a tendency to sing a flat 'Aaah' instead, I recommend the following exercise.

Strengthening a slack soft palate

One way to strengthen the muscles of the soft palate is to sing 'Ngggg'. Alternatively, you can hold a similar mouth position without actually making the sound; that is, with the soft palate supporting itself against the wall of the nasal cavity, the tongue lying loosely with its tip resting on the lower teeth, the lips gaping. The sound, if you do make it, is nasal, closed and buzzes in the head.

Sing or just hold this mouth position as often as possible. It could be done in the car, while cooking, in the shower... Another possibility is to sing 'Arng-arng-arng-arng ... ', since repeating this sound makes the soft palate move, so that each 'ng' hits the wall of the nasal cavity. This exercise increases your physical awareness of the muscles responsible for the function of the soft palate. Be prepared to yawn quite a bit.

A third exercise is to throw the tongue backwards and keep it there. That will automatically raise the soft palate.

If these exercises provoke resistance, you may need to take a deeper look at emotional issues, because in energy terms opening the throat creates a bridge up to the third eye. This connection is of great value to every person who wishes to develop spiritually here on Earth.

If you have no trouble singing 'Arng', you can also sing 'Huuh' on any higher note that feels good together with the vowel. The soft palate no longer leans on the nasal cavity wall, but is held up by muscles and the flow of air. The tongue remains lying with its tip resting on the lower teeth.

You could start by rolling the tongue (if you can) and pursing your lips on 'DrrrrUuuh' or by rolling the lips (if you can) on 'BrUuuh'.

Try to centre the sound in the third eye. When you can do that, your 'Huuuh' note will ring with overtones and have a rich, beautiful quality.

Depending how much practice you do, it will take one to three weeks for the soft palate to regain enough strength to be able to arch beautifully on an open sounding 'Aaar' or 'Haar'.

Note that tiredness and exhaustion also affect the voice. The soft palate will get slack. Therefore, sleep and relaxation are the best forms of 'song training' to start with.

THE NOTE FROM HEAVEN

The Note from Heaven is true. It is true because our personality/ego is not interfering with how it should sound. The note comes from above and overwhelms us when we relinquish all control.

As mentioned earlier, by absorbing yourself in your key image you can take a shortcut and experience the Note from Heaven without any sort of physical preparation. The experience of joy creates a feeling of gratitude and those two emotions combine to fill the heart with a devotion that allows us to surrender safely.

When we surrender, the body opens up and functions as if reborn.

The Note from Heaven puts you in a timeless state. When you have achieved this – which can take up to ten minutes following the actual surrender – it feels as if you could sing the same note forever. You are being sung and the voice resonates with wholeness. It does not feel as if it is you singing. You get the tangible experience of not owning your own voice. The voice is a wild and uncompromising animal that will always be most beautiful when it is free. Taming the voice in its free and natural form requires the proper bait and a loving attitude. Otherwise, you will conjure up the ego's fear and pretence.

The experience of the Note from Heaven is holy, because it is not constructed with the help of the ego. If you try to sing it in public, it takes quite an effort to stay clear of that little ego troll. If it is allowed to affect the sound even slightly, the whole thing falls apart on the spot.

Therefore, trained singers need to be aware of previously learned forms of expression. Only a very few singers sing with their natural voice. For example, most singers automatically add a vibrato to their 'Aaar'. This is true of both rhythmic and classically trained singers. Such deliberate interference with the sound might bolster their confidence enough to ward off performance anxiety, which every stage performer has to face, but, unfortunately, they will also miss the chance to free themselves from their ego, since it is built into the voice. At worst, the performance will be so polished and professional that it never touches the heart.

A person is most beautiful when stripped down to who he or she really is. Only in that state is it possible to take off with the Note from Heaven.

When you listen within to your sound, you will discover how artificial it is to bolster yourself with voice-makeup. It is just showing off for the crowd. The ego animates the ego in its audience. It may seem like success, but, spiritually speaking, it is the complete opposite.

I recently met a former fellow student from the Royal Academy of Music. I remember she sang opera fantastically and scored top grades in the mid-term exams. Now, meeting her again after fifteen years, she admitted she felt that she had cheated the examiners; that she had been play-acting. She had used her voice like a costume with which to please them. Towards the end of her studies, she gradually lost her ability to sing in tune, without anyone being able to figure out why. Today she still feels unable to trust her own ears; so much so that she decided to give up singing. What may have happened is that she became aware of her dishonesty, but neglected to deal with it and was thus caught between two poles – the ego and the soul. A strong ego can easily lead to success – although that kind of success has quite a hollow ring to it.

The primal sound behind the Note from Heaven

To get the primal sound behind the Note from Heaven to break through, imagine that you are a wolf howling at the moon from a mountaintop, or a gorilla that wants to win respect by showing off his powerful voice.

Deep down most people love to play monkeys. Just try saying 'Huh, huh, huh, huh' and scratch yourself under the arms, while bouncing at the knees. Most people really have fun, once they have overcome their shyness. It feels so good to come down to earth.

Finding the strength of your voice

Imagine that you are an animal or a primitive person. Close your eyes.
- Picture yourself setting a boundary. You do this with your voice, which will soon demonstrate the fact that you exist, and that you are capable of releasing your overwhelming, pure and terrifying power.
- Breathe deeply down in the stomach chakra, as this is the seat of power.
- Tilt your head slightly back and look upwards behind your closed eyes.
- Concentrate the centre of the sound in the third eye. Adjust the sound

to be ruthlessly sharp and nasal.

- Spread out your arms in a 'daredevil' way and raise your palms upwards, while you release the sound as if through the *sushumna*, the body's middle channel, on a 'Haaar'.
- Lower your arms when the tone ends. The sound becomes uncompromising when fully expressed and you can sing for an unusually long time on one breath. It can feel similar to shouting.

As children, many of us were taught not to make noise. Push that to the side. It is exceptionally delightful to shout and feel the power singing in the body.

Stop if your voice starts hurting. Check your breathing; do one or more of the physical exercises 12–15 on pages 86–88. You can try singing again when your breathing functions correctly.

The primal sound can be heard three times, a good way into track 2 on the practice download (with the volume turned down to avoid frightening anyone within earshot!).

The strength behind the weakness

When you have got to know your strength, then you are no longer at the mercy of your weakness.

Weakness becomes a choice. The same principle works in singing. You can express whatever you want when you know your strength. It turns into a conscious choice, which gives you a feeling of freedom. The freedom to choose to express yourself.

Some people have no problem at all in expressing themselves forcefully – quite the opposite, in fact. The difficult thing for them is to be weak, gentle and empathetic.

Someone who possesses such rigid strength is not truly free. The strength itself has become an entrenchment against the outside world. The heart is wrapped up tightly, because the ego is guarding it. It wants no more pain than it has already suffered.

Difficulty in singing gently from the heart is not due to insensitivity in the person. It is caused by a mental barrier blocking the way.

If you cannot sing beautifully when softly singing 'Aaar' on the root note, then you simply have not opened up enough yet. Open up, open up, and continue to open up, even when you think you cannot open up any more. Make sure that the sound is not 'Oorr', but really an open sounding 'Aaar'. Smile and let the teeth be as they are.

When you smile freely, everyone will see your smile, not your teeth. Get into the habit of smiling unreservedly in your daily life.

Singing the Note from Heaven with strength behind the weakness

With the previous exercise, you made contact with your strength. Now use this strength and feel the Note from Heaven through it. The note will become unusually long and it will feel as if a higher power is singing through you.

- Gradually bring the sensation of your sound down to the heart chakra. It helps to let the torso's point of balance (in the middle of the stomach chakra) and the head's point of balance (in the third eye) join in the heart. You can do that by surfing on the air current, as explained in the exercise to relieve tightness in the solar plexus or throat on pages 12–13.
- Choose a key image that envelops you in a feeling of love or caring. For example, the thought of a child, a pet or person close to you, can fill you with that wonderful feeling of wanting to give everything you have to another living being.
- Avoid sentimentality, because then you will be moved and will need to cry, which will close the throat. Look at the experience as a blessing that sets you free, since all self-importance disappears.
- Sing on 'Aaar' or 'Haar' and let the sound swell in your chest.
- While you are singing to your imaginary loved one, perceive your voice as soft and comforting, but with the security of the strength that lies behind it.
- With each breath try to open yourself up more and more to an acceptance of your outward sensitivity and weakness, while simultaneously feeling an immense strength on the inside.

- End by singing 'Aaar'/'Haar' freely and surrender to the Note from
  Heaven without any kind of conscious thought.

Once your body has opened up and understands the nature of the Note
from Heaven, you should be able to freely sing 'Aaar'/'Haar'/'Sa' on your
root note for a half hour to an hour each day.

Listening with the ears becomes the same as feeling with the body.
You simply are.

At this point I recommend that you stop reading and practise Part I,
since it is the basis and main message of this book.

In the following part of the book, I use musical expressions and
terms that readers who do not come from a musical background may
have difficulty understanding. I wish to emphasize that, by engaging
in the exercises on the practice download yourself, you will have the
opportunity to understand everything in your own way – just as most
of what I describe comes from my own experience. The problem with
putting this subject in writing is that words can never perfectly convey the
real experience of working with the Note from Heaven, since it can only
be experienced as a state. The sound, because of its very nature, speaks
for itself.

Should you find these musical expressions difficult to understand or
uninspiring, then ignore them. Whatever happens, the Note from Heaven
will still be there, a doorway through which you can find freedom.

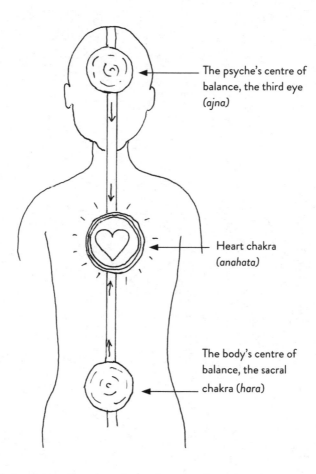

The psyche's centre of balance, the third eye (*ajna*)

Heart chakra (*anahata*)

The body's centre of balance, the sacral chakra (*hara*)

With the help of the in breath and visualization, the energy field at the hara is brought up to the heart chakra. With the help of the out breath and visualization, the energy field at the third eye is brought down to the heart chakra. After that, the sound will swell in the chest and it will be easier for the singer to feel devotion and, thus, be more able to express love.

PART II

SINGING WITH THE NOTE FROM HEAVEN

NOTE NAMES

Many Western schools use the tonic sol-fa/solfège system of naming musical notes: Do, Re, Mi, Fa, Sol, La, Si, Do. In India, they have corresponding names:

SA RE GHA MA PA DHA NI SȦ

Both scales correspond to a major scale (refer to track 11 on the practice download). Singing the note names helps you become conscious of tonal intervals.

It is easier to attract an animal if you know its name. The cow is no longer just a cow; it is a specific cow, named (say) Bessie. All cows can become specific cows, if we choose to have a relationship with them. The same is true for musical notes; in fact, it is the same for anything we become deeply interested in. By naming the notes, we get a conscious and, therefore, personal relationship to something as intangible as sound.

The location of specific vowels in the body

Since the Indian note names are mostly based on the sound 'Aaar', it is healthy to sing them in the speech register, which is the range of notes that mainly resonate in the torso. Do, Re, Mi ... 'Oooh' and 'Eeeh' are related, in terms of vibration, to the throat and head, which means it is easiest to express them with a free-flowing sound in the higher registers (falsetto and middle-range registers).

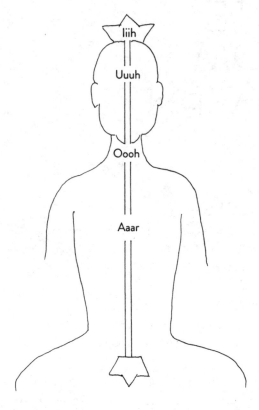

The location of particular vowels in the body in relation to where they resonate.

The illustration represents my experience of how sounds, vowels and body resonate together.

The deeper and slower a sound vibrates, the lower it resonates in the body.

Men with a good bass are usually down to earth and rarely considered 'flighty'. A deep voice has a soothing effect because it connects us to our roots, our foundation. Therefore, 'Aaar' is the spoken sound that vibrates most easily in the lower parts of the body, at a lower pitch. Other systems claim that 'Uuuh' belongs there. That is true, if you're talking about the over- and undertones of the sound. However, that is another matter.

For our purposes, the preferred vowels are 'Aaar' at the bottom, 'Oooh' or 'Uuuh' in the mid-range and throat, and 'Uuuh', 'Eeeh' and 'Iiih' in the falsetto, the third eye and crown.

The remaining vowels are also useful and necessary in soundscanning, and in the language we use in everyday singing and speech. However, we will disregard them in this first book, since they are more difficult to sing in a relaxed way. The body very seldom uses these other vowels in animated outbursts. 'Aaay', 'Uehh' and 'Eeem' are not usually very powerful and mostly relate to mental activity. 'Oorr' is close to 'Aaar', but is more closed and resigned in its expression. Some people have difficulty in singing 'Aaar' and subconsciously switch over to 'Oorr'.

When it comes to it, most of us find it easier to complain than to worship.

DEEPENING THE VOICE

In the classical North Indian *dhrupad* singing tradition, there is a rule about not singing higher than your root note for the first five years of practice. My Indian singing teacher, Mangala Tiwari, reassured me with this information when I asked her why she wanted me to sing as low as possible. It was simply in order to deepen my voice.

In ancient Indian singing it is a matter of getting the Sa *below* the root note Sa to ring out freely – that is, the note one octave below an already rather deep note.

When you are able to do this, your sound can also travel upwards freely. This is because your vocal cords relax completely when you make the deepest sound you can. As the vocal cords become free of tension, they become more flexible. The sound can, therefore, resound more freely when you raise it to the mid-range. The same is true of a rubber band or a guitar string. When the band or string is stretched, the sound gets higher, and when it is slackened the sound becomes deeper.

That is why it is worth beginning by developing the voice in a downward direction. You might say that we let the voice develop a strong, well-developed root system, which will help it absorb nourishment and grow big and strong.

Stretch your voice downwards at the beginning of each singing session, and especially in the morning if you want to reach really far down. (I touch on this only briefly on the practice download, because the depth to which people's voices can go varies greatly.)

How low can you go?

This exercise is for training your voice to go as low as possible. However, be careful not to push it beyond its limits.

- Imagine your voice as a rubber band that you stretch in a soft glide from the root note and downwards.
- Find a deeper note to glide down to and repeat the glide until it feels light and good.
- Then stretch it down a little further. Gently massage the deep notes by breathing fervour into them with your song. If it feels comfortable to sing the deep notes for a long time, then by all means do so.
- When you have reached the limit and your voice sounds like a hollow rustling in the trees, stop pushing yourself any further.
- If this depth exercise gives you problems, it could be possible, especially if you are a man, that your root note is wrongly placed at note A. In that case, refer back to the root note section on page 34.

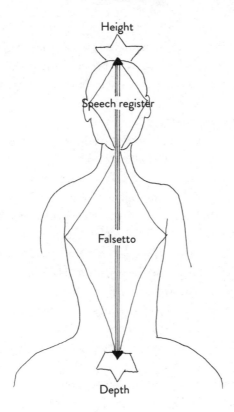

The pitch of the tone of a sound dictates where in the body the sound's resonance will be felt. The deeper the tone (the coarser the vibration), the further down in the body it is felt. The higher the tone (the finer the vibration), the higher up in the body/head it is felt.

Using the Note from Heaven to build up your voice

On the practice download first one note is sung (Sa), then two notes (Sa, Re), then three notes, etc., up to nine notes. The idea is to work one track at a time. For example, sing the combination of Sa and Re until:

- You are sure of how the note names function in relation to their specific tone.
- You have experienced the Note from Heaven spreading from Sa to Re.
- You are able to sing Sa and Re combinations on your own supported by the tanpura (track 21).

After that, you add the next track to what you have already worked with. Give each track the time it needs. Whether that be hours or weeks, do not hurry, because if you do your house will be built on a shaky foundation.

Example of a work method

Sing together with, for example, track 3 on the download, where the singing of the Sa and Re combination is led.

Repeat this track until the two note names have become second nature, which means the singing and the location of the sound feels natural, change to track 21 on the practice download. Sing exclusively to the tanpura accompaniment. If this feels difficult, return to track 3. By singing with the tanpura alone, you can really listen to yourself. It is here that the final expansion of the Note from Heaven, for example from Sa to Re, takes place. The expansion occurs when you sing on 'Aaar' and keep an awareness of the note names in the back of your mind at the same time. As with the examples of singing on the download, this is maintained by alternately singing the same phrases using the note names and on 'Aaar'.

By gliding from one note to another as slowly as possible, the opening through which the Note from Heaven reverberates can be expanded. Put yourself into slow motion during this process, because this will lengthen the pathway between the two chosen notes. The longer the pathway, the more details you can experience. The microtones begin to appear during this attentive listening. It is important to let go of the stairway perception of notes. Perceive Sa and Re as two points between which the voice draws an elastic line. The function of the note names is solely to define the working area, from one point to another point.

While working, you move smoothly into a heartfelt, floating state. It can be compared to caressing the notes as gently as you can.

I see the process as similar to making a hole in a frozen lake. The moment when the Note from Heaven breaks through is like pounding a hole in the middle of the ice. After that, it is important to expand the hole by softly melting it with utmost care. If we go too quickly, the ice breaks and we lose control of our work.

INDIAN NOTE NAMES

In the following section, I will give examples of experiences I have had with the individual notes. As mentioned earlier, these experiences have occurred as I slowly and gradually worked my way through the basic scale: Sa Re Gha Ma Pa Dha Ni. In Indian music theory, there are countless versions, and as many interpretations as there are authors, of what the tension values of these notes represent. One system perceives the intervals of the scale, which are always measured out from the root note, as corresponding to different animal sounds; in another system they correspond to different human organs, and so on. I don't think it really matters which version you follow. The main function of these stories is to inspire the singer. Therefore, it can be beneficial to create your own stories or visualizations for each note. By developing a subjective relationship to the notes, you can forget yourself. This is what lifts the music up to a spiritual level.

The subjective relationship is a type of converter, through which the otherwise indefinable sound can be captured and studied. The following description of my note experiences is completely subjective. It is only included to give you an idea of what this is all about. Please do not treat the explanations as rules that need to be learned by heart. The only important thing is that you become inspired to explore your own relationship to the notes. If it is difficult at first, by all means choose some elements from my experiences and draw on these until you begin to get your own ideas. As mentioned earlier, it is important to proceed slowly, note by note.

Sa

In Indian terminology, Sa is called 'the human sound'. Sa is an abbreviation of the name Shadja. Sa is the root note and can be any sound that suits your voice. So it is not predetermined at C, as Do is in the French sol-fa system.

When we establish a Sa, we decide on a starting point (for example, A) and tune the tanpura's strings accordingly. A field of tension is created with the help of the tanpura's drone.

To rest in Sa gives a feeling of being relaxed and well. You feel at home, because you 'agree' with the tanpura, since Sa is the tone quality of the tanpura.

If on the other hand you sing other notes, different qualities of tension will arise that clearly do not feel like 'home'.

In meditation and healing, Sa symbolizes the root chakra and is associated with the colour red.

A tanpura is an Indian stringed instrument. It normally has four strings and is made mainly from a half calabash, wood and a bridge of bone or ivory. The first string is tuned to Pa (fifth), the two middle ones to Sa (root note), and the last string to Sa. In some ragas/scales however, the first string is tuned to either Dha (sixth) or Ma (fourth).

The tanpura is used as a drone accompaniment by both singers and instrumentalists in enharmonic styles (i.e. where the harmony does not change).

The sound of the tanpura is loaded with overtones, which are created with the help of threads placed exactly where the string rests on the slightly arched bridge.

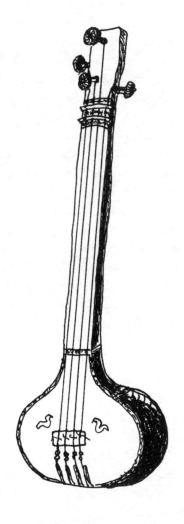

Re

This is the second note. In the major scale, Re is like the first step away from home (Sa), where everything is safe and peaceful.

Re is outgoing, like a traveller seeking new horizons. Still, you are not so far away from home that you cannot immediately change your mind and rest safely in Sa again.

There is an uplifted and timeless anticipation in Re: what is waiting out there in the future?

Re is an abbreviation for the name Rishabha, which means the big second (tonal interval).

In meditation and healing, Re symbolizes the solar plexus chakra and is associated with the colour orange.

Gha

This is the third note. In the major scale, which is sung on the practice download, my experience of Gha is similar to admiring a beautiful view. Via Re we come to a magnificent valley in glorious sunshine.

Do not hold yourself back when singing Gha (the big third). Many students hold back on this note. This may be a sign of low self-esteem. It seems as if the student is silently telling himself or herself: 'No, I don't deserve the many blessings of life. I will hang my head and hold myself back.'

Allowing yourself to believe that you do deserve all the best, the most beautiful, the most wonderful in the world will quickly cause Gha to compete in radiance with the sun. The tone becomes silvery and very moving.

Generally, Gha is the determining factor as to whether we sing in major or minor. It sets the trend for the tonality of the whole scale. The scale becomes major when Gha is big (*shud*, pure) and minor when Gha is lowered by a semitone (komal).

In Indian music there are microtones. If you sing Gha in minor and then lower it slightly further, the expression and feeling of the scale or melody changes noticeably. It becomes more serious, heavy, sorrowful.

If, on the other hand, you sing the minor third Gha a little sharper than it normally is in the minor key, then the expression becomes one of a sweet longing or weeping. In addition, the minor third symbolizes the feminine, introversion and the moon, and the major third represents the masculine, extroversion and the sun. A whole scale can become coloured by feminine or masculine energy merely from the tension around the third. Gha's important role in defining the tonality of a scale can be explained by the note's symbolic location in our body: the solar plexus, the centre of emotions. The colour of this centre is yellow and can be connected to Gha.

Ma

This is the fourth note in the scale and is called the fourth in Western terminology. Ma is an abbreviation for the name Madhyama. In my experience you cannot really rest at Ma. Ma is heartfelt, mystical, a little introverted and aspires both upwards and downwards (notice that it is placed in the middle, just like the heart chakra). The tonal cadence – the three basic chords of harmony-based music (children's songs, pop songs, classical compositions) – is built on Sa (tonic), Ma (subdominant) and Pa (dominant). The combination of these three chords contains all of the notes of the major scale. They are simply the building blocks of harmonic music. In Indian music theory Ma symbolizes the sound of the heart chakra. Ma is flighty and deep like love; she is our mother, 'Mama', and can be connected to the heart chakra's colours, green and pink.

Pa

Now, who would be number five then? Of course it has to be 'Papa', daddy, known in Western terminology as the fifth.

The cycle of fifths (our harmonic system) is actually built on the theme of 'father, mother and child' – Ma (fifth) Sa (fifth) Pa, with the child in the centre. It fits wonderfully well, doesn't it?

In Indian terminology, Pa is associated with the throat chakra. Among other things, this centre represents communication. Pa is the note that, in terms of tension, is closest to Sa. Here you can relax. Using the analogy of a field trip, Pa would be the point at which you would stop to eat your lunch. It can get a little boring to sing for a long time, though, as it lacks Sa's deep inner calm.

Pa is an abbreviation for Panchama and can be connected to the colours sky blue and turquoise.

Dha

Dha is the sixth note of the scale and is called the sixth in Western terminology. It is an abbreviation of the name Dhaivata. Dha is also on its way somewhere, while at the same time remaining in the comforting presence of the less tense Pa.

Just as Sa and Pa share some similarities in their chemistry, so do Re and Dha, although I do experience Dha as more bold than Re is. If we are climbing a mountain on our field trip, then Dha is the note that gets a whiff of the approaching summit. In its major form Dha is curious and upward reaching.

Dha symbolizes the third eye and higher consciousness. The note and centre can be connected to the colours violet and indigo blue.

Ni

Ni is the seventh note and is called the seventh in Western terminology. It is an abbreviation of the Sanskrit name Nishada. As Ni, in its pure form, functions as the note leading to Sa, it is difficult to remain with it. We seek the objective of the field trip, like the person in love longs for their beloved. It takes discipline to explore Ni and not rush through it in a flurry. For some, it can be almost painful to stay with Ni, as it is right next to Sa, the note with which the tanpura continually seduces our ear. Nevertheless, it is a good exercise to stick to your guns and your intentions: 'I will keep my focus, no matter how tempting my surroundings may be.'

You can even come to enjoy the tension in its own right. When it is finally released on the high Sa, at the top of the mountain, then the sensation is that much more powerful. Our field day has a 'happy ending'.

Ni is associated with the crown chakra and the soul. Notice that the 'i' sound makes Ni vibrate at the top of the head, where the seventh chakra is located. The colour is white or violet.

Writing the note names

The row of note names repeats itself endlessly, both upwards and downwards.

When we write notes that lie an octave below the basic scale of Sa, Re, Gha, Ma, Pa, Dha, Ni, one dot is placed under the note, two dots for two octaves lower, and so on. When we write the notes that lie an octave above the basic scale, a corresponding dot is placed above the note concerned. If we need to write down an even higher octave (which is normally not necessary in this context), then we place two dots above the note in question.

In Indian terminology, the lowering of a tone is called *komal*, which is shown with a line under the note in question, and the raising of a tone is called *tivra* and is written with an accent above the relevant note. Only the notes Re, Gha, Dha and Ni can be *komal* and only Ma can be *tivra*.

In this way, the Indian system is identical to the Western twelve-tone system, except that it is more simply expressed in the Indian single-harmony method of writing:

Sa R̲e Re G̲h̲a̲ Gha Ma Má Pa D̲h̲a̲ Dha N̲i̲ Ni

Benefits of the note names

One reason why it is rewarding to sing the note names is that you become aware of how to express yourself through sound. This training of consciousness is not only effective within the discipline of music; it can improve your whole life in the long term. By learning to be conscious of the note names, you can also learn to be conscious of other mechanisms in daily life. Starting out to develop our consciousness with something as innocent as singing is very beneficial because it takes us into an area that is like a playground. It is quite simply fun to sing. If we choose to stick our head straight into the hornet's nest of personal weaknesses and announce, 'Consciousness', we will usually bump into the wall that our subconscious mind has quite properly built to protect us.

In addition, singing on note names is excellent ear training. Knowing how the note names relate to specific tones, helps us to write them down and to read melodic passages. Besides that, note language is great to use in vocal improvisation. Here, the Indian note names sound catchier than sol-fa (Do, Re, Mi ...).

If you try to improvise without being conscious of the note names, the tonal material can get used up long before you manage to establish a true expression of any mood or feeling. By becoming aware of note names, you learn to distinguish the different 'wavelengths' from each other, and so you are able to use the available notes more economically.

With practice, you will not need to think any more. At any one time you will 'know' where you are in the sea of sound. Your ship will be the tanpura's constant ground note, saying: 'Here you belong, here is your home, take your soundings from me.'

In Israel, I had an immensely talented singer as a student. She sang enchantingly from the first lesson. However, this natural talent actually became a problem for her. The depth got lost. She was used to being able to impress people right away.

With the help of the note names, she learned to improvise, and through that, to tell a story. If a scale aspired upwards towards, for example, the high Sã she could now choose to heighten the tension by weaving around Sã for as long as the sensation felt good, before finally surrendering and letting Sã bring satisfaction. That student's singing gave you goose bumps.

We had some fantastic lessons together and gradually became friends, so that the teacher–student relationship eroded. She slid back again and never really developed her talents properly.

Suddenly one day she decided to live as an orthodox Jew. Nobody in her circle of acquaintances was religious and many people shook their heads ruefully. I did, too. Until the day she sang a religious song at a private wedding ceremony.

There it was again! Goose bumps all over. The tears trickled quietly down my cheeks. She had become religious; she had made a decision that went against her surroundings, and had finally found a structure through which she could breathe. A breakthrough had been made. She sang straight from the heart. Oh, what a joy to hear her sing!

This example shows me that true religious belief and having a conscious relationship with notes have something in common. It's to do with getting closer to authentic expression, deeper into the music. Away from the ego, into the soul. Finding balance between the chaos of feelings and the dictates of the intellect. Disappearing somewhere between these two states, and growing from that place through the music.

SCALE

In this section I will touch on the concept of 'raga'. To gain a true understanding of the raga, first you need to know the note names and their tonal vibrations in your body. If you are reading this book for the first time and have not yet worked with the note names, then feel free to skim over the sentences you do not understand.

The following explanations about the raga concept are partly meant to serve as an appetizer, and partly as an explanation of the Indian tradition's exceptional ability to link sound and emotion.

The primary purpose of this book is to liberate the natural voice. Therefore, it does not cover the raga concept in great detail. Should you wish to explore the subject more deeply, I recommend that you find an Indian song teacher.

What Westerners call a scale is known as a raga in India. However, the term raga also encompasses an overall form in which there is both improvisation and established melodic elements. The raga starts with an A-lap, which is a free improvisation without underlying rhythm, through which the notes of the raga are slowly presented in delicate slides and ornamentations. There is nothing to say exactly how long the A-lap should last. Its main purpose is to enable the musician to find a way to his or her divinity, and through that, to merge with a higher state. It is that aspect of the raga which this book deals with.

In the raga, the A-lap is followed by compositions and rhythmical improvisations that are technically very demanding. Therefore, for inexperienced players, the need to focus on technique can stifle the aspiration to reach a higher state. The tempo gradually increases, until the musician cannot play any faster. If the musician is gifted, this form can express a kind of ecstasy.

The vibration of a scale

In Ravi Shankar's book *My Music, My Life*, the raga is defined as 'that which colours the mind'.

The note is, in itself, a vibration. More notes together create a new vibration, an atmosphere.

Switch yourself on as a listener. You are a sensitive mechanism with thousands of nerves, which come into play like small buttons being pushed.

When there is total silence, the nerves are passive, ready to react to stimulation by any sound. The body is like a white screen. Each note leaves its colour, its form. For example, if a raga has five notes, then five different colours are applied to the screen, five different forms that, by interacting, create even more forms. A picture is created with a particular atmosphere. This atmosphere is dependent on how you combine the colours, and in which order you use them. The nerves are incredibly sensitive to tiny nuances. The aim is to express a feeling in as pure a form as possible by working with a scale whose vibration corresponds to, and thus affects, the relevant nerves. If you grope around among the colours in an unfocused way, the screen will become brown. You have to know the way the colours function in order to get them to glow.

So the Indian raga is not just a scale, but also a set of rules on how to treat the notes in order to express a distinct feeling (colour).

The source of these rules can be found all the way back in the Vedas (ca. 1500 BC).

During my studies in India, I asked Mangala what would happen if I sang one of the notes that is not part of the raga (they are called *vivadi*, or enemies).

'That is very simple,' she replied. 'Then it is another raga.'

I discovered that the rules give scope for deep concentration. They are hard to learn at first. For example, in a specific raga it is not allowed to go straight to Sa (the leading note must not lead directly to the root note) when you are in the lower pitch. There must be five notes in the ascending scale and six in the descending scale. There are special notes, which in certain situations may need a sliding, or a note may need to be sung a microtone above or below it – there are countless variations, depending on which raga you are singing into.

With practice, these rules gradually allow you to create an atmosphere that moves you and feels natural. By repeating a particular pattern of notes until you know it by heart, it becomes a part of you. This very same mechanism applies to the good and bad behavioural patterns that we unconsciously follow every day. We learned them once, but now they are automatic and that is why they feel such a natural part of ourselves.

Learning the feeling of a scale

The raga's *pakad*, or way of singing, is learned by repeating phrases sung by the teacher, and not through analysis and memorizing. It corresponds to a child's parrot fashion learning, which is an extremely quick way to learn languages (refer to tracks 3–10 on the practice download).

Simply by copying the patterns, with no pressure to sing them well, you will find that they automatically become impressed upon your subconscious. At some point, the patterns will have become so sustainable that you can just fall into them and the musical phrases will pour out of your mouth. Suddenly the raga takes you over and its core essence reveals itself to you through a surprising 'a-ha' experience.

It is wonderful to sing, floating around in a raga, to identify with it without being an emotional captive. You are both caught up in your feeling and, at the same time, master of it.

The feeling is legitimate, since it is not attached to any sense of guilt. It is beautiful when purely expressed. Frustrations, rejection, doubt, jealousy – the sides of our life and our self that we do not like – also have quality and can be beautiful. For when feelings are recognized in the raga, their explosiveness is defused and they become harmless.

You can spend your whole life exploring the raga concept, since there are as many ragas as there are nuances of feeling. New ragas (new note combinations) are still being made, in step with the new feelings that developments in society engender.

It is, fundamentally, a heart-searching effort that demands deep reflection and immersion.

The best way to work your way into the raga universe is to learn one raga as thoroughly and as well as possible. That can take several years of work, or, if you have the proper surroundings and can practise four or five hours a day, it can take less time. Some Indian singers practise for up to 12 hours a day. The song is their *dharma*, a way of life.

The raga, a state
Working with ragas, we learn how to disappear into them. The feeling of sliding into the raga, when everything you needed to learn has simply become the raga's soul and no longer needs to be remembered, corresponds to the feeling of the Note from Heaven. You are led to a sense of being present in the moment.

The question of how many ragas you can sing is irrelevant. What counts is what you are able to express from the heart at that particular moment.

In his book *The Mysticism of Music, Sound and Word*, Sufi master Hazrat Inayat Khan describes a sitar player who always played the same raga when he gave concerts. People were deeply moved and came to his performances again and again.

One day he was asked why he always played the same raga. 'Why should I play another raga, when I can play this one perfectly?' he answered.

That which touches the heart is never boring.

We come up against the same truth again and again. It is the essence that is important, not the story itself.

Common Western ragas
The major scale, which is presented on the practice download (see page 5), is familiar to most people in the Western world. The majority of our songs are written in the major mode, with fewer in the minor.

Examples of songs in the major scale: 'Row, row, row your boat', 'Happy birthday to you', 'For he's a jolly good fellow', 'Oh Susanna', 'What a wonderful world' ...

Examples of songs in the minor scale: 'Summertime', 'Greensleeves', 'Scarborough Fair' ...

So the scale is already familiar, which makes it easier to concentrate on listening to yourself. On the other hand, the weakness with this scale choice is that the note language is so straightforward.

The experience of 'being taken over' by a raga in the major scale can be difficult to provoke, because we are working without rules while dealing with a scale that does not have that many levels or facets to explore.

In India, the major scale is called *bilawal*. It is not used very much in classical northern Indian music. When I asked one classical northern Indian musician about *bilawal*, he told me he found it boring.

However, it is used a lot in Indian folk music where the theme is usually religious as, for example, in *bhajans*.

To compare Western and Indian note language is interesting, because it says something about our cultures. The use of keys in the West stays within a moderate number of scales, mostly in the major mode. The major is positive and we can hold problems at bay with a happy song. The question, however, is whether we can solve them with 'oompa oompa' rhythms and 'tra la la'.

In India, there are ragas that are suited to the seasons and to special occasions. They might, for example, use a particular raga when they need to call forth rain.

Even so, a raga or scale is normally associated with a particular time of the day. The major scale is associated with noon, when the sun is warm and high in the sky.

At this time there is no tension between light and dark. The light, the masculine power, has taken over. In cooler climates such as in northern Europe, a preference for the major scale could therefore be explained by a need for optimism in order to withstand grey, dark weather. This is hardly true of India, if one's state of mind is to be measured by the hours of sunshine.

Other scales

If you want to set about learning other scales to express different emotions, then I recommend you first go through this basic material. Later, it will be easy to change the scale, because the note names are already integrated. Perhaps you do not feel comfortable working with the major scale. Maybe you harmonize better, for example, with an introverted, intense atmosphere. In that case, the basic work can also be done using the minor scale.

When looking for the small nuances in our sound, we cannot be humble enough. Therefore, it is important to start with a scale that is relatively easy to handle. The degree of difficulty should be low enough not to impede the sense of well-being we derive from the musical experience.

Quality is found where the soul sings and the ego sleeps.

Scale exercises

Do not attempt the exercises outlined in tracks 12–20 of the practice download (see pages 96–99) until you are ready for them. The basic scale (track 11) is useful for everyone to memorize forwards and backwards at the beginning, whereas the rest of the exercises could be overwhelming for a beginner.

The exercises break the major scale into different mathematical patterns. These are very similar to the exercises that are known in both the classical and rhythmical schools of Western music. Feel free to make up your own combinations, if you want to.

Since we are now moving into the dangerous area of technique, it is exceptionally important to play with – and get into the spirit of – these tonal figures, rather than becoming addicted to a mechanical recitation of note names and sounds. For example, you could imagine yourself verbally explaining something to a person while practising.

The aim of learning the scale patterns is to stamp them onto your subconscious mind. Then these patterns can be naturally combined and grow into the melodic phrases of an improvised passage.

By singing the note names, you can train your consciousness to recognize the relationship between the notes, while also practising intonation and attack. Always work at a slow enough tempo that you can work accurately, avoiding mistakes of pronunciation and intonation. The brain is totally naïve in nature – it records all the information that it receives. If we record an incorrect piece of information, this error is hard to overwrite, which is why we tend to repeat the same mistakes over and over. Consequently, it is highly beneficial to work patiently at a much slower pace than we think we can handle.

After 10 or 20 correct repetitions, you can try to see if your technique holds at an increased pace. If there is just the slightest touch of hesitation in your expression, please return to the original tempo. And when you build up your own tonal pattern, avoid jumps that are too large or difficult between notes. They will be hard to express naturally in an improvisational context later.

By always repeating the scale exercises on 'Aaar', you will train the flexibility and the intonation of your voice. Just as it is possible to write with a pen without lifting it from the paper, the voice can express a long, unbroken line when it moves between the notes of 'Aaar' on an exhalation. It is an undulating movement, which is reflected in the visible up and down movement of the throat. This sliding angle of attack on the notes will, when sung at a fast tempo, result in a vibrato created solely in the throat. In Indian singing, this technique is called *gamak* and it is explained further on page 97.

PART III

CREATIVE MUSIC-MAKING

IMPROVISATION

Improvisation is the natural next step after you have learned to express
yourself in note language. We speak in notes. Everyone can improvise
– it is merely a question of adjustment and of rejecting the ego's fear of
surrendering to the divine.

When we connect to the Note from Heaven in our improvisation, the
sounds mingle without interference from the ego. When this succeeds
and is recorded, we hear the most beautiful melodies. Usually, the person
who sang them cannot remember what he or she expressed, which is
not surprising as the most beautiful melodies arise when we are 'lost'
in the moment. We are 'gone' in that state, and afterwards can seldom
recall more than that something good just happened. By perceiving
improvisation in that way, the improviser is prepared to let something else
sing through him or her. To create in the present moment means taking
a chance, jumping into an abyss, abandoning all self-restraint, making
room for the manifestation and birth of a divine expression. Mozart seems
to have worked in this way. He composed as if he were dictating straight
from heaven. The incredible number of notes he managed to write in his
short life (he was just 35 when he died) supports this theory.

Addiction to notes

I believe that the reason why so many Western musicians, including the most highly educated, feel inhibited when asked to take a creative, improvisational approach to music is that they depend so much on reading music.

When we sing or play melodies from notation, we are seeking to breathe life into what, hopefully, has been the composer's experience of a divine moment. The notes are the skeleton, which we then reanimate with flesh and blood.

The melodies that continue to inspire us, despite the changing styles of music over time, have, much like crystals, a clear and balanced design that somehow does us good. Some melodies make us share the emotions the composer experienced, when the holy fruit fell into his or her lap.

However, if you only play or sing music that has already been written you will not necessarily recognize and find your own divinity.

We tend to idolize fellow human beings whom we perceive to be geniuses. But then we feel inadequate in comparison.

The commandment 'Have no other gods than me' is vital in this context. It is all too easy to just give up on yourself and feel incompetent in the shadow cast by a brilliant person. It is like idolizing a guru who has developed a high level of consciousness. You can learn a lot from that kind of person, but idolizing someone else can prevent you from finding the same elements within yourself.

An authentic model of inspiration or guru does not need to be adored. Such a person knows that he or she is just a channel for a higher power and bows down in honour of this divine miracle.

When individuals express themselves, the expression is a mirror of their innermost self. Therefore, it serves no purpose to look at someone else's expression and compare it to our own. Doing that has a stagnating and limiting effect. We end up whispering to ourselves, 'I am not good enough,' or, 'Wow, look how good I am compared to ... '

In creative work, we express ourselves through, and thus train ourselves to unite with, the same channel used by the Note from Heaven, and by being inspired we surrender to the present moment and thus to the divine power within us. When a perfectly ripe fruit falls into our lap in the form of a poem, a melody, a painting, an idea etc., that which, paradoxically, makes us happiest is being moved and stimulated by a higher power. It is the deep-seated driving force behind all creativity – a yearning for divine expression, a yearning to vanish along with our ego and thus experience our soul as complete and from a higher world.

Considering that we all have the seeds of perfection within us, it is amazing how often we put obstacles in our own, and other people's, path.

During my studies at the Royal Academy of Music, I sensed, despite all my many positive musical experiences there, a constricted energy visible in the pale, anaemic faces of many of the students. I myself felt as if I were suffocating. The creative aspect was missing and it is definitely not a priority in most public institutions of classical music in Europe.

The experience of your own divinity is a great gift. It teaches you always to be daring in your musical expression. You can then fully understand what composers were feeling and the power they were channelling.

Without this understanding, the notes are nothing more than a series of small instructions, which first the eyes obey and then the ears hear: 'Did I read that right, it sounded funny, didn't it? Oh, yes, that was correct.' We blindly follow the orders and play correctly in order to please the ego, while feeling dissatisfied by any mistakes that we make. The childhood experience of conditional love and the associated fear of failure gets good soil to grow in when working in this way with notes. Consequently, our entire musical development ends up on the wrong track, and music becomes more of a battle of nerves than a surrendering to something higher.

All this gradually became clear to me when I took a period of sabbatical leave from the Academy and was introduced to Indian singing, where improvisation is the actual challenge and the written compositions function like small islands you can rest on while developing the nature of the raga through improvisation. According to the Indian tradition, the indisputable purpose of music is union with God.

Composition

As mentioned in previous sections, melodies can arise in improvisation. These moments of sudden beauty appear spontaneously and unexpectedly. We can all compose, if we allow ourselves the freedom to do so.

A recording is the best witness you can have when improvising a composition. Since the composition arises in the moment and vanishes afterwards, the singer is not usually able to remember it.

Another way to compose is to put text to music. I often use this form of composition with students, since it is clear-cut and easy to do. Everyone ends up writing a song, even those who resist at the beginning.

The interesting thing is that, by speaking a sentence out, you can sense how to direct the melody. It is a matter of relaxing and letting what comes come, while at the same time noticing whether it feels right.

In order to remember the song, it needs to be recorded in pieces, sentence by sentence. I know from experience that we tend to overestimate our ability to remember melodic phrases. Since they are part of the moment, they evaporate like morning dew. Always record every finished phrase, singing the song from the beginning to see if it 'stimulates' the later sentences. Then record the new part that is added and continue like that until the melody is finished. If you play an instrument, it is possible to have a coherent memory of the melody, due to the support from the underlying harmonies.

Sometimes when you are in the middle of some activity, a melody you have never heard before will suddenly come into your head. If this happens, drop everything you are doing and record it right away. If you are good at note language, writing the song down in note names could be an option. If you consider yourself tone deaf you will need help from a teacher. It is difficult to hold on to a melody when you're not sure about the notes. The teacher can sing or play back the student's melodic phrases and in that way, the student can correct any tonal misunderstandings.

Tone deafness

Funnily enough, those people who believe they are tone deaf have repeatedly surprised themselves, and me, by composing some excellent songs. Maybe this is because a self-declared tone-deaf individual has nothing to lose. Therefore, there is no reason to try to impress anyone. This eliminates the ego's influence, which leaves room for suggestions from the soul to break through.

In most cases, a tone-deaf person can sing their own melody in tune, because he or she has created it. Through that process, they have set their own parameters and, therefore, worked without being influenced by preconceptions as to what they should achieve.

As a result, the process of composing strengthens the student's self-confidence and reveals the source of the tone deafness as primarily psychological and fear-based.

Creativity generates a 'self' confidence that unfolds through the experience of inspiration, a word that derives from the Latin *in spiritu* – '*in the spirit*'.

CHILDREN, ADULTS AND VOICES

It is not surprising that presumed tone deafness or feeling inhibited about using one's voice, whether when singing or communicating, originates, in most cases, from childhood experiences.

For us as adults there are a lot more sources of noise than in the past. In addition to obstructers like the radio, washing machine, TV, stereo, etc., there is an abundance of electrical installations that influence us with radiation of microwaves inaudible to the ear.

Nevertheless, our nervous system picks up all these vibrations and gets irritated by them. The fact that we increasingly work indoors, sitting in front of screens such as computers, iPhones and iPads, reinforces radically the constant vibrational influence on the body and its energy field.

Then, when we spend time out in nature, far away from all sources of artificial noise, we discover that the body, quite inexplicably, calms down. We breathe a sigh of relief, or maybe even feel slightly uneasy in the silence if we are confirmed city-dwellers.

Our body and energy field suffer noise pollution in everyday life, so our level of noise tolerance declines. There does not need to be much noise before it almost physically pains us.

Children have a need to get to know themselves. That is why they experiment. The voice is a wonderful toy. The adult's understanding of the child, and the way the child expresses itself vocally, is enormously important, since the basis of the child's relationship to its voice is established in the first years. It is not only about singing in tune. It is also about maintaining contact with the higher centres in the head, which among other things connect the child to its intuition and self-confidence. If the child is forbidden to use the voice for experimentation, the body will seek to compensate for the blockage in the flow of energy in the throat.

Then, the energy can only flow freely in the five lower chakras and this pent-up energy will try to express itself through bursts of anger, nervousness, crying, violent behaviour, apathy, hyperactivity or screaming and yelling, which are the lower chakras' way of communicating. Thus, a vicious circle is created, caused by the adult's misunderstanding of the child's attitude. Try to imagine that you are doing something that feels good and completely right, and then someone tells you that what you are doing is wrong.

Let us say, for example, that you have been sitting singing and are totally absorbed in the Note from Heaven and then someone interrupts with, 'What are you screaming for?' or 'Stop that noise!'

How will you react to that? In many cases, a blockage will occur, because, when you have just surrendered yourself to the moment while singing, you are in a completely soft and open state, like an infant. At the very least, the response will have a negative effect, even though, with our adult intellect, we can rationalize the situation and understand that our hinderer didn't understand what we were engaged in.

Children sing the Note from Heaven quite spontaneously. Small, healthy, natural voices fill and rip through a room with their vitality. When my sons were young and I had students at home, I could her them singing along in the distance. Children love to sing long notes on 'Aaar'.

In the early years, children see their parents as gods. If we tell them to keep their mouth shut when they are in the middle of truly loving their own voices, their self-confidence becomes damaged. What can they trust, if their own evaluation of what feels good is wrong? Experimenting with one's own voice becomes tinged with guilt.

You don't need to just swallow your irritation and let your children be noisy. The idea is to subdue the noisiness in a constructive way by listening to the child's sound and then communicating on an equal footing, if not through language, then through sound.

With regard to the infant years of both my sons, I have experienced how happy babies become when you understand their sounds correctly. A sound based on an understanding of what the child is doing when they scream, for example, is strengthened by the listening work described in this book. You learn to sense and listen intuitively to whether the child is really sad, angry, setting limits... or just playing with its voice. Parents ought to use their instincts, and just take the time to stop and listen attentively to the child's sound, rather than immediately reacting with irritation and trying to quieten the child down.

The trick is to give the child the stimulation that the sound calls for.

Calming a noisy child

If a child is screaming for no apparent reason, you can assume that the child is playing with his or her voice. To calm the child down, I would lift him or her up in front of the mirror and try to copy their sound without ridiculing them in any way. By seeking the child's sound, I tune into his or her level of consciousness and, through that attitude, develop a true acceptance of the unfolding of the child's voice. I try to hit the note the child is expressing and after a while draw it up and down in slides with my voice.

The child will do the same, as children love to imitate. When that exploration has been exhausted, you can make the notes break into a melody that the child is fond of and then you are singing a song together, after which the child will very likely become interested in playing with something else. This method is also effective for situations where the child takes a small tumble and starts crying.

A method for calming children who are able to talk is to let them know that you are sensitive to sound right now, and would like some quiet time. Maybe suggest that they scream outside, but say clearly that you know how much fun it is to use your voice in this way.

In general, singing has a calming effect on people, which is why we sing lullabies. So perhaps doctors and nurses should learn a repertoire of songs to suit different types of patients.

Our son broke his leg when he was two and did not like getting his cast cut off by a noisy, vibrating and rotating knife blade. Both we and the medical staff were worried that a trauma might develop. To cover up the noise and the crying, we started singing his favourite children's song with all our strength. The doctor and nurse joined in spontaneously. He stopped crying in sheer amazement at this meeting of his own fear and the festive spirit of the singing. It was a beautiful experience to stand there and sing together with these two people in their white coats. The masks and barriers completely vanished. Our son still whimpered, but the worst of the fear had been warded off by the singing and, in the meantime, the cast was being cut through and removed.

Understanding through imitation

Why do we find it so funny when a comedian imitates a well-known person's voice?

It seems to me that what makes us laugh is that we can so clearly sense the character of a person through the vocal caricature. Children constantly copy voices in the first years. Not only do they learn language in that way, they also acquire knowledge about their parents' personality. Children perceive a grown-up's 'tone' of speaking and integrate it subconsciously into their own personality. It is, therefore, not so strange that in later life you discover traits from your parents in yourself, traits that you thought you had left behind long ago. These character traits, which are learned through intuitive intonation, are well embedded in our behavioural patterns, whether we want them to be or not.

Essentially, we learn undesirable behaviour patterns through active listening. The good news is that we can also listen them away again. This is what happens when we work with the Note from Heaven. It enables us to experience an opening, a glimpse of ourselves in full bloom. After that, it is entirely up to us whether we wish to express our true self through our voice. When the voice opens up and becomes increasingly natural and active, negative behaviour patterns break up while, at the same time, corresponding expressions of sound in the voice disappear. The fewer inhibiting behaviour patterns, the more flexibility and freedom can be experienced, both in the sound of the voice, and in the mind and body.

CREATIVE TEXT WRITING

All inspiration comes from the same source, the higher self. As a channel of the higher self, the Note from Heaven can be recognized in all creative work. Just as it is valid in improvisation and composition to let something higher sing through you, the same is true for writing texts.

The only thing you need is a certain level of writing ability, combined with an openness to believe in your higher self. Just like singing the Note from Heaven, it is a matter of opening, opening, opening... in order to give space, let go of your need for control and drop every judgmental attitude.

You can capture a particular emotional experience and express it in words that evoke that experience every time you read those words. When the words are also put to music, the effect becomes even stronger. This makes the creative process an excellent tool for self-understanding and self-examination.

You don't need to write a cogent account if you don't want to, although that is one valid approach. You could end up writing a series of images that make no sense at all at first. However, by looking closer, you may find that they reflect your reality, rather like a dream does.

The story itself is unimportant. It is the fact that we are developing our consciousness that matters.

There are myriad approaches. I am suggesting one possible course of action to get you started if you are not used to writing.

An approach to creative text writing

- Sit in your singing position. It is important to keep the spine straight so the body's energy can flow freely.

- Have a pen in your hand and a piece of paper or cardboard within reach so you will be able to write as soon as the words come.
- Close your eyes. Breathe air into the sacral chakra (*hara*, a hand's width below the navel) and press the stomach gently inwards with each exhalation.
- Concentrate on your third eye. If there are thoughts, let them remain there. Open the space in the third eye outwards like ripples in water. Let each thought float in its own ring. There is stillness in the centre. Try to stay there.
- When you feel peaceful in your mind (perhaps like a silent helicopter with so many thoughts rotating and disappearing out to the periphery and yourself resting in the peaceful emptiness of the centre), move your awareness down to the *hara*.
- Let the third eye fuse together with the *hara*. It is as if your body is disappearing between the two centres. It is a wonderful feeling.
- Sense the two centres' collective space. Observe the space. Ask to have some words sent.
- The words can come in the form of pictures or feelings. Describe what you see or feel. If there is something you want to know more about, ask and wait, observing the space.
- Seize the inspiration when it comes, write and don't hold back. It is up to you whether you do so with open or closed eyes.
- Take a break when you have emptied your mind. Later you can go over the material and make any necessary adjustments to ensure it makes sense to you. Usually, you will develop a fuller understanding of the written work during the editing.

If you want to put the text to music, go back to the section on composition on page 72. When processing text into music, be prepared to polish the material further, as the rhythmical relationships between the words are of greater importance here.

PERFORMANCE

When you find a form of expression that brings you joy, you will naturally wish to share it with other people. This is a spiritual law: joy is like fire. When you pass it on and it is accepted, it spreads. To experience giving yourself and being gladly received is a basic human wish. Such an experience can change our lives fundamentally. It strengthens our self-worth, affirms that we have something to offer to others, affirms, in fact, that we have a mission here on earth. Therefore, a successful performance can be a great boost, especially if our relationship to our voice has been warped by repeated unfortunate experiences.

As mentioned in the section on performance anxiety, the danger with performance is that the ego can take control. It craves the applause from which it gains a false sense of self-confidence. An authentically successful performance is, therefore, one in which the soul is strong enough to outshine the ego.

By experiencing situations that call for the best in us (the soul, the higher self, the divine), we can learn to recognize the difference between control by the ego and control by the soul. Above all, when we are governed by the soul, time seems to disappear, the words and sounds flow naturally from our lips, we feel warmed and touched deep in our hearts, and we are overwhelmed by a feeling of devotion, joy and safety. The more the soul has the chance to influence us through such experiences, the stronger its hold on us will be. That is why it is good to sing the Note from Heaven for hours. The soul will eventually overwhelm us with its irresistible power of love.

Sometimes students drop the Note from Heaven before they have completely absorbed it into their body, and switch to a familiar, well-known song. The voice, which was free-sounding and whole before, all at once sounds meek and fearful. This is because the familiar song represents the world we were born into, including all the old behaviour patterns, which are what create performance anxiety and a feeling of unworthiness – 'Just who do you think you are?' we ask ourselves.

It is possible to transfer the effect of the Note from Heaven into a familiar melody, but to achieve this you need to have become convinced, deep down in your heart, of your own divine power. This is because we are most beautiful in our natural form. Sing the song as it is without adding artifices and extra frills. Let it live, fill it out; let it lead you to the Note from Heaven. Be the song instead of performing it.

Singing for each other in a group is the very best way to train performance while allowing the soul's message to come through. This audience is conscious of the forces the performer has to deal with – if the ego wins, it is no defeat, because everyone present understands what it is like to deal with the mechanisms of the ego.

You can keep on trying, and when you finally succeed in singing from the heart, everyone receives a great gift. An atmosphere of devotion descends upon the room because everyone present has been deeply touched and, quite frankly, healed. Sacred moments like this are charged with a natural, loving atmosphere and complete calm, which in daily life can only be maintained by faith – an inner conviction, whose function is to preserve the essence of those moments in which we have felt blissfully whole and well-functioning.

Experiences like that happen spontaneously. They do not arise from talking to others about our inner truth, so maybe we would do better to stop talking and start singing instead. Song is a beautiful way to communicate, because no one is betrayed. Its power is unmistakable and it makes no wars. It gently sprinkles its loving frisson onto us all, cutting across all barriers.

The trees, the snow, the sky, the silence of nature. I, a tree, stretch my arms up towards the sky's milky-white arch and touch a moment of eternity. My heart becomes suffused with gratitude.

EPILOGUE

Tree

Tree you are me.
I am a tree,
Each of your leaves'
green lights relieve believe in me.
Under your crown 'I' becomes 'We',
A sceptre of love,
A bridge to eternity.

Tree you are me.
I am a smile,
Open to be –
two eyes one sight burning to Thee.
Inside your crown an embryo grows,
A sceptre of fire,
A key to divinity.

Tree you are me.
We are one,
A moon and a sun,
a miracle where the end has begun.
Over your crown a union of light,
A sceptre of truth,
Balance the day, bless the night.

Githa Ben-David, 2013

APPENDIX

PHYSICAL EXERCISES

Face

Exercise 1

Make faces and hold each grimace for a few seconds. Feel free to include the tongue in your creations.

Exercise 2

- Do lip rolls, quick vibrating movements with your lips, so that you sound like a helicopter or a snorting horse. Make the movement as relaxed as possible, both with and without song sounds.
- When you have got your lips vibrating easily, it will not be long before other facial muscles become involved. After about five minutes, the nose begins to vibrate. It is a simple way to give yourself a facial massage.
- If it is difficult to vibrate your lips, try pressing the corners of your mouth together with the index fingers. Another possibility is to splutter explosively, similar to a baby spluttering its food. You might want to hold your hands in front of your mouth to avoid spitting everywhere!

Just a few rolls are enough to get a sense of the exercise. Then practice whenever possible. It can be fun to do when driving or cycling, for example. Sooner or later the jaw muscles loosen up and the lip roll becomes relaxed.

Exercise 3

- Tongue rolls vibrate further down in the throat. Roll your tongue while you sing through the whole register of notes. Be sure that the tongue rolls lightly up against the hard palate. It is easiest to start further back. Not everyone can make tongue rolls. If you have problems, exercises 5–8 may help.

Neck and throat
Exercise 4

- Head rolls, as done in yoga. The whole exercise is done to a gentle and, preferably, very slow tempo. Tilt the head to the right, then to the left five times. Breathe in deeply with each stretch, and feel the muscles letting go with each exhalation.
- In the same way, let the head go forwards and backwards, five times in each direction. Note that in these initial stretches, you can support your head with your hands, especially if you have a weak neck or back.
- Now turn your head in gentle, slow circles or half-circles, whichever is more comfortable. There are some people for whom it is not advisable to turn their head in complete circles, as this can injure the vertebrae in the neck. Repeat the movement five times in each direction.
- After this, breathe in deeply through the nose. Hold your breath, then while lifting the right shoulder up to the right ear, breathe out. Do the same with the left shoulder. At the end, lift both shoulders up at the same time and release them on an exhalation.

Tongue, jaws and neck

Exercise 5

- Hold the tongue in the right side of the mouth as long as it feels comfortable, relax and do the same on the left side.
- Stretch the tongue as far backwards as possible and hold the stretch while looking upwards with eyes closed. Relax.
- Stretch the tongue out of your mouth as far as possible, while looking upwards with eyes open. Relax.

Exercise 6

- Make circles in the air with the tongue in both directions. Stretch the tongue down, hold the position, then upwards towards the nose, hold. Relax.
- Make the eternity symbol – a horizontal 8 – in the air with your tongue. It is also possible to do this exercise inside the mouth. Relax.

Exercise 7

- Write your full name in italics in the air using the tip of your nose. You can imagine that you have attached a little pencil there. Notice the pleasant sensation in your neck.

Exercise 8

- Massage the joints of your jaw and feel free to grunt and make baby sounds at the same time. The jaw joints, or hinges as they are also called, can be found by opening and closing your mouth and, at the same time, placing your fingertips in front of your earlobes.
- After that, massage your jaw muscles. Do this vigorously with both hands. Start from the middle of each jaw, then draw the muscle out to both sides – up towards the ear and down towards the chin at the same time.
- Try to yawn. Note that the temples are activated as well. The fine muscles that attach the jaws to each other are to be found here. Therefore, massage these small indentations with your thumbs as well.

Shoulders, neck, chest and spine

Exercise 9

- Stand with your feet shoulders' width apart with loose knees. Breathe in through your nose and stretch your right arm up along your ear and backwards, while following it with your eyes. Allow your arm to continue describing a backward circle while breathing out.
- Repeat with your left arm.
- Roll both arms backwards and let your neck fall all the way back while breathing in through the nose. Bend your knees a little.
- Continue the circular movement as you exhale, while moving your arms forwards and upwards and slowly raising your neck.|

Do this exercise as often as you wish. If you get dizzy, bend your head forwards as in exercise 10.

Exercise 10

- Imagine that your arms and head are a heavy burden for the rest of your body, which in this exercise is a crane. The 'burden' is hanging and dangling downwards. Do not overstretch your knees, but be sure to have some feeling of stretch at the back of the knees.
- Hang there and feel gravity working. Do not press your hands towards the floor, allow them to hang totally relaxed.
- Now let the crane pull the load up as slowly as possible. Lift one vertebra at a time, starting from the bottom and moving upwards. The slower you do this exercise, the better it feels.
- When you are standing again, bend the neck backwards while rolling the stretched arms up over your head, and letting them go backwards as far as possible on an inhalation. Continue the circular movement by returning the stretched arms to the front and slowly raising the neck while exhaling (as described in the third step of exercise 9). If you get dizzy, bend your upper body forwards and relax in that position.

Yoga exercise that benefits the eyes, the ability to concentrate and activates the third eye

Exercise 11

The maximal visual angles that our eyes are capable of when they move to their extreme positions can be described, as in this exercise, in terms of the numbers on a clock.

- Look up (12 o'clock) and look down (6 o'clock), five times in each direction.
- Look to the sides (3 and 9 respectively) five times in each direction. After that, look to 2 o'clock five times and then to 8 o'clock five times.
- Repeat for 10 o'clock and 4 o'clock.
- Draw circles with your eyes trying to describe a round, soft arc. If the eyes tend to jump, try giving them extra time in those places where they jump. Make five circles in each direction.
- Hold your thumb 10cm (4 in) from your nose. Focus on the thumb, and then focus on a point in the distance. Do this five times.

Warm your hands by rubbing them together and cup them in front of
your eyes. Let your eyes relax in the darkness.

Breathing, posture, spine, tense solar plexus and awareness of the *hara*

Exercise 12

- Get down on your knees and bend forwards in the foetal position.
  Let your arms rest in front of you in a relaxed way. Breathe deeply
  (preferably through your nose). Try to place your hands on your back
  (or better – get someone to do it for you). Note how you are breathing in
  your lower back and sides. Put your hands down again.
- Relax in this position, keeping your attention on the breathing in
  your back.
- At the same time, bend your tongue backwards, while you look gently
  up with eyes closed.

Exercise 13

- Do the reverse of exercise 12, by lying on your back with your knees
  pulled up to your chest.
- Hug your calves with your arms and press your thighs in towards your
  body. Sense the breathing in your lumbar region again. Breathe out
  and make the sound 'Tssss' or 'Kssss' and note which muscles become
  activated.

Exercise 14

This exercise is effective for people who usually breathe in their chest.
Do it very thoroughly and with concentration. Stop if you are unsure of
when the stomach should go in or out. Clarify this and then continue the
exercise.

- Sit on the edge of a chair. If possible, rest your face, chest and stomach
  on your knees. The arms are hanging limply alongside the legs.
- Breathe in and let the flow of the in breath push you into a sitting
  position. Hold your breath.

- It is important to exhale with the help of the stomach muscles alone. Keep your concentration on the balance point, which is a hand's width below the navel.

Push the air out in small amounts whilst saying: 'Kssss, kssss, kssss ...' Sense how the muscles around the balance point under the navel are actively pushed inwards with a small thrust every time you say 'Kssss'. Every time the sound stops, the muscles relax and move outwards.

Exercise 15

Seesaw breathing (Moshe Feldenkrais)
The following exercise is very helpful in enabling the Note from Heaven to break through. It activates energy flow in the five lower chakras and simultaneously strengthens awareness of the breath. It can have a releasing effect on a tense solar plexus and breathing problems in general. At the same time, the inner organs are massaged.
- Lie down on your back with your knees bent and feet on the ground. Be aware of your back. Your whole spine is now in contact with the mat.
- **Breast:** Breathe deeply through your nose, fill your body with air, hold the breath and push all the air up into your chest. Pushing your stomach inwards does this. Pull your pelvis up. Press your chin down, which closes the throat. Notice how the chest muscles are stretched out front and back. Hold the breath as long as you can. Breathe out. Repeat five times.
- **Stomach:** Now do the opposite, so that the stomach instead of the chest is pushed out. Breathe deeply through your nose, fill the body with air and push the chest muscles downwards in order to make the stomach as big as possible. Hold your breath and enjoy the feeling of the stretched muscles in the stomach and lower back. Close off your throat and pelvic floor as in the previous step. Hold the breath as long as you can. Breathe out. Repeat five times.
- Now the two parts of the exercise are combined. Breathe in through the nose, fill the body with air, close off at the top and the bottom, as before. Slowly push the air from the chest to the stomach area, back and

forth in a gentle, rocking movement. Note how it goes up and down the spine, how your organs are being massaged and are very likely making sounds. You may be able to hold your breath for an extremely long time in this position.

When the above exercise can be done easily, you can choose to do the whole exercise, or just parts of it, without air. This means exhaling and then closing off the pelvis and throat. Doing the exercise in this way is more demanding. It is not advisable to do this exercise just after a meal.

Exercise 16
Yoga relaxation

- Lie on your back with your legs outstretched and your arms by your sides with the palms turned upwards. Roll your feet from side to side and feel how your legs roll with them. Stretch your insteps downwards, hold the tension, then relax. Draw your feet towards your body and press down with your heels, relax. Tense the whole buttock area, holding your breath for as long as you can, then relax.
- Tense the chest muscles, hold your breath, then relax. Tense your shoulders up towards your ears, hold your breath, then relax. Clench your fists, hold your breath, then relax. Squeeze tightly every muscle in your face, purse your lips, then relax. Now open your face wide, stretch your eyes open and stick out your tongue as far as it will go. Relax.
- Stretch your whole body downwards. Chin, hands, arms, legs and insteps are stretched as far down in the direction of the soles of the feet as possible. Hold your breath, then relax.
- Slowly and gently roll your head from side to side. The head is a ball or a bubble gently bobbing in water or on a current of air. The slower you do the roll, the deeper the effect. Centre your head comfortably and relax.

Neck, breath, energy flow and suppleness of the spine

Exercise 17
Shoulder stand

- Lie on the floor with your legs together and your hands, palms down, by your sides. Inhaling, push down on your hands and raise your legs straight up above you.
- Lift the hips off the floor and bring your legs up over and beyond your head, at an angle of about 45 degrees.
- Exhaling, bend your arms and support your body, holding as close to the shoulders as possible, thumbs around the front of the body, fingers around the back. Push your back up. Lift your legs.
- Now straighten your spine and bring the legs up to a vertical position. Press your chin firmly into the base of your throat. Breathe slowly and deeply in this pose, keeping your feet relaxed.
- To come down from this pose, lower your legs to an angle of about 45 degrees over your head, place your hands, palms down, behind you, then slowly roll out of it one vertebra at a time. Among other things, this pose encourages deep abdominal breathing, because it limits the use of the top of the lungs.

Exercise 18
Plough

This exercise has the same starting position as the shoulder stand, but the legs are stretched backwards over the head instead of upwards.

- Support your back with your hands, keeping the elbows as close to one another as possible. If your feet comfortably reach the floor, walk them as far behind your head as you can. Now clasp your hands together and stretch your arms out behind your back. Breathe slowly and deeply in this position. Use the shoulder stand rollout (exercise 17, last step) to come out of the position.

Exercise 19

Fish

This exercise is pre-training for the Fish pose and a counter exercise to the Plough and the shoulder stand.

- Lie down on your back with your legs straight and your feet together. Place your hands, palms down, beneath your thighs.
- Pressing down on your elbows, inhale and arch your back, resting the very top of your head on the floor. Exhale. Breathe deeply while in the position.
- To come out of the pose, first lift your head and place it gently down again, then release your arms.

Stomach muscles

Exercise 20

The stomach muscles play an important role in singing. Therefore, this exercise is invaluable unless you already have a trained body. Many women believe they cannot do this exercise. I too felt that way at first. The point is that the breathing helps you to get up. Without the initial inhalation, you cannot move at all.

Note that this exercise is not suitable for people with back problems.

- Lie down on your back with your knees bent and the soles of the feet placed on the floor. The arms are stretched down alongside the body.
- Breathe in through your nose and, in an extension of the inhalation, lift your upper body up and forward while trying to reach down between the knees with the tip of the nose.
- Breathe out and roll back to the lying position. Aim to do this exercise five times, then relax and try to do it five more times. Regulate the number of repetitions according to your physical strength. It is essential to pause in the middle. In addition, women need to pull the bottom of their pelvis up, because of the pressure on the uterus.

A more difficult version of the exercise is to do it with your hands folded behind your neck and/or with outstretched legs.

Balance, awareness of the *hara*, activation of the body's energy flow, posture

Exercise 21
- Stand with legs slightly apart and note your point of balance, the *hara*, a hand's width below the navel.
- At the same time, fix your eyes on a specific spot in your surroundings.
- Let the two points merge in your awareness.
- Stand on your right leg and, with your left hand, take hold of your left instep. Pull your leg back and up into a horizontal position. This presses the lower leg down, which pulls on the arm.
- Besides the stretch in your thighs, you can also feel how your shoulder blade is pressed inwards. Keep the position as long as possible and keep your focus concentrated on the inner point (*hara*) and the outer point (in the room) the whole time. The free arm is used as a balancing bar. Breathe deeply in this position.
- Change sides. If your ears buzz and everything goes black afterwards, bend forwards with your head and arms, as in exercise 10.

If you want an even greater challenge, hold the instep with both hands.

Opening the chest, relieving pain between the shoulder blades

Exercise 22
- Lie on your right side, bend your left knee, slide it forwards and down to the floor. Put your right hand on the bent left knee. Then stretch the left arm back. The arm will be up in the air for most people. You will feel a wonderful stretch in the chest and the whole shoulder area. Breathe deeply into the tension around the arm. Try to relax in this position. Take your time. You can relax the muscles by letting the arm rest in front of your chest for a moment, after which you roll back into the stretch.
- Lie in the position until the hand touches the floor on its own.

Eventually it will, although it may take some time. After that, turn onto your left side and do the same exercise with your right arm.

This exercise is frequently used in yoga and relaxation.

Sealing off uncontrolled air in the voice

Exercise 23

This is a classical glottis exercise. The glottis is the narrow opening between the two vocal chords. When there is a lot of air in the voice, the glottis can become a bit loose. It doesn't close enough when you want to make a distinct or sharp sound. The following exercise needs to be done very carefully and, to begin with, preferably together with a teacher, who can make sure that you are using the muscles correctly.

You start by not actually clearing your throat, but by being just about to do so. Instead of an explosive and unhealthy clearing, there will be a delicate little click. It feels as if you are creating small, crispy bubbles that float out of your throat like pearls. The sound of a creaking door, which is easy to make instead, is much coarser in sound. If you creak, then try to split the sound up into small, isolated bubble sounds.

Do not do the exercise for more than five minutes at a time. It can be done inconspicuously in almost any situation.

THE PRACTICE DOWNLOAD

I have attempted as far as possible to tailor the download to each singer's individual needs. As stressed in Part I of this book, the idea is to start by singing Sa, the root note, only. This is the principle behind tracks 1 and 2, and later track 21.

When you have worked with a point of the download (except track 1) I recommend that you repeat for example singing Sa Re alone with the tanpura on track 21. That is the only point where you will be totally confronted by your own sound and, through that experience, develop your consciousness and self-confidence.

If you start by playing the download and trying to sing along with it all the way through, you will have begun at the finishing line. You are meant to gradually add more points to your singing practice until eventually you are able to use the whole download.

If you follow the procedure described above, then, by the time you have finished the download, you will be able to improvise similar sequences yourself without any support other than the tanpura accompaniment.

Once you have learned to sing the note names fluently, you can go on to connect the notes to colours and chakras (see the diagram on pages 100–101) and in that way give your body a sound-healing. The healthiest way to sound-heal your own chakras is to see them as a coherent energy flow, where a slow vocal gliding between the notes can cleanse the connections between the corresponding chakras. A balanced flow is thus created through which the energy can run more freely. The result is that your voice becomes more beautiful and that you feel more whole as a person. When concentrating sound on a single chakra in isolation, be careful not to do it for more than five minutes at a time.

The range of notes on the practice download stretches up to a one-stringed A – that is, right up to the place where most women's and some men's voices begin to change gear from speech register to falsetto, which in many instances results in the voice breaking.

I have chosen this pitch mostly because one of the basic premises of this book is that the muscular support needs to be mastered and completely assimilated in the body in the speech register (the lower part of the voice) before you move up to the higher notes. This is where the 'space' gets increasingly narrow, making correct location of the note even more important. It is impossible to maintain such full awareness if you are simultaneously concentrating on developing your body support.

A second reason is that you risk injuring yourself if you practise the high tones without guidance from a singing teacher. This is especially true for those inexperienced in listening to themselves and their body signals.

Track-by-track comments

Track 1

Before you move on to anything else, you need the Note from Heaven to break through on the root note. Track 1 is a preparatory guide for singing the Note from Heaven. You can discard this guidance when you have found your own key image and when good habits of body posture and breathing have become a natural way of being for you.

Track 2

Track 2, where I sing with you on the root note, and track 21, where you can sing alone with the tanpura accompaniment, give you an opportunity to practise the Note from Heaven. I have included my voice on this track as support. The idea is that you sing over my voice using the rhythm of your breathing. You are not meant to sing after me.

Halfway through track 2, I sing the primal sound behind the Note from Heaven (see page 43) three times. The volume of the note has been reduced to avoid startling unnecessarily. You can sing the primal note yourself, if and when you need to find your power.

You should repeat track 2 several times while you are in the first phase – trying to open yourself to the Note from Heaven.

Tracks 3–10

This is a slow improvisation, where the major scale is introduced in different combinations. Each phrase is followed by a pause so you can repeat the phrase.

The same phrase is always repeated two times, first in Indian note language and then in 'Aaar'. This activates both brain halves and enables you to learn both the note names and create a beautiful sound.

With each track, another note is added to the improvisation, so that you can proceed as slowly as you wish. Note that it can easily take weeks to learn note combinations when a new note has been added. With daily practice, it can take a year to learn to sing along with the whole practice download.

What is important is not how good you are at note combinations, but how well you feel when you sing.

Practise each track by listening to yourself singing alone with the tanpura accompaniment. Do not rush through it, wanting to be able to do it all at once. For example, try to practise two notes (track 3) and then improvise by yourself with the tanpura (track 21). See also the example of a method of working on page 54.

Tracks 11–20

These ten tracks provide outlines of the flexibility exercises to give you an idea of the melodic sequence of the exercises.

Practise these exercises at your own speed with the support of the tanpura accompaniment (track 21).

Track 21

If you are unsure whether you are singing in tune, it is a good idea to turn up the sound of the tanpura. Let yourself be enveloped in its tones and glide into the landscape with your sound. Soon you will come to recognize when you are singing in tune. If you are still in any doubt, ask someone you trust to give you feedback.

Choose a volume level that enables you both to hear yourself and safely lean on the tanpura's supportive tapestry of sound.

Contents of each track

Track 1 – 8:24

Introduction – establishing breathing and concentrating on the key image.

Track 2 – 5:10

1 note: Sa (sound A)

Track 3 – 3:54

2 notes: Sa, Re (sound A, B)

Track 4 – 5:14

3 notes: Nị, Sa, Re (sound G#, A, B)

Track 5 – 6:15

4 notes: Nị, Sa, Re, Gha (sound G#, A, B, C#)

Track 6 – 4:17

5 notes: Nị, Sa, Re, Gha, Ma (sound G#, A, B, C#, D)

Track 7 – 10:16

6 notes: Nị, Sa, Re, Gha, Ma, Pa (sound G#, A, B, C#, D, E)

Track 8 – 5:54

7 notes: Nị, Sa, Re, Gha, Ma, Pa, Dha (sound G#, A, B, C#, D, E, F#)

Track 9 – 6:27

8 notes: Nị, Sa, Re, Gha, Ma, Pa, Dha, Ni (sound G#, A, B, C#, D, E, F#, G#)

Track 10 – 6:45

9 notes: Nị, Sa, Re, Gha, Ma, Pa, Dha, Ni, Sả (sound G#, A, B, C#, D, E, F#, G#, A)

Track 11 – 0:51

The first basic exercise is to sing the scale with the note names.

Organize your method of breathing according to your ability. For example, upwards on a breath, up and down, twice up and down or three times up and down.

When you can sing the scale twice on a breath with note language and 'Aaar' respectively, you can go further.

Sa, Re, Gha, Ma, Pa, Dha, Ni, Sả – Sả, Ni, Dha, Pa, Ma, Gha, Re, Sa

Track 12 – 0:24

Sa Sa, Re Re, Gha Gha, Ma Ma, Pa Pa, Dha Dha, Ni Ni, Sả Sả
Sả Sả, Ni Ni, Dha Dha, Pa Pa, Ma Ma, Gha Gha, Re Re, Sa Sa

Sing the note names first and then 'Aaar'. Move your breathing according to your ability, but always sing slowly enough to be able to enjoy your singing.

Note that the passages between the quick 'Aaars' always flow within each breath, just as when you write with a pen without lifting it from the paper.

To glide in that way, you approach the note by gliding downwards a little and then up again. This glide is quick and imperceptible and fluctuates by approximately a third.

This technique is called *gamak* in India. It is a movement that takes place only in the throat.

To practise *gamak*, try to say 'A-haar', as if you were suddenly realizing something.

On the last part, the 'haar', glide from above and downwards within the tone of your voice. Note the effect on your own throat. It should also move downwards on 'A-haar'.

Try to say 'A-haaraaraaraaraar' as a wavy movement.

The technique can be practised separately throughout the whole scale. It is beneficial to practice the glides in slow motion and then slowly increase the tempo. Notice that the note, your fixed point, is always totally pure. It is like a well-memorized fact in your mind. You can pull at the fact, which is elastic, but, when you release the elastic, it springs back to its starting point.

It is particularly beneficial to practise *gamak* in exercises that use repetition of the same tone. For example, exercise 12 (Sa Sa, Re Re...) or exercises where there are movements in thirds, for example Sa Gha, Re Ma, Gha Pa ... (see exercises 17, 18, 19 and 20).

Track 13 – 0:24

Let's sing tones three and three:

Sa Re Gha, Re Gha Ma, Gha Ma Pa, Ma Pa Dha, Pa Dha Ni, Dha Ni Sá
Sá Ni Dha, Ni Dha Pa, Dha Pa Ma, Pa Ma Gha, Ma Gha Re, Gha Re Sa

Track 14 – 0:25

After that, you can permeate the spine with the same exercise pattern using four notes:

Sa Re Gha Ma, Re Gha Ma Pa, Gha Ma Pa Dha, Ma Pa Dha Ni, Pa Dha Ni Sả

Sả Ni Dha Pa, Ni Dha Pa Ma, Dha Pa Ma Gha, Pa Ma Gha Re, Ma Gha Re Sa.

Track 15 – 0:26

Gha Re Sa, Ma Gha Re, Pa Ma Gha, Dha Pa Ma, Ni Dha Pa, Sả Ni Dha

Dha Ni Sả, Pa Dha Ni, Ma Pa Dha, Gha Ma Pa, Re Gha Ma, Sa Re Gha

Track 16 – 0:41

You can do it in both directions:

Sa Re Gha Re Sa, Re Gha Ma Gha Re, Gha Ma Pa Ma Gha

Ma Pa Dha Pa Ma, Pa Dha Ni Dha Pa, Dha Ni Sả Ni Dha, then do it backwards

Track 17 – 0:27

Another classic exercise is to do every other note, which is breaking the scale into thirds:

Sa Gha, Re Ma, Gha Pa, Ma Dha, Pa Ni, Dha Sả

Sả Dha, Ni Pa, Dha Ma, Pa Gha, Ma Re, Gha Sa

Track 18 – 0:25

Or in reverse:

Gha Sa, Ma Re, Pa Gha, Dha Ma, Ni Pa, Sả Dha

Dha Sả, Pa Ni, Ma Dha, Gha Pa, Re Ma, Sa Gha (Ṇi Re Sa)

Track 19 – 0:23

The two previous exercises combined:

Sa Gha, Ma Re, Gha Pa, Dha Ma, Pa Ni, Sả Dha, Ni Rẻ, Ghả Sả

Sả Ghả, Rẻ Ni, Dha Sả, Ni Pa, Ma Dha, Pa Gha, Re Ma, Gha Sa

Track 20 – 0:48

Sa Re Gha Gha, Re Gha Ma Ma, Gha Ma Pa Pa, Ma Pa Dha Dha, Pa
Dha Ni Ni, Dha Ni Sả Sả

Sả Ni Dha Dha, Ni Dha Pa Pa, Dha Pa Ma Ma, Pa Ma Gha Gha, Ma
Gha Re Re, Gha Re Sa Sa

Find your own combinations, write them down and practise them in
track 21.

Track 21 – 9:00

The tanpura tuned to Pạ, Sa, Sa, Sạ (sound E, Λ1, Λ1, Λ).

In addition, see pages 34–36 on the root note.

APPLYING THE TANPURA ACCOMPANIMENT
TO THE PIANO

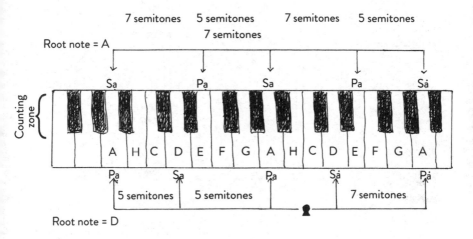

This is an example of the calculation of the accompanying notes for a root
note in D = Sa.

A half-note step is a movement from one note to its nearest neighbour
on the keyboard, whether black or white. It is easiest to count the half-note
steps correctly when you count closest to the keyboard in the counting zone
where the black keys are.

CHAKRA OVERVIEW

ASSOCIATED CONCEPTS	SENSE	CHAKRA
Intuition, soul, the divine aspect, spirituality, inspiration	INNER LIGHT	CROWN CHAKRA
Higher consciousness, overview without emotion, manipulation, psychological point of balance	INNER SOUND	THE THIRD EYE
Communication, connection to intuition, enthusiasm, influence on own life	HEARING	THROAT CHAKRA
Devotion, love, gratitude, empathy	TOUCH	HEART CHAKRA
Emotions, ego, control	SIGHT	SOLAR PLEXUS CHAKRA
Energy, desire, appetite	TASTE	HARA CHAKRA
Instinct, survival, reproduction, grounding	SMELL	ROOT CHAKRA

ASSOCIATED NOTES	COLOUR*	ELEMENT	DEVELOPMENT/ EXPERIENCE	FORM OF SUBLIMATION
NI	VIOLET/WHITE			
DHA	BLUE/VIOLET		INDIVIDUAL	INSPIRATION
			PERMANENT EXPERIENCE	MEDITATION USE OF THE VOICE
PA	SKY BLUE/ TURQUOISE	ETHER		
MA	GREEN (ROSA)	AIR	PERSON	CARE AND CREATIVITY
GHA	YELLOW	FIRE		MOVEMENT
RE	ORANGE	WATER	IMPERMANENT EXPERIENCE	FOOD
SA	RED	EARTH		INSTINCTIVE REFLEXES, SECRETION

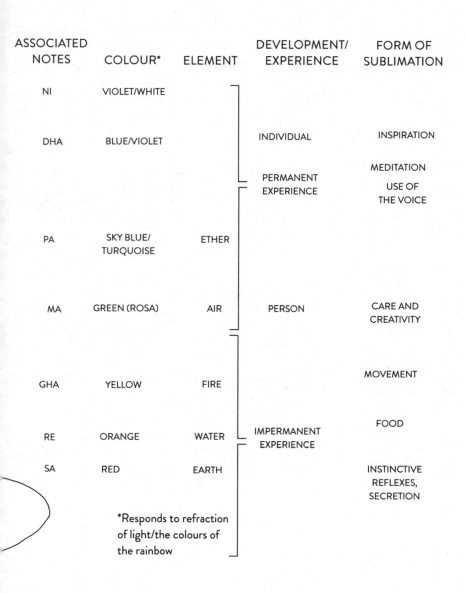

*Responds to refraction of light/the colours of the rainbow

The Note
from Heaven
Book II

Sing
Your Self
Free

Dedicated to Péleh Ben-David

INTRODUCTION

My second book on the Note from Heaven focuses on a new method called regressive cell-singing, in which you can sing your self free from traumas that have their origin in this life, the womb or previous lifetimes.

Emotional stress affects our whole organism and causes it to go out of tune. We are all born in tune, with a beautiful composition in our cell structure, a matrix which contains our full potential and which is reflected in our voice.

In regressive cell-singing the Note from Heaven is used as a tuning fork to retune cells to their former harmony.

My view of trauma is as a tension that blocks the free flow of energy in the body, a blockage that weakens the life force and thereby, if left untreated, causes imbalance and illness.

In regressive cell-singing any notes, sounds or outbursts that genuinely express the Note from Heaven can release blocked energy imprisoned in the singer's body as trauma. The process starts a cell-dance, which reorganizes the body into its original balanced matrix.

The method can work alone or in combination with any other kind of therapy. Essentially, when you sing your self free you spit out the poisoned piece of apple and return to life, just as Snow White did when the prince kissed her and woke her from her deep sleep in the glass coffin.

PART I

COLLECTIVE TRAUMATIZATION

'There is no sin. It is you who make sin exist ...'
Gospel of Mary Magdalene

Dear reader, in order to bring to your attention one of the biggest collective traumas in the Western world, I will refer to a number of quotes from the apocryphal writings, especially from the Gospel of Thomas. These writings, which are an expression of Gnostic wisdom, were banned in 324 AD by the church fathers who selected the texts that we know today as the New Testament.

When the Gnostic scripts were found hidden in caves in the mid-twentieth century, scholars surmised that some of the authors had probably been disciples of Jesus, and that their writings reflect his original message: a teaching based on self-knowledge and self-development. Orthodox Christianity's dogmatic use of sin, shame and judgment seems to misinterpret this message of love.

We humans are much more influenced by our historical, religious and cultural roots than most of us realize. Orthodox Christianity conditions us to feel that we are 'not good enough' and to cultivate false humility, which limits our belief in our own essence. This perception immediately rules out the Note from Heaven as a possibility because we do not feel worthy of the light!

These collective religious traumas lie deeply stored in our subconscious mind and act as the main gateway in the process of release. If a person is in contact with his or her inner divinity, then it is usually easy to find resonance. If the gateway is closed, then as a healer you can at best scratch the surface a little. 'I carry my burden with a smile.' If a person doesn't want to throw off their burden, then no healer can wrest it from them.

For centuries, Christianity and other religions have suppressed the feminine powers. These include holistic thinking, compassion, intuitive knowledge and wisdom and a natural tendency to cooperate. Religious authorities have also undermined the sacredness of eroticism through condemnation and punishment, making believers feel guilty for the sexuality that we are all born with. The fact that more and more people are now rejecting these controls is for me a sign that we are ready to open ourselves up to a higher level of consciousness which can only be reached by unfolding the feminine divinity within.

Overcoming the historical traumas, however, is a challenge, for fear is all-encompassing. A woman who has become traumatized after being attacked by a man may find her trauma reactivated by contact with any other man. Similarly, our experience of any form of religiousness and, therefore spirituality, is affected by these universal, archetypal religious traumas. I believe that spirituality is an expression of the intuitive abilities we all innately possess. However, the historical traumas have stunted our self-development and undermined our confidence in our intuition and innate divinity. The traumatized cornerstones that our cultural heritage is built on must be dug up and brought to light. The most effective tool for this purpose is sound.

The path
'You must burn in order to shine'
Lars Muhl

Our destiny can feel like a bumpy ride on a dirt road full of potholes, but when we look back on our journey the higher meaning of all the trouble becomes clear. It turns out that the dirt road leads to a very beautiful place, which we have been destined to reach from the beginning. Some people have high ambitions, they get famous and we think they have accomplished everything. But, in fact, worldly success does not count on the other side of life. What does matter is that you find your path, and that you gain the courage to pursue it with dedication.

We all know people who seem to have found their calling: a wonderful kindergarten teacher, a waiter or sales clerk who has just the right feel for the customer, effortlessly sensing what they need and how best to serve them, a checkout assistant at the supermarket who gives you a smile that sends you home feeling good. To encounter people in their right element is pure joy.

When your light shines, you activate the light in others, and help them to remember that they are complete beings.

Anybody can shine! It is a matter of choice. If you wish to set your light free, then you need to unfold your wings. Let the wind carry you, and be prepared to land on both feet so you can fulfil your destiny on earth.

'Dull birds. The cage door is open and you do not even dare to fly. I am scaring you in order to make you fly.'

Gitta Mallasz, *Talking with Angels*

The pain body

The pain body gives us licence to project unacknowledged emotions onto our surroundings. It is the ego's mouthpiece and the shadow's storage space for emotions.

You may be wondering what it is that keeps us from walking our path on earth, and why many of us subconsciously prefer to remain in the shadows.

The key to understanding this behavioural pattern can be found in the pain body. We all have a pain body that in a stressful emotional situation offers us an amnesty, which temporarily puts our adult self-knowledge on hold. Wounded, we isolate ourselves in the pain body to recover our breath and restore ourselves. Here everything is black and white, as we regress to the level of a small child and dwell on a self-justifying 'pity me!'

The pain body's function can be compared to a big black umbrella that we can open for protection against a sudden storm. Sheltering under the pain-body umbrella, the mind gets time to compose itself and figure out how to regain control of the situation.

Temporary use of the pain body as described above is healthy and natural. But it can become a chronic and unhealthy habit. We can end up permanently hiding in a safe, secluded, deep, dark lake, where we drown our light in a soothing abdication of life's demands and responsibilities.

By staying continuously in the pain body, a person identifies with the role of victim and achieves a negatively charged status that separates them from the surrounding world, which they blame for their situation.

When people isolate themselves from their surroundings, they simultaneously exclude themselves from the oneness level. They justify their pain and their self-perception as victims through a judgmental attitude that says, 'I am here and you are there.' The 'pain' confers a special status around which they base their identity as victims. They complain, but do not want any help.

The four primary archetypal feelings that bind us to our pain body are:

I am not good enough (I am not lovable).
I do not belong.
I am not allowed to be here.
I do not wish to be here.

These negative thought patterns prevent us from taking part fully in life. They are caused by the fears of the ego and are usually already integrated as a part of our identity in the womb or in early childhood.

The pain body is our challenge, the wood for the fire that will raise our consciousness.

Will you be swallowed up by the darkness or be lifted up towards the light?

It is all about taking responsibility for yourself.

Adults, subconsciously trapped by choices made as infants, are not able to take full responsibility for themselves until they realize what programming they are suffering from.

Without being aware of it, we shackle ourselves to a post and move around in a circle like a chained dog, moaning and groaning or quietly whimpering as we cast longing glances at the horizon, sadly gazing at all the lovely things that are out of our reach.

The best tool to break the chain that links an identity to its pain body is awareness. The awareness is a matter of choice: will I be conscious, or will I not? Will I stay in prison or will I break free? Do I fear freedom? Who do I want to see in the mirror – the familiar little self or the unknown big self?

Fear of the unknown causes most of us to prefer the pain we are familiar with, because we know what we have, but not what we could get.

Those who acknowledge their own shadow see the light.

A dark cloud can be experienced from two perspectives: you can remain inside it and become blinded and overwhelmed by despair, or you can see the cloud from the outside and recognize that it is merely temporarily hiding the sun.

In order to lift yourself outside the cloud, the consciousness needs a moment of stillness. This stillness will appear the moment you stop panicking, take a deep breath and embrace your pain body in total acceptance.

'I am ugly, I cannot sing, I had a terrible childhood, nobody likes me...' By repeating such mantras, you blow great black clouds in your own sunny way, and the pain-body illusion manifests itself in reality. It is true that *you are what you think*'. As our perception of life will always be an illusion and we can think whatever we like about ourselves, why not create a positive, sunny illusion and let that manifest itself in reality?

Plus power

The higher and lower selves can be seen as two separate parts: shadow and light. This perception causes pain, because it divides the whole. The whole self is unified: where there is light, there is shadow. In that way any minus can be changed to a plus by adding a single vertical line to it.

In the plus sign, the horizontal line symbolizes the dualistic world of good and bad. The vertical line symbolizes the oneness level (fire – consciousness), which you can reach by lifting your 'self' up above the horizon level (water – feelings). Embrace your emotional condition and seek a moment of stillness; this will bring you to the centre of the cross, where you can raise your level of awareness.

In the rebalanced 'plus' you see the positive part of the negative and can contain both parts within you: the pain body is fully accepted, because your consciousness observes everything from a higher perspective.

The small self (the pain body/ego) and the higher self (consciousness/the soul) are symbolized by two dots on either side of the horizontal line in the minus symbol. In the plus symbol, the two selves are connected and merged into oneness. The ego (master of the underworld) and consciousness (master of the upper world) collaborate, with the result that the heart literally opens its red velvet curtains in the middle of the chest. And who appears on stage? The true you!

Every human being on earth is able to create oneness in their life, to change all the minuses they have experienced into pluses, simply by singing themselves into oneness. When your heart opens, your whole organism becomes aflame with enthusiasm and passion – a passion for walking your path in life.

' ... seek, and ye shall find.'
Matthew 7:7

'When all is said and done, it seems meaningless to dig into the past
again and again in order to find the reasons for one's lack of self-
confidence. At a certain time, everyone must take responsibility for
their own life.'
Carl Gustav Jung

'When I take responsibility for my own life, I stop looking for
someone else to blame for my suffering. The responsibility opens
my eyes to the possibilities that I alone have.'
Anselm Grün

'Rise up, take your stretcher and go home.'
Mark 2:11

How to truly listen to your self
'Blessed be the one who hears the call from the minaret of their heart.'
Hazrat Inayat Khan, *Gayan, Vadan, Nirtan*

When you hear you use only your ears, but when you listen attentively
you use all your senses.

By training your ability to hear microtones, over- and undertones,
you are fine-tuning your sensitivity at all levels of your organism. Your
awareness of careful listening is the only true master. Through listening
to the feeling in the colour of a voice, you develop your intuition and start
to pick up messages that you were not aware of before. You sense people's
energy and feel what is good and what is not good for you. Besides this,
you improve your ability to be present in the moment.

When you sing yourself free of a trauma, the Note from Heaven will
sound spontaneously the very moment you sing at the right frequency.
When it appears, hold on to the sound that expresses the Note from
Heaven until the physical tension connected to your trauma is released.

If there are any other traumas or tensions in the body, just focus your attention on the affected cells and glide slowly up and down with your voice until you catch the Note from Heaven again. Let it guide you, just as you would follow a beam of light.

PREPARING FOR REGRESSIVE CELL-SINGING

The essence of all life is vibration. When you strike a tuning fork tuned to 440 Hz, any other tuning forks in the room that have been tuned to the same frequency will also start ringing at an audible level. This effect is caused by resonance. If you stop the sound of the first tuning fork it will fall silent, but the others will continue to resonate.

This simple example demonstrates one of the most profound laws of nature: all vibrations in our universe influence each other. So when a frequency finds resonance in your body, it will set the resonating part of your cells in motion.

The question is, what is happening when a sound resonates in our body? Are the cells dancing? Are our bodily fluids resonating? Is it a kind of electrical process, triggered by a sound impulse?

The voice, which can affect us in the most ingenious ways, appeals to our senses, works from within us, and is far more sensitive than the most sophisticated computer, has still not been thoroughly and scientifically investigated. And none of the research that has been carried out has been accepted by mainstream science or brought to the attention of the general public. The main explanation for this is perhaps financial – the healing effect of the voice is a free medicine that cannot be monetized. Also, each person's voice is unique and the workings of the voice are so complicated that present-day scientific instruments can only measure certain aspects of it. So we can only rely on our own practical experience.

Trust your senses by listening attentively to even the smallest signs from your body, and be aware of the particular circumstances in which they occur. Respond to your body's signals. You know better than anyone else how you feel, but you might not have given yourself the necessary attention because our world values the external over the internal.

When you act on what you feel, you listen to your 'self' with the result that your 'self'-estimation grows. By listening to your whole self (including the ego's acceptable needs), you project 'self'-respect into your surroundings and they will, in turn, respect you.

'A sower went out to sow his seed: and as he sowed, some fell by the wayside; and it was trodden down, and the fowls of the air devoured it. And some fell upon a rock; and as soon as it was sprung up, it withered away, because it lacked moisture. And some fell among thorns; and the thorns sprang up with it, and choked it. And others fell on good ground, and sprang up, and bore fruit in hundredfold. And when Jesus had said these things, he cried: "He that has ears, let him hear."'
Parable of the Sower, Luke 8:5-8

Through physical exercises, healthy eating and respecting your basic psychological needs, you can ensure the Note from Heaven is sown in fertile ground. Through faithful listening to the self, you care for the seed and give it the right amount of water it needs to grow.

The soil symbolizes your pain body, the shadow. There is a lot of potential energy hidden there. You can see traumas as bank boxes that can only be opened by a specific key in the form of a certain frequency. The moment you open the box, the energy becomes free and available for use.

A heavily traumatized soil will have so much energy stored in it that it can be compared to pure compost. Only a limited range of plants will be able to grow in it. So, in order to normalize the soil the traumas must be opened and transformed one by one. At first, potatoes will be able to grow there and in that way the core trauma is transformed, then the next step is to grow squash, signifying the healing of the wounded heart that gradually reopens. Only then is the ground ready for more delicate plants like carrots, beans, salad vegetables, parsley and peas.

Some people who have been in therapy for years may have managed to open their trauma-boxes but not succeeded in withdrawing the blocked energy. In such cases, regressive cell-singing can work like a miracle: all the energy will be withdrawn in one go. The Note from Heaven unites the energy and opens up to its flow, as it casts its beam of resonance into the darkness. It can feel like striking oil or winning millions in the lottery. Some people even experience a spontaneous remission of serious illness when this kind of release happens.

The inner experience of resonant sound 'knows'.

God is sound. Nada Brahma.

> 'You can only truly believe what you have perceived through your own experience.'
> **George Harrison**

Your ability to believe is equivalent to your ability to listen unconditionally.

> 'Belief is not a foundation or a state within me. Belief is motion and mobility. God as voice and the human as ears.'
> **Jesper Blomberg**, priest in Udby, Denmark

Faith is a sound that moves our body and soul. Fear causes atrophy and opposes faith.

> 'Everything is given. All that has been hidden will be exposed. And that day is NOW! The illuminated consciousness is NOW and forever.'
> **Lars Muhl**, *The 'O' Manuscript*

The Note from Heaven – a gateway to oneness

In recent years my work with singing has provided me with an increasing number of opportunities for personal development. The Note from Heaven is the key factor common to all of them. My personal understanding of the concept of the Note from Heaven is continually expanding and changing, because contact with that state of mind is a constantly unfolding process which seems to stretch all the way out to the quantum physics of the infinite universe. The Note from Heaven is a doorway to the 'moment'.

'The disciples asked Jesus, "When will you reveal yourself to us, and when are we going to see you?" Jesus replied, "When you take your clothes off without feeling shame and when you take your clothing and put it under your feet and step on it, like small children. Then you will see the son of the living and you will not fear."'
Gospel of Thomas

Once someone has experienced the state induced by the Note from Heaven breaking through, they will usually search for it again. As described in Book I, the path through the undergrowth to the awakening Sleeping Beauty needs to be trodden many times before a permanent pathway is established. Then the Note from Heaven is yours forever. It will sing through you and influence you in far broader perspectives than you can possibly imagine.

Grounding

'The human body is an electrical system. It is able to transport an electrical charge with a strength that is carefully adjusted to the resistance that nerves and glands are equipped with in relation to electrical currents. The stronger the body is physically (the meridians' state of purity), the greater the electrical charge it can handle.'
Dr Stephen T. Chang, *The Complete Book of Internal Exercises*

For an electrical system to be able to function safely, it needs to be earthed. In the same way, being grounded is also a prerequisite for the body's electrical system to be able to support an influx of energy.

From experience with sound-scanning and regressive cell-singing, I know that the stomach, hips, legs and feet correspond to our roots and those deep tones/undertones resonate well here. The higher up in the body the sound moves, the higher the tone, the finer the amplitude, the stronger the electrical current. The way to work safely with strong electrical currents is to have the means to discharge them through grounding.

When the voice cracks and won't function at a high pitch or you get sore from singing, it's a sign that you may have lost your grounding – both physically and energetically.

The voice protects us, like a fuse that blows, ensuring the organism doesn't get burnt. At a physical level, the muscles in the stomach (*hara*) and root chakras are crucial for grounding the sound. Without this support system, the body compensates by tensing the muscles of the chest and throat.

A person with weak grounding should not be exposed to high overtones without preliminary grounding. This applies to people suffering from stress, for example, as well as those in crisis and highly sensitive souls. Therefore, it is good practice to always start by working at the deep end of the vocal pitch, as that helps to ground the body and mind.

The experience of being sung by a higher power

Anyone who experiences the Note from Heaven will know what it feels like to 'be sung'. Below are some typical comments made by participants on my courses:

> 'It feels as if it isn't me singing!'
> 'I thought it was everyone else's voices, but it was me.'
> 'Where did that sound come from? Was that me?'
> 'I could have kept on singing forever.'
> 'Don't you have to breathe?'
> 'It felt as if I was an open reed, a channel.'

Here is an example of a longer feedback:
> 'It's hard to describe, but the way I experience it is that the release which took place at the course in regressive cell-singing just kept going and going … I still have the sensation of volume that I felt in

my *hara* chakra while singing ... maybe not the whole time, but I can
return to it when I consciously think about it. I don't think I have ever
been present in that part of myself before, if you know what I mean ...
suddenly I was three-dimensional. There was a little white shiny
tube sitting in the centre of my *hara* chakra that went up through
my throat and switched on a light on the top of my head... and I felt
a sense of grief for having hidden my power and my light away for
such a long time ... And then the grief just disappeared and I was
pure sound.'
Response from a course participant (Liselotte).

Contact with the Note from Heaven

'The ego will not surrender before it recognizes a higher power.'
Ramana Maharshi

You are advised to open your voice according to the instructions in
The Note from Heaven Book I before you practise the following sections.
    When you sing yourself free of deep traumas, you should work with
a 'listener'. A listener is a kind of midwife–therapist who supports the
singer in the process of regressive cell-singing. In the first year of my
two-year course in vocal sound therapy, participants are trained to be
good listeners. The first thing a listener must do is support the singer in
breathing correctly.

BREATHING AND THE NOTE FROM HEAVEN

'The vocal expression of our soul can only come into being as
movement of air through our respiratory passageways.'
Dr Audun Myskja, *Music as Medicine*

Our breathing is inextricably connected to our psychological state.
When we get a shock, we gasp. When we find ourselves in a dangerous
or stressful situation, our muscles tense, our senses become heightened
and our breathing becomes shallow, part of the innate fight or flight reflex.

Peter Levine describes in his book *Waking the Tiger* how the gazelle instinctively stiffens and plays dead when a lion drags it away as its prey.

Surrendering to its fate creates a potential opportunity for the gazelle to get away the second the lion lets go of its 'dead' prey and maybe looks the other way in a moment of distraction. When, and if, the gazelle does escape, it will then react by violently shaking itself, as if it is shaking the experience off. Afterwards the gazelle is, apparently, not traumatized.

Although this response is incredibly useful in an actual emergency, for many of us it becomes chronic, which causes problems. When we tense up, we almost completely stop breathing. Our fight or flight mechanism instinctively cuts off the connection to the digestive system for the purpose of gathering as much energy as possible to be able to run away and survive an emergency. A lot of people walk around with a frozen breath like tense gazelles that never ran away and never shook off the tensions from their traumas.

During a complete inhalation, the lungs are filled to the maximum. The organs are, therefore, pushed down to the stomach, which then bulges out. The stomach is a big gift. Don't make it smaller than it is.

During an active exhalation, the diaphragm and stomach muscles are pushed inwards, and the organs are pressed up towards the lungs, which are emptied of air. You can, of course, empty the lungs of air without using your stomach muscles, in a sigh where you 'let the air out of the balloon'. But for effective singing and emotional release, you need to activate the 'support' from your stomach muscles.

Your body's 'accelerator pedal' is located in the area under the navel. You can feel it like a slanting plate that slopes from the beginning of the lower abdomen and up under the navel. The 'fuel tank' is located in the *hara*, the stomach area. To send energy out into the body's circulation system, you have to press the accelerator pedal – the abdomen and stomach muscles.

Everyone carries shock or trauma of some kind. A traumatic experience in our past can cause an instinctive reaction that results in shallow, chest breathing without active use of the diaphragm. The four primary archetypal feelings (see page 110) can also influence our breathing from an early age.

When you do not feel that you are good enough as you are, you naturally try to change yourself: the full breath is restricted, the shoulders are pushed way up to the ears, breathing is superficial and confined to the chest and throat, while tensions in the solar plexus act as a check.

In an attempt to compensate for the feeling 'I am not allowed to be here', you breathe like this to make yourself as small as possible.

As children, many of us were told to be quiet when we were just about to test our full breath by shouting. Children love to shout, because they feel their strength when the breath unfolds completely and functions optimally.

Very few adults recognize or appreciate a child's vocal sound quality when it naturally, and with great vitality, opens up with the Note from Heaven. The majority of grown-ups have themselves been scolded for making loud noises and, therefore, consider shouting to be undesirable. Thus the pattern is inherited and happily and unconsciously passed on in the name of good parenting.

Women may feel the need to conform to the idea of 'the weaker sex'. We push our bust up and hold in our stomach. But by doing this, we cut ourselves off from our power.

Breathing uneconomically is like driving a car in the wrong gear – you end up using twice as much fuel as you need to. In Indian philosophy, life is measured according to the number of breaths we take. If the breathing is the best it can be, one lives optimally and the organism is strained as little as possible.

The breath testifies to the inseparability of body and mind. Every thought sets a process in motion in our physiology. Every physical stimulus influences our psyche.

Shallow breathing reinforces feelings of inferiority: we are never good enough, because we feel we are hiding something away. To hide who we really are is to deceive. Imagine, what if someone finds out? How disgraceful! And so the vicious circle continues.

Living a lie can sap our energy and in most cases we don't even know the cause or identity of this falsehood. A full breath is like a liberating sigh: 'I give myself permission to be who I am.'

The challenge in taking that step can be overwhelming if you are one of those people who is like a car that is only getting a few miles to the gallon. Being asked to inhale 'correctly' deep down into the stomach can feel totally disorienting. Fortunately, the body has maintained the function. A shortcut to experiencing the full breath is to 'let go' in the moment, to leap, to live out your emotions.

When we are overwhelmed by genuine feelings or when we yawn, the full breath functions the way it is meant to. It is like an oasis, where you can be yourself. Many of us breathe deeply when we sleep regardless of the quality of our breathing during waking hours. However, I have come across people whose trauma has infiltrated so thoroughly that their breathing reflexes do not function properly even during sleep.

How a listener can support the opening of a traumatized breath

- Invite the singer to hold his or her hand on your stomach while you at the same time put your hand lightly on their stomach, if that is OK with them. Breathe simultaneously. In the role of listener, show the singer how the stomach moves out on the in breath and is pressed gradually inwards while exhaling. This tactile and sensual experience through touch can do wonders.
- Guide the singer through breathing exercise 14 from Book I (see page 86–87).
- Stand behind the singer. If they permit you to do so, support the singer's neck (this soothes the autonomic nervous system/reptilian brain) and place your left palm *lightly* on their forehead (this activates the anti-stress points in the forehead).
- As the reptilian brain, which governs instincts, heartbeat and breathing, and is associated with the flight or fight reflex, is helped to relax, the singer will sigh relieved and lean their head slightly backwards as the breath starts to open. Urge the singer to open their arms and express whatever sound feels comfortable. When the Note from Heaven breaks through, the breath is fully unfolded.

How a singer can work alone with a traumatized breath

- Concentrate on a physical tension and express the feeling of that tension in sound.
- Lie in a foetal position and breathe, hum quietly and comfortingly to yourself and note how your breathing gradually gets deeper. Undertones and low tones ... sing what feels good.
- Perhaps take a teddy bear or some other soft thing and imagine that it is you when you were a baby. Hold it close to your heart and sing to it. Have fun with it. Notice that your breath becomes deeper. Eventually take the teddy with you wherever you go in the house so you can nurture yourself.

IMAGES AND THE NOTE FROM HEAVEN

In the first years after I explored the Note from Heaven, I taught singing with the aim of bringing the singer into contact with his or her natural voice. I usually cheered the singer on when their voice started to open up to an authenticity and ease that touched my heart.

It was during this type of teaching that I once came across a highly educated woman with an unusually strong resistance to opening up. She had a determination that was difficult to tackle.

From childhood I have seen images flowing through my mind when I relax. I never took much notice of them, as I always thought they were a kind of dream or flight of my imagination. When I was getting nowhere with this particular woman, despite all my efforts, I got a sudden urge to use these inner images. It felt like quite a big step for me to do this, so I asked the singer, hesitantly, if she wanted to hear what I saw. She agreed.

I described to the singer the image of a woman slowly walking down the aisle of a large cathedral with her unusually long hair let down, trailing behind her like a gown (the course participant had a short page boy haircut). At the altar she meets a priest who orders her to put her hair up.

I addressed the singer directly and asked her if she would agree to put her hair up in that situation. She replied emphatically, 'Heavens no! Why should I submit to the priest's demands for piety?'

The imaginary priest then calmly explains to the woman that it will be much easier for her to open her voice, if she puts her hair up. After that the woman agrees to roll up the whole lot of it onto the top of her head.

The very moment the singer imagined the woman with her hair all set up on top of her head, the Note from Heaven broke through.

I clearly remember this episode, because it opened up completely new avenues for working with the Note from Heaven. The story and use of images in relation to the singer's sound expression led me to devise the vocal release format, which later evolved into regressive cell-singing.

WE ARE TONE DEAF AND WANT TO BE ABLE TO SING IN TUNE

I established regressive cell-singing during the Christmas season of 2003. Several tone-deaf people had participated in my sound-healing and singing courses. One day, one of them called me and told me it had been nice to experience that her sound could be healing, but she also wanted to be able to sing along to Christmas carols without feeling embarrassed. 'Can you make a course where we learn how to sing in tune?' she asked.

I had previously had good experiences with one-to-one singing lessons for supposedly tone-deaf people. Feeling safe in this environment, they experienced moments when they forget themselves and sang completely in tune. It was already one of my hobbyhorses: everyone can sing. Tone deafness is a blockage that can be removed. I had no idea how, but I firmly believed that it was possible.

Before I knew what had happened, there was a group of five totally tone-deaf people. I had no idea how to design the course. One thing was for sure, though: no more than five participants. Three days before the course, I received the revelation that to this day is still the core of regressive cell-singing:

- A blockage is stored in the body's cells.
- Cells can be energized and purified by sound.
- By activating the emotion that has created the blockage, the appropriate cells are contacted.

The unresolved emotion is reactivated through code words: particular thoughts, images, sounds, words and expressions that touch the traumatized person emotionally.

The moment the emotion is activated, it is transformed into a sensation and affects the singer's physical state in the form of tension, pain, discomfort, difficulty breathing... symptoms of the suppressed discomfort that a trauma or shock have caused.

The outward, physical symptoms are the therapist's only way of measuring the degree of release taking place during regressive cell-singing. When recited at the end of the session, the code words that caused discomfort at the beginning of the session should now be demonstrating no, or at least only minimal, physical reaction.

When a person's tone deafness or other trauma originated before he or she started speaking as an infant, playing with baby sounds can bring the adult human back to a bodily experience of that preverbal state.

The sounds can easily spark off reflexes such as sucking, kicking, crawling and grasping, especially if the practitioner is lying on a mattress on the floor. They should be encouraged to give free rein to these responses; perhaps by being nursed or maybe even tickled a bit.

Parts of the tone-deaf person's identity have been kept on coat hangers in the pain body's dark closet. Some of the outfits are for formal and official use – for example, 'I can't sing in tune, so I will keep my mouth shut' – but there are also moth-bitten clothes lurking in the recesses of the closet as forgotten hopes: 'The teacher told me to stop singing, maybe he was mistaken?'

As the listener, I am fully convinced that the teacher was probably right that his student was singing out of tune at that moment, but at the same time I know he was wrong to leave that student alone with their self-perception, 'I can't sing.' My antidote to that is: 'Yes, you can sing! No matter how hard you try to convince me that you can't, I won't believe you. I know you can! What you are suffering from is a certain type of trauma, which is a frozen sense of powerlessness that has become a reflex. This means that every time you are about to sing, the "chained dog" inside of you starts howling, telling you that it is pointless to try.'

The day of the course came. We played with the body's sounds and in that way slowly got closer to the five participants' blockages. After we had worked for four hours, finding and vocally releasing the blockages at the root of their tone deafness, and looking at each individual's specific difficulty, I sat down at the piano. We had not practised singing in tune at any time.

I'll never forget that moment. I thought to myself, they must realize that this is an experiment; if even one of them manages to sing in tune, I'll be more than happy.

I played two notes. The whole group repeated them together. Each one of them could do it. It continued like that. In the end, I went so far as to sing children's songs with them. Yes – they could even hold the tone when I added in a second voice. So we threw ourselves into singing in canon. The atmosphere was thick with energy and several had tears in their eyes. We sang and sang. Finally, each of them plunged into singing solo. They each chose a particularly cherished song that they had dreamed of being able to sing their whole life. I remember one woman in particular who sang 'Edelweiss' without going off track at all. She and all the other participants achieved what is normally considered as 'singing in tune'.

This experience became a decisive turning point. If singing therapy could dissolve blockages of tone deafness, then surely it could be used to dissolve other types of blockages.

PART II

REGRESSIVE CELL-SINGING

PRINCIPLES AND PRACTICE

'Jesus said: "If you bring forth that in yourselves, this which is yours
will save you; if you do not bring forth that in yourselves, this which is
not yours in you will destroy you."'
Gospel of Thomas, log. 7

In regressive cell-singing, the listener supports the singer in singing his
or her cells free of the energy trapped inside them. When the energy is
liberated it reveals itself as the Note from Heaven. In order to listen to a
singer empathetically, you need to accept their state completely.

Sound is mere being. No judgment exists here.

The deeper you are able to listen to another person's sound, the stronger
the presence, the greater the sense of safety and human intimacy
that can arise. In regressive cell-singing all feelings are equally valued,
because, in terms of sound, they all have energetic potential.

The purpose of the process is to set free the specific frequency that
every true emotional expression embodies, to acknowledge and express

these sounds and let them ring, so the earth shakes. Those listening are delighted, uplifted, and wish for more and more. Sing more for us.

A suppressed feeling is an emotion. A feeling is 'felt' in the body. An emotion is transformed into a feeling when it is acknowledged. A feeling is transformed into an energetic state when it is exempted from judgment.

Listener and singer

In regressive cell-singing, the person singing him or herself free is called the singer. The responsible therapist is called a listener. The listener's main purpose is to listen carefully to the singer's expression of sound and reflect on what they hear; partly through practical advice about the sound and the physical aspects of its production, and partly through encouragement and passing on useful intuitive input and/or images.

Overview of a one-day course in regressive cell-singing

First contact between listener and singers

When someone registers for a session or a course, I ask for a few general details, but a minimum of personal ones. Occupation and education are the usual factors that bind a person to an old identity. Therefore, it is best that no one knows in advance who each person is. This will avoid prejudgments based on people's status.

In the case of heavily traumatized course participants, it is nevertheless important for the listener to know briefly what the case is about by privately discussing it with the singer. Avoid going into too many details about the trauma, as that can weaken the effect of any subsequent 'storytelling' (see page 159). The listener should reassure the participant that it is possible to take part without having to reveal which trauma is responsible for the sonic release. If embarrassing situations come up in a singer's story, never ask for an explanation or response. This discretion ensures that the focus stays on releasing the trauma. The actual nature of the trauma is of secondary importance. Anyone can participate, except for people suffering from a delusional mental illness.

Course participants who are taking medication are obliged to inform the course leader in advance. Antidepressants and psycho-pharmaceuticals place a 'lid' over the crown chakra, making it more difficult to get in touch with feelings.

Course structure
- Introductory talk (primary feelings, wishes, code words, body tensions)
- Contact with the inner child through sound and/or movement
- Breathing exercises
- Surrender to the Note from Heaven
- Regressive cell-singing
- Relaxation
- Sound-healing/healing

What to expect during regressive cell-singing
- Storytelling (the listener sees images and shares them with the singer)
- The singer sees colours/images
- Regression to past lives
- Regression to the spiritual state between lives
- Healing by the spiritual realms
- Sound-healing through the listener/group
- Supportive singing from the listener/group
- Changing of the story behind a trauma
- Others in the group can be deeply touched and respond to the singer's expression
- The singer's body reacts with spontaneous movements of the sphincter muscles
- The singer is confronted with a choice and has to decide in order to move forward
- The singer receives a symbolic tool to help them in daily life
- The singer comes in to contact with the spirit of a dead person
- Forgiveness
- Contact with a master/spiritual group that can clarify important issues

Providing a comfortable environment

During regressive cell-singing, the energy in a room always becomes intensified, no matter how big the space is.

Therefore, remember to air the room during breaks and agree with the participants that they are free to open and close the windows as they wish. Everyone is responsible for his or her own well-being. This means that if you are in a draught, don't just sit there and suffer while looking complainingly in the direction of the person who just opened the window. Swap places. Or close the window again. Or borrow a blanket, if that isn't enough. We are on a course to release the pain body, not to cultivate it.

Most people get warm when they are singing them self free. Quite a few articles of clothing get thrown off during the process. Afterwards the singer can feel cold, so it is imperative to have blankets ready. These have a symbolic protective significance. They also make people feel cosy after having been 'on the spot'. So the conditions of the room have to take account of widely differing needs.

Sensitivity to the density of the energy in the room varies. Everyone must take responsibility for him or herself and let the others know if they have difficulty in breathing or develop other problems.

If the course is taking place in an urban environment where the vocal activities may disturb other people, then the windows will have to remain closed. The best thing you can do in that case is to notify the course participants that the energy will get heavy and that the room will be aired between each release. If someone needs air, then they should feel free to leave the room for a while.

An expression of feeling from a singer can cause breathing difficulties for a fellow participant if their cells resonate with that particular problem. If a person's cells begin to sing along uncontrollably, this can arouse fear and cause tension in the throat or solar plexus.

The most suitable location for a course in regressive cell-singing is somewhere isolated. For a singer to have the courage to totally surrender to their sound, they need to feel confident that no one outside the room can hear them.

The listener's role

'To listen is to let go of oneself and surrender to a voice that is talking to you. It is to be open to being told a story.'
Jesper Blomberg, *priest in Udby, Denmark*

The listener's role is to support the singer in finding an opening in the sound of their voice through attentive listening.

The following tools are useful, but do keep in mind that no two situations are completely alike and sessions may take place where the opening occurs in a new way, which is the only possible way to overcome that particular singer's fear and self-control. When a person develops their ability to listen, the ability develops on all levels. For instance, their intuition will be refined and sharpened.

There are methods of treatment that are good and necessary to have as a platform, but intuition, compassion and love for your fellow human beings are the most important qualities of all. These are the qualities that develop through working with the Note from Heaven. A natural consequence of the work as a listener is that 'belief' is overtaken by 'knowing'. This knowing fills your heart with gratitude and happiness and urges you to serve the Note from Heaven dedicated with the deepest respect and humility.

'If you will come towards us, we will bend down and lift you up.'
Hazrat Inayat Khan, *Yayan, Vadan, Nirtan*

The amount of energy a person can bear is dependent on that person's ability to step aside and trust fully in a higher consciousness. If the singer is able to rise above the personal level, then they will not have to expend their own energy when singing. On the contrary, the singer will become recharged through the expression of the Note from Heaven, which gives access to an unlimited energy source.

Love for our fellow human beings, humility and gratitude are naturally awakened through work with the Note from Heaven. They are gifts that appear spontaneously and keep the listener and singer in ethical balance.

While listening closely, the listener becomes aware of the singer's feelings through their sound, and opens up to the singer's world: I hear you. I understand you. You do not need to isolate yourself with your feeling anymore.

When listened to unconditionally, the singer feels safe and opens up even more. In the purely listening state of consciousness there is no judgmental attitude, since all feelings are expressions of our humanity.

We are all equal and a part of the same whole.

If the listener is able to view the singer's outbreaks of emotion as archetypal, they will both be lifted above the purely personal level of the pain body. If, however, the listener becomes personally affected by the singer's problem and feels pity, contact with the Note from Heaven will be lost.

Meditative vocal work with the Note from Heaven naturally develops the abilities the listener needs. Regressive cell-singing can be carried out responsibly only by therapists who have listened to themselves thoroughly and, as a natural result of that, have purified themselves emotionally to such a degree that they can recognize the archetypes in themselves. This means that they can, at any time, rid themselves of restricting emotions like anger, fear and powerlessness by surrendering to the Note from Heaven. This opening stimulates the development of clairvoyance, clairaudience and clairsentience. When used with humility, these tools can in many cases be instrumental in pricking a hole in the festering boil to get the energy moving and ready to be released.

As a listener, it is an advantage to have knowledge of regression and other associated therapeutic tools, because these can support a singer in relieving traumas from earlier incarnations.

Another advantage for the listener is familiarity with working in 'between life' states. These can arise during sessions and it is important to be able to recognize them.

Sound-healing and other types of healing can be necessary if the singer gets stuck or needs help during the process. All sessions of regressive cell-singing finish with sound-healing, administered either by the course leader or by the course participants who take turns to give each other sound-healing. The purpose of this is to reinstate the protective energetic field around the body and to fill the emotionally released cells with light.

Important qualities and skills for the listener
- Ability to express the Note from Heaven
- Intuition developed through work with the Note from Heaven
- Listening without judgment
- Understanding physical navigation signs
- Experience with the methods of Regressive Sound healing;
    Regression Therapy
    Sound healing
- Respect, humility and ethics
- Love, compassion and presence
- Humour
- Authority, responsibility and vigour

Ethical considerations
Regressive cell-singing is based on respect for what 'is' at the present moment. The singer's voice must not be pressured to express more than the organism can handle, either physically or psychologically.

Crude provocations that cause the singer's instincts to go into emergency mode may break through the body's natural defences, but if an emotion is chased out of its protected hiding place, it has not genuinely been released. The singer's voice will be marked by desperation, anger and rage that are not the result of the release of a trauma, but instead are the body's reaction to being provoked. Pressure creates more pressure. If we violently yank at the chains that bind us to the pain body, we will cause deep wounds. It is better to allow the chains to be bathed in the light of consciousness. Sooner or later they will fall to the ground.

The fruit falls when it is ripe. It should not be shaken off the tree.

Forcing out emotions risks re-traumatizing the body. For example, I have heard of another singing therapy where people's spines are hit to prod out deep-lying emotions. This is not something I would ever contemplate doing.

In regressive cell-singing, the listener, like a mother bird, leads the singer to the edge of the nest, but the leap to freedom must be made by the singer alone.

The listener can cheer them on and encourage them, 'Come on, let go, jump!' But pushing the singer into the abyss before they are ready to use their wings will never lead to any good.

Although most people do make contact with the Note from Heaven during a one-day course, there are also some who do not. Those people, and especially those who carry the trauma of having being ignored very early in life, will have to remove carefully one protective layer at a time. The breakthrough will come unexpectedly one day, like a gift from heaven.

As a listener, you develop your intuition through confidence in working with the Note from Heaven, but you must still stay on your guard. The ego is always poised to enter the arena. The more skill and knowledge you acquire, the greater the temptation to take on the role of a guru and consider yourself superior to your clients.

The taste of power tempts the ego to boast and use the Note from Heaven for personal advantage: 'I am born with special clairvoyant abilities and am never wrong.' That is when everything falls apart.

The Note from Heaven serves the healer as long as the healer serves the whole.

Anyone who abuses power sinks down to a lower frequency, where their ears become deaf to the ring of truth.

It is natural for some people to see images, because they have easy access to the astral planes of consciousness. That does not mean that the person is grounded or that what they see is useful.

It may seem simple to sit and sing on one note with a group of people and pass on what you, as a channel, see. The problem is that if what you see or sense derives from your ego, then you are an abuser of energy – not a listener.

The key to becoming a good listener is the preliminary, personal, deepening work with the Note from Heaven. By training your ability to surrender, you will stay grounded by the *hara* chakra, which functions like an anchor. This grounding is what keeps the listener's ego in check. The sound speaks for itself: once you have experienced the Note from Heaven, you will always recognize the state intuitively. It is therefore pointless to use the intellect to analyze the power and information that you can access through the Note from Heaven.

The message has to find resonance in the singer. When a sound resonates, its effect is the validation of its truth. When images, messages, symbols, and stories activate a healing vibration in the singer, they are truthful.

Resonance is truth.

The divine is constantly embracing us and is at our disposal at any given moment. The question is whether we are resonant with the moment. I usually say, 'Take what works and forget the rest.'

Truth and falsehood do not exist at the oneness level. There are no polarities there, only being.

Listeners may convey intuitive messages, for example in the form of images, to touch the emotions hidden in the singer's pain body. The moment the singer receives a divine message whose deeper meaning only they can understand, a miracle takes place. Belief becomes knowing – 'The light is there for me, I am good enough.'

The miracle is the spark of trust – a trust that can open the gate and allow a release to take place. Belief and trust in the divine can pierce any armour. If the singer has a deep spiritual experience, and is able to take it in and integrate it into their life, then they can make a great leap in a matter of seconds.

The oneness level

Poor is the one who does not acknowledge being enriched.

The oneness level is the blissful state to which the Note from Heaven leads us. A plane where we are all part of one greater, higher being and become overwhelmed by a deep compassion, love and gratitude for everyone.

No one is alone. We are all part of the same source and belong to a shared power. There is no death, in that we are a connected whole. There are many names for this higher plane – the *akasha* field, *nirvana*, the zero-point field ...

When we are in touch with the oneness level, we can feel so wrapped up in love energy and so integrated that we experience ourselves as enlightened.

The Note from Heaven leads you to a plane of consciousness where you are illuminated, because your energy level is raised and your light therefore becomes stronger. 'I am enlightened,' the ego can now proudly cry out – but with this, the light bulb shatters and from the oneness level you plummet down to earth like a shot bird.

We are enlightened when we are illuminated. When the light is switched off, we are no longer illuminated. We are darkness, we are light. We are what we are.

To look for boxes to put ourselves into and labels to give ourselves is an expression of fear. What if you were enlightened and didn't know it? What if you thought you were enlightened and were actually in darkness? The light is given to us. You can't tie it down or capture it. Look for it in humility and maybe, then, you can stay there for a while longer. Who knows?

Trust and faith

'True faith is independent of reason.'
Hazrat Inayat Khan

'Faith doesn't begin with a person needing to think or make something up. No, faith is like when we were children and we listened to a story: "Once upon a time … ""

Jesper Blomberg, *priest in Udby, Denmark*

The process of regressive cell-singing normally starts with the participant making a wish, giving, in a way, the higher energies permission to work. This declaration is important, because neither the listener nor the power of the spirit has the right to infringe the integrity that the singer establishes through this initial wish.

Before the formulating process starts, it is useful to establish where the singer's true trust lies.

Does the singer feel secure leaving their wish as 'the release of what is most important right now', implying that they trust in an all-knowing power that knows best? Or does the singer need to control part of the process and express their own specific wish?

Most participants have no doubts. Some will have complete confidence in the higher plane, but the majority will feel more comfortable formulating a personal wish or prayer.

The degree to which the singer trusts the listener will depend on how much contact he or she has with the Note from Heaven. Can the listener support me if I fall and need to be picked up? What characterizes a good listener is that they have full confidence in the Note from Heaven.

Getting in touch with the Note from Heaven will dissolve any fear of the unfamiliar and supernatural, because the higher powers are integrated as a natural and positive part of our consciousness. We are never alone. Help is always available. The higher powers are cherishing us and we can contact these powers at any time. They are our superstructure, our internet.

Before a singer's consciousness can expand, his or her pain body must be ready to let go, so that it will be able to resonate with the higher-vibrating frequencies. I have seen several examples where course participants have had heaven placed at their feet, but they were not ready to embrace it.

'But the kingdom is in your centres and is about you. When you know yourselves then you will be known, and you will be aware that you are the sons of the Living Father. But if you do not know yourselves then

you are in poverty, and you are the poverty.'
Gospel of Thomas

Once the ego is flexible enough to relinquish control to the soul in total devotion, the Note from Heaven can work without the limitation of the participant's wishes. This lack of expectation makes the singer truly receptive.

Beauty is wholeness.

Any flower loses its beauty when dissected.

The resurrection of a torn flower reveals the miracle of its wholeness.

Before the dissection we didn't see the innate miracle, but the resurrection opens our eyes.

The flower's parts must be gathered together again before this can happen. Similarly, the Note from Heaven doesn't lead us 'forward', but always back to our original self, so that we, from within the shadows of the lost, can see the light and retrieve our whole self.

Only through the process of separation can the veil covering the face of divinity be withdrawn. A soul is born into the dualistic world and its longing to return to the oneness level awakens the consciousness, which can view its origins only through such separation.

There arises the possibility of a conscious reunion – a conscious moving between the two worlds. Two notes unite and a new note is born from their harmonious resonance. Wholeness is duality as well as oneness – to be a point and a wave at the same time.

The placebo effect

'Placebo, "I shall please" from placeō, "I please", is a simulated or otherwise medically ineffectual treatment for a disease or other medical condition intended to deceive the recipient. Sometimes patients given a placebo treatment will have a perceived or actual improvement in a medical condition, a phenomenon commonly called the placebo effect.'
Wikipedia

Most illnesses are caused by a general weakening of the organism. The petals of the flower are lying spread all over the floor, the stem is broken ... what a mess.

Placebos are usually referred to dismissively with a sceptical smile. 'He took a calcium tablet, which he believed was such and such and got well.' Belief is invisible, but it is belief that makes the connection to self-healing powers. Belief gathers all the petals back together. The immune system's ability to rebalance the body is nurtured by the patient's *belief* that he has the possibility to get well.

Doctors have taken on the role of priests in most of the Western world. They radiate authority and the patient gives a trusting sigh of relief: thank goodness, the doctor will know how to treat me. Sick people crave authority to give them hope and pull them out of the pain body's black waters. It is no wonder, then, that witch doctors in tribal communities have a role that covers both doctor and priest – for the one who can activate divine powers can also heal.

'Angels exist only if you believe in them.'
Gitta Mallasz, *Talking with Angels*

The Internet works only if the computer is hooked up to the router. You have to turn the television on before anything appears on the screen. You have to knock on the door for it to be opened.

In its meeting with the Note from Heaven, the soul is healed as the participant's trust in the higher self grows. This trust activates the placebo effect, which contains every belief's sparkling and healing strength – a power that at all times strives to regain wholeness for the body and soul.

WISHES AND PRIMARY FEELINGS

A session of regressive cell-singing starts with the singer uncovering his or her primary feeling in order to formulate a wish in writing.

By directing focus to the singer's primary feeling, the listener can help the singer to understand the core of an emotional problem or pattern and so to formulate a precise wish. During the formulation process it is the listener's responsibility to prevent the singer from spilling out their whole life story – first, because it is not energetically wise to do so, and second, because too much background knowledge given in advance can weaken the effect of any intuitive images or stories that the listener might receive.

Bear in mind the following considerations when working with primary feelings.

Painful and negatively charged emotions like hate, anger, jealousy, aggression, suppression, self-pity and so on can act as primary feelings because they are connected to the individual's self-identity.

Seen from a personal viewpoint, emotions usually arise from the subconscious as feelings of powerlessness, as a result of our personal boundaries being violated. In reality they represent frustration with our inability to command respect:

Why are they treating me like that? What am I doing wrong? Why do I let it bother me at all, when it must be their problem that they are so rude? Or is it me? Why didn't I say the right thing? Why did I cry? Why did I lash out? Why wasn't I able to control my emotions?

Seen from a higher perspective, primary feelings are linked to a survival pattern in the reptilian brain: to be abandoned by the tribal community means death. You cannot survive as an outsider. Arvin Larsen, scientist and heil practitioner, calls a primary feeling 'the neurological template'. Author and biologist Bruce Lipton calls it 'programming'. This programming is set in early childhood when the child instinctively submits to the environment's demands simply in order to survive.

So our primary feeling is the foundation upon which we form our perceptions about life and death; which means that if we need to change it, we also need to replace it with something else. By exposing our primary feeling, we awaken our awareness of its existence. From that awareness and self-reflection, we can gradually dissolve a negative, damaging feeling and substitute it with a positive, healing replacement.

The four primary feelings

1. I am not good enough
Indications

I feel ashamed, insecure, lacking in self-confidence. I fear failure, being exposed, being inadequate. I feel afraid of my own power. I am not lovable. I am ugly. I am stupid. I am wrong. I can't live up to what's expected. I feel anxious when I need to perform. I find no joy in life. I want to be admired. I want to be perfect. I am not good enough to be the light – not worthy of joy and happiness. I mustn't think I'm anything special.

Commentary

These kinds of thoughts go round in circles incessantly like toy trains on a track.

We all have a potential master within us.

For the light to reside within our bodies, we first need to let it in. If we feel unworthy, we keep ourselves in the shadow.

Positive implications

In your attempts to fit in with your surroundings, you can develop an understanding for your fellow human beings. As a result of your own insecurity, you need to try out identities that are not your own. When you land back in your own shoes again, you are able to see through other people's clumsy attempts to be good enough. The fact that you have been there yourself gives rise to care, compassion and empathy. You will be the last person to take advantage of someone else's lack of self-confidence. Power games and controlling behaviour are just not part of your repertoire.

2. I don't want to be here
Indications

I want to escape. I want to hide in a hole. I don't belong. I feel powerless.

I am jealous that everyone else has an easier time than me. I feel hurt. I lack grounding. I long for another dimension and I don't feel at home here on Earth.

Commentary

This primary feeling is often experienced by people who have been abused in childhood, where their soul has been at the mercy of an overpowering person and the child has found a way of coping by escaping into a psychological nonexistence. A classic example is when a neglected or ignored child dreams him or herself away.

Another case is the beautiful and rich child who has been given everything a heart could desire, except for true love and attention. The implications in 'I am not good enough' and 'I don't want to be here' are quite similar. The difference between the two feelings is nevertheless striking.

The former is all about staying and doing your best to fit in, which entails an endless effort to be good enough. For who is going to decide what is good enough? Is it your father, your mother? Society? Who has the right to decide, if not you?

The latter is about escape. You don't want to be here, because you don't fit in. The implication is that you'll fit in somewhere else, so you'll wait for an opportunity to get away.

Positive implications

The instinct to 'run away' – spiritually as well as physically – is essential in life. By spiritually running away from a harrowing experience, you remove yourself psychologically and thereby reduce the pain and dampen down the trauma.

On the surface, you are good at protesting defiantly. It's an expression of a frayed and vulnerable, yet persistent self-respect that you will fight for to the end. Somehow you know that there is another world somewhere else, because that is where you have a refuge. This knowledge can be used in connection with spiritual work.

'Jesus said: "Blessed is the man who has toiled, he has found the life."'
Gospel of Thomas, log. 58

3. I am not allowed to be here
Indications
I don't feel welcome. I try to make myself invisible. No one listens to me.
No one sees me. No one notices me. I am nothing. I don't mean anything.
I don't want to give anybody any trouble. My children, my husband/wife –
I am here for their sakes.

Commentary
People who have this primary feeling may have felt ignored or unwanted
as children. They may have felt abandoned by their closest relatives and
left to their own fate. Siblings may have arrived on the scene, leaving
them feeling marginalized. They have difficulty noticing what they feel.
Delusions of grandeur often go hand in hand with self-effacement.
   If the feeling of abandonment is associated with the death of a parent
or sibling or another loved one at a young age, this can also result in
feeling 'I don't want to be here.'

Positive implications
You are good at avoiding drawing attention to yourself. From this hiding
place you can observe the world without being disturbed. Therefore,
once you can feel entitled to be in your environment, you will have the
advantage of understanding it well and it will be easy for you to see
through the games people play with each other.

'He who understands everything but himself understands nothing.'
Gospel of Thomas, log. 67

4. I don't belong here, I am different
Indications
I don't fit into society. I feel alone. I yearn for something I cannot express.
I'm afraid to show who I am. I feel like an outsider. I'm afraid of my power,

because it can reveal who I am. I wish I could be like everyone else.

Commentary

These feelings are often a sign that a course participant has made good contact with their spiritual abilities. To confirm whether that is the case, the listener can inquire if the person had experiences as a child that would conventionally be regarded as abnormal. Be aware that the participant will probably consider these experiences to be normal. So it is the family members' response and reactions you have to ask about.

In regressive cell-singing, participants with this primary feeling are often shown glimpses from past lives: witch-burning, hanging, torture, stoning ... the ways society showed its fear and distrust of people who found their own way to the light.

When dealing with such violent traumas, it is essential that the singer is exposed to his or her agonies without getting emotionally lost in them. To do this, the listener should support the singer in surrendering to the Note from Heaven, so that the singer's soul can rise up to the light and be healed there. From this higher perspective, the singer can be shown their path here on earth and with that come to understand the meaning of life.

Positive implications

You know how to wait for the right moment and are humble in relation to power. The fear of revealing who you are causes you to hide behind different roles. The pain of recognizing this self-betrayal leads you deeper into loneliness. If you can acknowledge the loneliness as a positive teacher, this will lead you to the awareness that we are all separate (living in duality), as well as connected (united in oneness). Loneliness can lead to the recognition of unity.

> 'The mote that is in your brother's eye, you see, but the beam that is in your own eye you see not. When you cast the beam out of your eye, then you will see clearly to cast the mote out of your brother's eye.'
> *Gospel of Thomas, log. 26*

The listener's access to the formulation wish and primary feeling

The purpose of the articulation process is to come into contact with feelings in the body. Without expressing your emotions, without making a cry for help, you cannot be heard. The wish needs to be felt in the body. In some cases, the client is already so moved during the articulation phase as to be close to tears. As becoming moved and overwhelmed by a feeling can lead the sound directly into the cells, the listener, if possible, should push everything else to one side and urge the client to sing him or herself free right there and then.

In some cases, you really do only get one chance. If you don't seize the opportunity when it's there, you risk losing it. It's like fishing. You have to reel the fish in when it takes the bait.

If a feeling in the singer is ready to surface, you may observe physical signs such as shiny eyes, red spots on the throat and cheeks, restlessness, lips pressed together, a thick, throaty voice.

Rely on the slightest hint from your intuition. Don't wait, but act on your impression. Ask the singer, 'Can you sense a feeling inside you?'

If the singer whispers yes or is moved even more, then you must add wood to the fire: 'Where is the feeling located in your body? Go into it, sing it out! Let go! Every sound is welcome... in this space everything is allowed. Nothing can scare me. I want to hear all that you are! I love to hear your voice!'

In this situation, the listener is welcome to be as enthusiastic as they wish!

During the articulation process, the singer should be made aware that you get exactly what you ask for. Some course participants are under the impression that the articulation process is an opportunity to get as many presents as possible in their 'Christmas stocking'.

This is not the case. You usually get pretty much what you ask for, but not always in the way you expect and never more than the voice (the soul) is able to carry home from the 'Christmas party'.

Examples of formulating wishes

Each participant brings his or her unique set of experiences to the course and so the list of possible wishes singers may formulate is endless. However, the following is a guide to the kinds of wishes a listener will most commonly encounter.

Wishes to alleviate physical problems
- I wish to have the pain in my left shoulder released.
- I wish to have the main cause of my life-threatening disease released.
- I wish to get rid of my headache.
- I wish to have my bronchitis/my tinnitus/my reduced hearing ... released.

Wishes to alleviate psychological problems or undesirable life patterns
- I wish to have the feeling of not being good enough released.
- I wish to have the obstacle standing in the way of my trust in God, the universe and myself removed.
- I wish to have the feeling of being different released.
- I wish to have the feeling of not wanting to be here released.
- I wish to have the feeling of not being allowed to be here/of not being heard/of having to be invisible released.
- I wish to have the pattern that is preventing me from realizing my dreams in life released.
- I wish to be able to sustain a relationship and have the pattern that prevents me from doing so released.

Wishes for personal development
- I wish to serve a higher consciousness and have the barriers that prevent it released.
- I ask for what is most important, right now.
- I ask that my feminine/masculine powers be expressed better.
- I ask for my feminine and masculine powers to become mutually balanced.
- I ask for help in defending myself less and daring to show who I am.

Musical wishes

- I ask to be able to let go of all performance anxiety when I am on the stage.
- I ask to be able to express myself fully when I sing or play.
- I ask to let go of the need to control and to become able to surrender to the music.
- I wish to have the obstacle that makes me tone deaf removed.
- I wish to find the natural pitch of my voice.
- I wish to sing better in the high/low pitch.

Code words

In the process of articulating a wish, the singer listens attentively to his or her body and, with support from the listener, searches for their code words, which are those words that provoke strong emotions in them. A strong emotion always causes the muscles to tense up and hurt in some part of the body. It is the listener's role to observe and note down these physical tensions and the specific code words that trigger them.

The code words are not necessarily part of 'the wish', but are excellent initiators for the listener to use if the singer gets stuck in performance mode when singing. It is important to use the singer's exact wording, as it is this specific composition of words that provokes a reaction.

For example, I had a case in a seminar where a woman's code words were, 'You are just like Ruth!' This sentence wouldn't have worked if I, as a listener, had said, 'You are similar to Ruth.'

The code words really got the woman's voice going so effectively that the other participants were laughing their heads off while she sang herself free. Nobody knew who Ruth was or what the background story was, but the code words worked and the woman (who was not named Ruth) experienced such a release that tears rolled down her cheeks from both weeping and laughing combined.

As the listener, I added wood to the fire by repeating the code words again and again until their effect wore off. At the end of the course, I let the singer hear that sentence just one last time. The words no longer caused tension in her body. She smiled gratefully and gave me a hug.

So, during the process of singing free, the listener uses prearranged code words designed to help the singer get in touch with genuine emotional reactions.

At the end of the session, the listener enquires about the tense areas of the body that were noted and that had reacted to the code words before. If the body still tenses up when the associated code words are recited, the singer is urged to sing into that area again. If listener and singer conclude that the trauma has more than one layer and needs to be released over several sessions, it's time to finish for the day.

The expression in the singer's voice can also tell you whether he or she has had enough.

The listener may intuitively decide to attempt just one last contact in a new way. Frequently, an unexpected breakthrough occurs when the singer has already given up and, with a shrug of the shoulders and no expectation of success, tries one last time, despite believing 'the voice is finished'.

If the tensions have disappeared after the singing and have been replaced with warmth, tingling and relaxation, a healing has occurred in that particular location. In such cases, the singer's face is usually radiant, the eyes sparkling, and seriousness is replaced by ease and a readiness to laugh.

The pain may have disappeared and the singer feels a blissful peace and sense of well-being. In some cases, a permanent healing takes place. In others, the pain returns after two to ten days. The reason for this is that the body produces pain-relieving endorphins during devoted singing, which can continue to be effective for several days afterwards.

After a process of release, the singer can continue on their own by singing devotedly in their daily life. Perhaps the listener and singer arrange a programme together to continue the work.

Examples of code words

Wish: I want to release the pain in my left shoulder.
Code words: You are powerless. You are not worth anything. You are not good enough. You will never be able to contact the divine powers.

Physical reactions: The singer's arms get heavy; there is a pressure in the head, pain between the shoulders.

Wish: I want to release the feeling of not being good enough.
Code words: You are not worth loving. You are afraid to be revealed. You should be ashamed of yourself.
Physical reactions: The throat tightens up, speechlessness, a hard tension in the solar plexus.

Wish: I want to release the feeling of not wanting to be here.
Code words: You have nothing to contribute. You can't be part of the group. Everyone hates you.
Physical reactions: The throat tightens up, the body stiffens, shortness of breath, tension in the stomach and lower abdomen.

Wish: I ask to be able to serve the higher consciousness and have the blocks released that are preventing me doing this.
Code words: You are afraid to show your true face. You are afraid of others' reactions. You can't stay centred.
Physical reactions: The throat closes off completely, a sense of strangulation, tensions in the solar plexus.

Cold hands may be an indication that the singer was burned at the stake in an earlier incarnation.

Navigation signs

A navigation sign is just as important for the listener as headlights are for a car driver on a narrow country lane in the dead of night. Navigation signs tell you whether you are on the right track or not. They appear as physical reactions that vary from person to person, and are a precious tool. A listener merely needs to be aware of certain physical reactions in their own body.

My green (i.e. positive) navigation sign is a kind of 'heart orgasm' – my heart expands and I surrender with a sigh. I feel moved and overwhelmed with gratitude. I yawn and gasp. If you have the same navigation sign, I suggest you explain to the singer in advance that when you yawn it means something good is happening, not that you are bored! My eyes often water during the yawning, especially the left eye.

So, for me, a 'heart orgasm' tells me I am on the right track and that I should continue and be patient. The meaning will be revealed later.

My red (negative) navigation signs are heavy arms and a feeling of powerlessness and fatigue across the shoulders.

When I feel these signs of exhaustion, I know I need to stop, because I am no longer on the right track.

To find your navigation signs, follow these three basic steps:

- Ask to have your navigation signs shown to you.
- Pay attention to your physical reactions when you or others are in contact with the Note from Heaven.
- Ask for the meaning of each navigation sign: is it a green light or a red light?

At a larger sound-healing course for therapists, several of them found that tension in the neck was their red navigation sign.

Some clients are difficult to get through to. There may be lots of images coming to you, but the singer can't relate to them. There just doesn't seem to be any resonance. 'How long should I continue? Am I heading in the right direction?' Those kinds of questions pop up in the listener's mind. It is good that they do, because a listener can never be completely sure that what they see or sense is pure. And, even if it is, if the singer can't receive it, then it makes no difference.

If I receive a green navigation sign, I continue with confidence, even if the story seems totally absurd and is not having any noticeable effect on the singer.

In cases like this, what sometimes happens is that the singer lets his or her defences down for a few seconds. In that moment, the connection in the story will 'ambush' them with such conviction that they will suddenly start to feel trust and, with that, open up to the Note from Heaven.

If I do not receive any navigation signs, I silently pray to be shown the way. In some cases, the story then takes a completely different turn. In other cases, it's necessary for the whole group to provide support and sing with the singer. Maybe a certain way of touching the singer will cause the barricades to fall – especially when dealing with experiences from infancy. Or the listener may need to use his or her voice in a way that speaks to the singer as a small child. Or maybe the singer needs sound-healing.

RIDING ON FEELINGS

The driving force in regressive cell-singing is feeling. The feeling rises just like a big wave, and must be caught at the right moment in order to be able to surf it all the way to the shore.

In brief, the process is: you awaken the emotion, catch the feeling, ride it ashore and in that way liberate the cells.

When a feeling is revived, the body's memory of a given moment awakens and the suppressed reaction to an old, unexpressed emotion will be poised and ready to surge through the organism.

Many of us have 'stopped up' our throats and find it hard to express strong feelings. The essence of the Note from Heaven is deep peace, brotherly love and gratitude.

Before we can get to that point, the bottleneck needs to be cleared, so that the excess pressure of carbon dioxide in the shaken fizzy drink can be released.

Regressive cell-singing is a quick method of release, where things can change dramatically from one minute to the next. When long-repressed feelings are released, it often happens with a wild, penetrating force. This may take the form of screaming or angry shouts, often accompanied by corresponding physical gestures.

Although dramatic, the process is profoundly liberating for the singer, so there is no reason for onlookers to be alarmed. However, they may still feel uncomfortable, not out of concern for the singer but because of Resonance with Domino Effect (see page 233).

In cases of screaming and other intense reactions, I have one golden rule: *it takes one to two minutes at most for the excess pressure to be released*. After that, it is the listener's responsibility to lead the expression up into the light for it to become musically beautiful as the Note from Heaven's nourishing energy transforms and celebrates the return to life of what was hidden.

If the singer is allowed to wallow in their feelings for longer than those two minutes, there is a great danger that they will, out of habit, surrender to the pain body and get lost in the trauma. If that happens, the feelings can become stuck and turn into a kind of self-perpetuating floorshow that can be very difficult for the listener to stop.

How to lead a singer up to the light

The listener listens intently for a strong sound in the singer's expression of feelings and emphasizes this sound by singing along with it. In this way the listener pulls the singer up onto a life raft in the middle of the surging sea of feelings. Turbulent feelings can be transformed effectively through 'cry-toning' (see page 155), where the tones coming through in the crying are reinforced and sung out.

If the singer refuses to follow the listener – and accuses the listener of disturbing them – it is almost always a sign that their pain body has taken over. I have been accused of re-traumatizing a singer, because they had wanted to scream in front of an audience and I had stopped them. The singer tried to get the other course participants to feel pity and draw them into a power game. The result was that everyone present was sucked dry of their energy. The listener's responsibility is to stop the process immediately by stating the truth: 'You are expressing your pain body – not the Note from Heaven.' In such a case, your navigation sign will be flashing red.

Expression

'We need to express what is within us to make it real. And we also need the right kind of response. When our expression is rejected, it feels as if we are being wiped out, annihilated – we become unreal.'
Audun Myskja

From the earliest age, we are conditioned to restrict the expression of our feelings. We have learned that it is wrong to yell, scream, be angry or hysterical. Boys are often told that it is embarrassing to cry. Feelings are held in check and tucked away in emotional boxes that are stored in the vaults of the pain body.

Children as well as adults sense the unspoken and unexpressed in the atmosphere that surrounds them: the air is heavy and breathing is withheld. People feel ill at ease when they are prevented from flowering as human beings. As a means of avoiding disapproval or censure, children learn to adapt how they express themselves according to the restrictions they are subjected to. If the adaptation happens early on in a child's life, it will become an integral part of his or her developing identity and that child will learn how best to attract love.

It is vital that a child's expression receives an open response, because true expression connects the child to the higher self. If adults continually reject the child's expression because they 'know best', the child will stop listening to their own feelings and lose self-confidence.

Let any expression of the self through vocal sound, truly and spontaneously, be legitimate and praiseworthy. An easy way to meet children's need to express themselves freely is to encourage them to cleanse themselves through sound. Where can the emotion be felt in the body? What does the feeling sound like? Sing it together with the child. As cleansing through sound comes naturally to most children, they usually feel much better straight after the outburst.

When adult and child join together in sound, they create an atmosphere of intimacy and closeness. The child feels completely heard, while the process may also allow the adult to release hidden emotions from childhood. Deep love emerges, whereas aggression, irritation and telling the child to 'shut up' (so the feelings can't come out) would have spoiled the day.

When we accept someone's expression of a feeling, we deny their pain body's appetite and help them to avoid suffering.

Imagine for a moment a crowd of people going berserk. This reaction could be incited by their football team losing, a perceived injustice, racial hatred or opposition to the government. According to the pain body, it is always *someone else's fault*. Just a single spark can be enough to ignite our bone-dry emotional kindling; the pain body's fuel is self-pity, provocation, projection and suffering.

When the pain body is activated and turns its black, foaming inner side outwards, all hell breaks loose.

However, through conscious vocalization of our feelings, we can regain self-confidence and shine light onto the pain body and heal its wounds.

When a feeling is expressed through sound, a surplus of pure energy is released. The rocket is fired off, but not aimed at anyone. It's more like a vibrant firework display. The energy fills the room and enriches everyone present with joy. They purify themselves in the moment by surrendering to the sound, singing up to the heavens and freeing themselves and their fellow human beings from the grip of emotions.

Unfortunately, there is a tendency to label people who relieve their feelings through sound as crazy, because they seem to be out of control emotionally. In the worst cases, they get admitted to psychiatric care, where they are heavily medicated and rendered harmless before they can activate too many unexpressed feelings in the 'normal' people's pain body.

For eons, tribal societies have instinctively released stuck emotions by making vocal sounds. The Sami, for example, go out into the wild and sing themselves free of surplus anger, joy and grief.

It is just as natural to cleanse yourself emotionally as it is to wash your hands when they are dirty. Holding back reactions for a long time is undesirable, not only for the individual but for society as a whole.

Repressed emotions tend to affect us differently depending on whether we are predominantly extrovert or introvert in nature.

Extrovert expression-pattern

An extrovert will, sooner or later, need to release the pressure caused by pent-up and festering emotions. The lid blows off and the pressure is relieved through an explosive expression of distorted, deformed feelings. This may manifest itself in, for example, obscure complaints, anger triggered by trivial matters, unjust and inappropriate aggression or physical violence.

Introvert expression-pattern

An introvert will exude reticence and will be difficult to figure out or relate to. Audible as well as inaudible bad vibrations become 'rancid' through being kept hidden too long instead of being addressed as soon as they occur. The result is a slow, leaking expression of repressed emotions that are projected onto the person's surroundings through instances, for example, of bitterness, irritation, anger or psychological violence/psychopathic behaviour.

Public recognition of the impact emotions have in our society could save humankind from a lot of its suffering. Just imagine if there was a public sound room in every city for the purpose of clearing out inappropriate feelings! 'Go to the sound room and let your emotions out, instead of snapping at us and making yourself ill from keeping your mouth shut ...'

All feelings are worth their weight in gold. The bad ones as well as the good. When you express a feeling openly and it is acknowledged, you can surf on it, gliding like a whale rider and, through the expression of your voice, escape from unnecessary burdens. It happens all by itself in a space where we can make unrestricted sounds in joy and safety. Emotions only do harm when they are imprisoned in the flesh.

Free-flowing water carries all of the vital nutrients around in the body. Movement is life. Still-standing water gradually becomes stagnant. In order to survive we need to drink clean, oxidized water; drinking polluted water can kill us. It is the same with feelings.

Freely expressed feelings enliven the organism. Trapped emotions poison the body.

Cry-toning

As a listener, it is possible to harness the power of crying to help a singer to release pent-up emotions, because the weeping brings out tones that resonate with a given emotion. The art is to get the singer to hop onto the wave of weeping at the right moment: just as the weeping starts the singer consciously strengthens their sounds and in a way dramatizes them by singing on long 'sobs'.

How to stimulate cry-toning

The moment a singer is moved by a feeling, the listener needs to sustain contact with the emotion, because most people have been taught to hold back their tears. Let intuition and sensitivity rule here. The goal is that, if possible, the volcano should erupt and the excess pressure be released.

On the physical level, if the singer has an open mouth and holds his or her arms up in a gesture of surrender, this will help to stimulate the weeping. This is to be done while the listener recites the code words that trigger the feeling. It feels good to throw out our arms in a devil-may-care manner. To begin with, if the singer is dealing with pent-up rage, he or she may clench fists. Later on, the listener will need to invite the singer to open their hands and turn the palms upwards. In that way, the body becomes receptive to an exchange of energy with the higher planes.

Participants who are scared by the inner forces that are breaking through may clench their teeth (a natural defence). This considerably reduces the power of the voice and the chances of crying. During singing of the vowel 'Aaar', the tongue must be relaxed and lie forwards in the mouth, with the tip resting on or just behind the lower teeth. With deeply felt cry-toning there are usually no tensions in the tongue.

If the singer struggles with their crying, it is the listener's task to catch the most penetrating and clear tonal gifts that the crying brings out. The listener can briefly emphasize and sing along, 'crying' on the notes, to inspire the singer to give in to the cry-toning.

Once the singer experiences the liberating, exuberant power that cry-toning awakens in them, they will be able to keep going.

It feels simply wonderful to release the weeping in a fire of song. After just one or two minutes, maybe less, the serious atmosphere is replaced with one of absurd comedy and opens into euphoric bliss, maybe even hearty laughter. No singer will be allowed to break down in tears. With cry-toning you sing on the crying tones, which releases much more energy than normal crying.

In cry-toning there is no self-pity.

You enjoy the weeping as a long-awaited downpour and use it as a gateway through which to access the Note from Heaven.

Cry-toning in action

For one female participant, weeping was a well-known and safe territory. She cried in the session like a little child who wanted to be heard and yet was not quite sure if it was really allowed. No really clear tones came forward – her voice whistled around in the weeping, like a swirling wind that couldn't quite collect itself to produce a powerful gust. Light puffs of wind don't get the fire going. If you observe the singer's breathing in that kind of halfway-crying, it will be gasping and short, instead of long, deep and dynamic.

At this point I, as the listener, needed to reflect back what I was hearing. The woman's role as 'the little one we should feel sorry for' felt safe because she had been playing it for years.

If the weeping is tearless, then the singer is almost always playing out an unconscious, learned role.

The listener needs to be non-judgmentally honest. 'What kind of crying is that? Can we get some feelings out in the open here? It's not good enough to hide behind sniffling, I want to hear genuine sound in your crying.'

People are used to negative reactions when they cry. Here it is a party. The weeping is a gift. And when the weeping gathers force it is immediately expressed by singing. If the cry-toning is authentic, the feelings remain and now we can get the fire going that will burn the cells free of physical and psychological trauma.

This singer stated that it was a conscious choice for her; she allowed herself to play up her feelings and let the weeping flow so freely that it could turn into sound. Not everyone is able to do that. As the listener, you will then have to gamble and give the singer a little push so they can make the run-up and take their leap. In most cases it works, but if the person is not ready to let go of their role there is a danger that they will close off instead of continuing.

The singer is faced with a choice. Do I want to passively watch the embers come and then go out or am I ready to actively take the step to consciously blow life into the embers of the trauma and go through the fire of transformation? Am I afraid of my powers? That precious fire, will I let it go out?

A transformation can happen immediately if the singer dares to let go.

Cry-toning can be used for acute personal clearing out of accumulated painful emotions, as demonstrated in the following account. While out driving with my then husband, we started arguing. Our son, four years old at the time, had a sensitive disposition and wasn't used to conflict. When my husband angrily stopped the car on the shoulder of the highway and went to the side to urinate, my son and I also got out of the car. Our son was obviously as upset as I was. We opened the boot, stuck our heads inside it and cried and screamed out our frustrations. Our son thought it was fun. We yelled out full blast on long tones. My frightened husband came running back with his pants half open. He stood there for a moment and looked at us. Then he stuck his head into the boot as well and screamed. We were all in a better mood for the rest of the journey. The air was still shaken, but cleared.

If you want to test cry-toning yourself and there are other people in the house, it can be done into a pillow in the bedroom or, even better, find your own secluded cry-toning place or take a trip in the car and express your cry-toning there.

Cry-toning works so well because the body's instinctive reactions are brought into play. The breathing muscles open up and do everything right. If the weeping and expression of feelings are genuine, you can clearly hear and sense when the real expression comes through. Cry-song is a prayer from the bottom of your heart. The energy is unmistakable. If you are in doubt, then the Note from Heaven has not come through. As humans, we can instinctively recognize the energy that manifests through the Note from Heaven. The power enhances us and makes us happy.

Although the expression can seem very intense, you don't run any risk of psychological or physical injury, because a genuine cry always comes from the pit of the stomach. This means that the expression is grounded and secure.

STORYTELLING

Some listeners see inner pictures when a singer expresses him or herself vocally. You can develop these images into stories and tell them to the singer to encourage the release of blocked emotions. The ability to see inner pictures develops gradually, as your trust in your intuition grows stronger. If you see colours, that is also good.

Storytelling reflects the subconscious mind, where the singer can be liberated from the wicked fairy's curse of petrified princes and princesses – in other words, traumas. Traumas are energetic impressions of events. Like footprints in the sand, these energetic impressions are blotted out when consciousness shines its light on them.

The particular benefit of stories is that they can slip past our defence mechanisms unnoticed as, like dreams, they seduce us into forgetting ourselves and thus pave the way for the light of consciousness.

The plot can lead in numerous directions. Almost all of them lead to heaven, but before this destination is reached, the singer can be led down into the dark recesses of the subconscious mind in the form of regressive experiences in this life, the embryonic stage, or past lives. Maybe they sing themselves to states between lives and get in touch with a spiritual master and receive healing there. It is also quite common to receive a parable that is full of symbols.

The listener is not supposed to try to understand or interpret the meaning of the story as it unfolds, but solely to rely on navigation signs (see page 149–151). The reason is, that the listener's ignorance preserves the singer's integrity and the story's validity and impact.

During the storytelling, the listener can ask the singer whether the story means anything to them if it's not obvious whether the singer is reacting to the images. The singer often nods slightly, completely absorbed in their song, and the listener takes encouragement from this, even though they don't have a clue what's going on.

Story examples

These stories are all genuine, but due to my professional confidentiality I have excluded distinctive characteristics and specific personal statements.

Story 1: Back to nature

Here is an example of a story in which the sound expression was so overwhelmingly pure that the atmosphere in the room turned completely devout.

Gender of the singer: Female
Wish: I ask to be shown my path in life.
Primary feeling: I feel different. I yearn to belong.(I don't belong here.)
Code words: You are not good enough to work with sound. You can't find your way. You are fragmented.
Physical reactions: Pain in the lower abdomen and right hip.

The story

Everything is white. *The sound opens up.* There is drifting snow. Strong wind. The Inuit. *The sound becomes melodious and sorrowful. The singer's face lights up.* A leather sled with a child tied to it. The child is wrapped in furs. The man is fighting his way through the mounds of snow. He and the boy have been out hunting and were surprised by a sudden change of weather. *The voice is fighting stoutly and bears witness to images of a strong, beautiful nature. The Note from Heaven has come through. Survival. The images are unusually clear.*

Thanks to the man's good sense of direction he makes it home. He is worried whether the child has survived the journey. Everything appears white and impenetrable, but then a crack in the rock appears. The man and child enter through a curtain in the form of several hanging furs. The feeling of relief at meeting the tribe in the long, deep rock cave. The warmth. The child is handed over to the women. The feeling of unity. Acceptance of nature and the will of the higher powers. Song of thanks.

The song is more beautiful than ever. Where before it was powerful, it now glows softly with gratitude. The men around the fire. A clear division between the genders. Laughter in the corners. Children, odours of people, dogs. The smell of food. Finally home.

What happened next

The singer was deeply touched and said that she had always been fascinated by the Inuit. She was only visiting Denmark. Normally she lived with her First Nations husband on a small island in western Canada. Her lower abdomen and right hip were now free of pain.

The unusually beautiful song expression in the story described above inspired me to record a CD of regressive cell-singing. My intention was to produce something that would help the singers and would also be a supplement to this book. The course participant kindly agreed to travel several hours to my home a few days later. I had prepared a studio and wired up. The same code words, the same wish. The woman's pain in her lower abdomen had been gone since the course. The expression in her voice sounded different now.

This time the images I saw were extremely blurred at best. We were both affected by the recording circumstances and 'performing' gradually took hold of the singer. Even though her singing was still beautiful, the expression was no longer authentic. Slightly disappointed, we had to acknowledge that the release had already taken place.

You can only express what you are.

An expression of feelings is unique and can't be repeated.

On a later occasion, I tried to capture sound expressions in the moment of release. With the participants' consent, I installed the studio on the course premises.

The course went well and then I started editing the recordings. Somehow I felt uncomfortable with this. Some of the participants had come through more clearly than others. Was I trampling on holy ground? When I shared my misgivings with the participants, they urged me to continue. So I decided to keep my promise and complete the project anyway.

When the editing was almost finished, the hard disk in the studio went down and all of the recordings disappeared. That was the first time such a thing had ever happened in the whole existence of the studio. Since then, I have never dared to record regressive cell-singing.

Story 2: Strengthening Faith

Gender of the singer: Female
Wish: I wish to release the behavioural pattern that is preventing me from forming a long-term relationship.
Primary feeling: I am not good enough.
Code words: You're jealous. You're not sure if you want to have children. You're frightened of being rejected. You feel powerless.
Physical reactions: Tensions in the solar plexus and heart.

The story

A woman with her hair wrapped up in curlers. *The vocal expression is going back and forth and isn't making much headway.* She ties a scarf around the old-fashioned curlers on her head. I say, *'What is the woman doing? Take me there with your voice.'* She is weaving. There are baskets of wool in the room; she is spinning her own yarn. She is weaving and weaving.

I wonder what all this weaving means and therefore pray to the higher powers to lead us to the core issue. The voice opens up a little bit more. The Note from Heaven has not yet broken through completely.

The weaver now goes out to a little yard to feed her sheep. The sound opens up a bit more. A change of scene: the woman has dressed up and brushed her curled hair. She is cooking and setting the table for two. A man walks through the gate into the yard. He has fair hair, steel spectacles and is dressed in dark trousers, jacket and white shirt. A young priest, a student? The woman is uncertain of his intentions.

They eat and she tries to catch his eye. She senses that he hardly hears what she is saying. He is shovelling the food into his mouth. The others in the parish must not find out about this. He was late, because he tried to avoid being seen. The woman winces at the feeling of his not wanting to acknowledge her. After the meal, he sits on the sofa and reads the paper while she clears the table. Afterwards, the woman also sits on the sofa, but on the edge and at a proper distance from her guest. She feels uncomfortable. Suddenly the man throws himself at her and kisses her hard on the mouth. He tears at her clothes. The woman resists and gets enormous strength. *Now the Note from Heaven breaks through.*

The woman stands up, pushing the young man away so that he falls to the floor. She runs out into the yard, through the gate and looks for help. Just then she sees a man with a cap and big wooden clogs covered in clay come striding across the fields in the direction of her farm. The man clearly leads an outdoor life, he must be a farmer or something similar. The woman is crying and the man comes willingly towards her and asks what has happened. He comforts her. He carries her resolutely into the house. They know each other.

I have always wanted to have children with you, he confides. Will you marry me?

This question opens up a choice situation that the singer has to respond to. So, as the listener, I ask her directly: 'Do you want to marry him and have children with him?'

The singer answers that she feels it is too soon after what she has just experienced (the young man is gone now), but she can see that the farmer is kind and open. Nothing is held back. 'The man wants to dance with you. Do you want to dance with him?' The singer replies, 'Yes.'

What happened next

Afterwards I was still unsure whether the big release had taken place.

The singer already had a good voice and even though the Note from Heaven broke through, she was still not sure whether to continue her relationship with the farmer. It looked as if she needed more time.

After resting, the singer, slightly shaken, explained that she did weave, that she kept sheep (not on a farm, but in her garden) and had spun the yarn herself and woven with the wool. The young man seemed to be an image of her former boyfriend and the farmer was a gardener she knew who was her weekly dance partner. He had recently told her just what the farmer said in the story: that he would like to have children with her. They had not yet become lovers.

Story 3: Dissolving a social phobia

Gender of the singer: Female

Wish: I wish to get into contact with myself.

Primary feeling: I don't want to be here.

Code words: You've lost your expression. You're afraid of being noticed. You panicked when you had to speak in school. You're afraid of any kind of social contact. You don't feel you belong here. You want to get away from here.

Physical reactions: The whole body stiffens. Throat contracts.

The story

A dead woman is hanging, naked and mutilated, by her neck on a big hook as an example and warning to the local villagers. *The singer agrees to go backwards in the story to dissolve it.*

Now the woman is being tortured by the men of the church. Her two children also, so that she finally admits to being a witch. *We go quickly backwards, only pausing at the violent scene long enough for the singer to make contact with the cells that are bound to the trauma. I sense from the singer's sound and reaction that it's not the violence itself that is the main source of the trauma.*

I ask her directly what she senses the trauma is about. 'The feeling of being let down, not the torture itself,' she replies.

It's the villagers. She had been their wise woman. It was to her they had all come when they had a problem. She had always been there for them. Being let down – the feeling of being totally let down. Their evasive glances. They bear witness against her. The help she had given them now turned into accusations of witchcraft. Was Jesus Christ perhaps involved? She had been associating with the devil, that's for sure, according to them.

The singer's feeling is clear: I don't want to be here on earth. I want to get away from here. I don't want anything to do with you all. The Note from Heaven rings through the air like a sword. The singer totally manifests her power through her sound. I ask if she would like a tool to help her rediscover the power she is now in touch with. The singer agrees. 'Close your eyes and ask for a tool. The first thing that comes to you is your tool, no matter how absurd it seems.' The singer picks up a flower.

The singer decides that she wants to change the story and, with that, the trauma's energetic imprint. I give her suggestions which she accepts or rejects until the story is just the way she wants it:

The woman is taken off the hook; we rewind the story as if it were a red carpet being rolled up. We come back to her whitewashed house with the beautiful garden full of herbs. She walks in her garden in a light-coloured dress. The children are playing. The woman is reborn. The villagers come by one at a time and ask for forgiveness. They bring flowers to her. A man offers to be her gardener. No, she will take care of the flowers herself, but he can help with the vegetable garden. When the villagers have gathered and are all kneeling in a circle and full of remorse, the woman forgives them.

She doesn't want anything to do with the priests, but she wants the church premises preserved. A spiral energy form sucks the priests up and they disappear for ever.

To avoid the fear of new, possibly hostile priests in the church, we put an open-minded priest into office. His attitude to the woman and her work is gentle and full of love and respect. He sees that she is a pious woman, who with her good deeds is following Jesus's true message.

What happened next
A week later, the singer informed me that during the past week she had sensed her body in a whole new way and that she now experienced the world differently, much more positively: 'This is the most releasing treatment I have ever experienced.' (She had taken early retirement because of her social phobia.)

SITUATIONS THE LISTENER MUST BE PREPARED FOR

The storytelling element of regressive cell-singing can throw up a number of situations that the listener must handle with particular care to avoid impeding the singer's emotional release.

When a choice needs to be made

Almost all stories lead to one or more situations where some kind of choice needs to be made. At these points the singer has to decide how they want to continue – if they want to go this way or that, whether, for example, to forgive, embrace, defy, fight, answer a question ...

When these situations arise, the listener must always interrupt the story and ask the singer what he or she wants to do, even if they themselves have a clear sense of what would be best for the singer. By all means discuss the options if the singer is unsure. The listener can give good advice and weigh up the potential consequences of this or that choice, but should never make the choice for the singer.

Example

A singer comes to a halt in the development of his or her expression when the story takes them to an old white house. The expression just goes round in circles, becoming monotonous and evasive. At the same moment, the images stop. The sound expresses the singer's insecurity about going into the house. 'Do you want to see what's inside the house?' the listener asks.

This is a gentler question than 'Do you want to go into the house?' and it helps the singer to recognize how they are feeling. 'I'm afraid to go into the house. I can feel my throat tightening.' They go on: 'The house isn't important; there's something behind the house in the garden. I'm afraid to go there.'

The singer starts to shake and cry at the recognition of the emotion beginning to surface. This creates an opening for the Note from Heaven. Situations that present a choice often lead to such openings in the energy field, so the listener really needs to have a sure instinct and good ear for these moments. As no one is out in the garden behind the house and the sound shows no trace of the Note from Heaven despite the opening, the singer appears to have evaded the issue with this manoeuvre. The listener then rephrases the question: 'I would really like to see what's inside the house, would you like to go inside with me?'

The singer doesn't dare, so an adult comes walking by to accompany the singer into the house. This can work particularly well if the singer's persona in the story is a child who needs to be released from something frightening – they will feel safer if they have someone to hold their hand.

'A hunter is passing by, is it all right if he goes inside with you?'

'No, I want to go inside with my uncle. I feel safe with him.'

When the path to a trauma has been cleared, the singer must be ready to meet the trauma. When faced with such a choice, anyone would be uneasy about opting for the dangerous path. So, as the listener, you must remove any 'land mines' in advance. If bodyguards are needed, provide them.

When other feelings obscure the primary feeling

There are several layers of emotion bound to a person's issues. In some cases, however, one emotion can be so prominent that you can't get around it, even though the course participant seems to have asked about something completely different.

For example, a woman came with a wish to have some heavy traumas from her childhood released. But grief about her dear old dog Spot dying a month before was uppermost in her mind. She hadn't mentioned the episode, but the little tail-wagging, black-and-white spotted dog was the very first image that appeared. This started a veritable hurricane of emotions.

The singer told how the dog had been mentally ill and its illness had filled most of her life. The image of the dog functioned like a needle piercing a hole in an abscess, so the infection could finally flow out.

We just managed to get a glimpse of a big black thorn wrapped in pink robes, before the hole closed up again: there had also been mental illness in her childhood home.

When a singer wants to tell their life story

A personal interpretation of a problem can become so integral to someone's identity that it prevents contact to their primary feeling and bars the way to any fresh insight.

For example, a person who has suffered from abuse may have retold their story so many times that they become trapped in the role of victim. This role entitles them to attention which sustains and reinforces the trauma; it also gives others the right to feel sorry for them and to feel superior. No one chooses such a role. It gradually becomes integrated into the pain body and the person is taken over by it, and becomes dependent on it. In this situation the listener needs to break the pattern and stop the singer before they assert this role in the group. As previously discussed, in regressive cell-singing the less the listener knows about the singer's personal life, the greater the chance for the therapy to have a releasing effect.

The listener will need to use intuition to draw the line between information that is important and information that will inhibit the process of release.

Issues of confidentiality

The listener and group members must respect the confidentiality of all participants.

In cases where a singer has been subject to serious abuse in this life, it is advisable for the listener to be briefly informed about it in advance, especially if the cell-singing is taking place in a group. If the singer feels insecure at the thought of singing in a group, the listener must consider whether it would be beneficial for the person to be confronted by their fear in front of other participants. If they decide it would not, a private session should be offered.

Sometimes I have had clear pictures indicating that a singer has been abused, without actually knowing whether this is the case. At times like this, it is especially important to take care not to overstep boundaries.

- A listener must at all costs avoid empowering the singer's pain body.
- Negative thoughts tie up a person's energy.
- Pent-up energy is poison for the body as it imprisons the affected cells.
- The listener's knowledge of the cause of a singer's trauma is only important if it supports the process of release.

Listeners can really set the cat among the pigeons if they are not careful. A singer might, for example, begin to suspect on the basis of the listener's images that they have suppressed the memory of abuse in their childhood.

I have known course participants who have received this type of information from clairvoyants and who walk around with a dreadful 'secret' that they dare not tell their aged father or mother about, a secret that can very easily get mixed up with other, totally different problems they are already struggling with. Close relationships are easy to poison: 'Did I sit on Dad's lap a little too often?'

To protect a singer's confidentiality and avoid inadvertently revealing embarrassing details during storytelling, it is important that all the participants are aware in advance that the listener's images and stories are to be understood as symbolic, archetypal dreams. I normally merely hint at any images relating to delicate subjects. If the images keep coming, I discreetly enquire about the theme or wait until I can do so privately.

If the listener is in doubt as to the story's meaning or validity, the singer's personal integrity can be preserved by the listener asking them to describe their own experience.

Example

Once in a story, a woman was so strongly attracted to another woman that she deserted her husband-to-be in the middle of their marriage ceremony. The two women then made passionate love. The story was set in the Middle Ages.

What can one say to that? The singer sang just as passionately and let go completely ... I asked carefully: 'Can it be true, that it is two women?' The singer nodded and seemed to become even more aroused in her singing expression, despite being happily married to a man. We never delved deeper into details. The images led to a release in the voice and thus served their purpose.

The advantage with regressive cell-singing is that the stories, just like dreams, can be interpreted symbolically or as past lives. They camouflage reality, so only the singer is able to draw on the essence of the story. That gives total freedom.

A FEW COMMON SYMBOLS

Animals

Birds

It is quite common for birds to feature in regressive cell-singing stories. I encounter birds of all kinds: eagles, swans, storks, pelicans, parrots, seagulls, owls, pigeons, falcons and small sparrows. Sometimes I see a bird with distinctive features but I have no idea what it is called. In such cases, I describe the features for the singer.

Birds act as messengers between heaven and earth. Sometimes they symbolize a person known to the singer, who passes over and gives advice. Sometimes it is the singer who becomes a bird and experiences the freedom of flight. For someone who is trying to go up towards the light, what could be better than to have a set of wings?

Riding animals

Pent-up powers can appear as horses or other strong animals like dolphins, whales, bears, lions, tigers, elephants, rhinos, hippos and gigantic spiders that break out of their captivity. In that moment, one doesn't know if it is the story or the Note from Heaven that comes first. The Note liberates the animal, and the animal sets the Note free. The type of animal depends on the type of trauma and on the singer's inner experience.

For example, a singer faced a challenge (or so I thought) when she was invited to sit up on a gigantic, black, hairy spider. Without a murmur she mounted the spider and rode it happily through the world while singing and exuding strength. 'I have always perceived the spider to be a sacred animal of power,' she said afterwards.

In Hinduism, every aspect of God has its mount. For example, Ganesh has a mouse, Sarasvati a swan, Shiva a tiger. It is interesting that these mounts also appear again and again as archetypes in regressive cell-singing. The animals carry us onwards from one state to another. They strengthen us with their trusting approach to life.

Embracing animals

When self-confidence is low, having the courage to embrace a formidable or repulsive animal can change everything. Kiss the frog and redeem the enchanted prince or princess. Beauty and the Beast. We all have fairy tales inside us. Here is an example from regressive cell-singing:

An Indian is standing outside a dark forest. The sky is dark grey and there are no leaves on the trees. The earth is frozen and covered with a fine layer of snow. The Indian is reluctant to go into the forest. Fear. Then he hears shots coming from the forest.

The sky becomes red. *Now the singer's voice gets warmer.* The hunters mustn't shoot the Indian's beloved animals. He finds a big stick and, filled with anger, goes into the forest. The shots stop, the Indian is in the middle of the forest and feels the fear creeping over him once more. The anger is replaced by frustration at not being able to find the hunters.

Suddenly he finds himself in front of a huge, furious brown bear. The stick would break like a matchstick in its mighty paws. The bear is up on its hind legs in the semi-darkness with its yellow-white teeth glinting. *Here the singer must make a decision: 'Do I meet the bear head on or try to escape?'*

In the event the singer chooses to run away, but now it is the listener's responsibility to point out that running away may signify death whereas meeting the bear head on, looking the beast in the eye, may represent the singer overcoming and releasing her fear.

The singer needs to be persuaded, but as soon as she decides the Indian should stand his ground the Note from Heaven breaks through. At times like this, when great courage is needed, the other course participants and/or the listener can sing their support.

After hesitating for quite a long time, the trembling Indian takes the first couple of shaky steps towards the angry bear. *You can be sure that's what's happening by the expression in the singer's voice. You would be able to tell if she were pretending and just telling you, 'Yeah, yeah, I'm doing it' – the whole organism has to be engaged.*

When the Indian is standing up close to the bear's body, it embraces him tenderly and he surrenders to the mighty beast. *The singer's voice expresses a fullness of power in its grateful unfolding of the Note from Heaven.* The Indian and the bear melt together in a column of light.

The sound moves us all and it gives the woman clarity about her path here in life. Now she has the strength to withstand her fear.

Thinking about the image of hugging the bear will always give her a feeling of power and wholeness. By recalling how her body felt in that moment, the woman will be able to contact the Note from Heaven whenever she wants.

Crosses

Crosses naturally carry religious associations. They often occur in classical stories set in earlier times (for example, regressions taking place in monasteries, churches or during the age of crucifixions). Many singers' stories culminate in release before a church altar, with a cross (or Jesus, God, Mary, Mary Magdalene, the Divine Mother...) leading the singer up to the light. Here are two stories of release with the cross as the theme.

Union of ego and soul

A heavy drawbridge must be taken up to prevent a threatening and heavily armed army from forcing its way into a monastery. A group of monks succeed in hauling up the drawbridge at the very last moment. *The singer's voice has low undertones, which continue.* Now they are safe. The enemy can't get in. A monk or priest is clearing up. He dresses himself in a fine cloak, puts a pope-like hat on his head and goes in to pray in the vestry. A big, heavy cross is lying on the stone floor in front of him, upon which a bluish, bald, naked figure is lying, unable to move. It looks like an alien.

As the priest is about to pray, the blue creature opens its eyes. They glow with a blend of precious stones and magnets. They are good eyes.

'Priest, you must unite with me,' the bluish, hermaphrodite figure says. After all the priest has gone through, only to be faced by this! Not quite what he had planned. Rather reluctantly, the priest tries to sing strength into the figure. Without success.

'Take your cloak and hat off, so we can meet in purity,' the blue figure says.

As the priest stands humbly and without the trappings of his power, the beautiful blue creature rises up from the floor. *The Note from Heaven breaks through with its marvellous, luminous overtones.*

The singer experiences total acceptance of the soul (the blue creature) by the ego (the priest). The blue figure unites with the priest. The cross now stands upright, pure and penance-free.

Freedom from an austere upbringing

A young woman is standing by the sea on a bridge. This is the time of Columbus. A merchant ship is approaching the shore. A young man rows out from the ship in a small boat and picks her up. He takes her back to the ship. Her parents and brother stand on a cliff and wave goodbye (*it turns out later that they represent the singer's own family*).

The woman sails off to find adventure. She resolves to marry the young man, but not primarily for love. The ship lands on an island, where the couple go into an imposing, square house with columns. They enter a hall with a high ceiling. In the middle of the hall stands a large cross.

'You must dance with the cross.' *I am surprised when the singer's face at once becomes tearful.* As the woman dances with the cross, it comes alive, its contours soften and it transforms into her fiancée. Now she can love him... the light breaks through and the cross gets its own place in the room, while the two lovers dance around freely.

Deeply moved, the singer later revealed that she grew up in a religious family that belonged to an austere Christian sect. She had left the sect as an adult. This had cut her off from her family, but her rigid upbringing still weighed heavily within her. That is why she had to dance with the cross, to soften it with her own hands and make it her own, in order to be set free.

REVEALING THE LIGHT IN A SINGER'S VOICE

Light symbolizes contact to the higher, healing energies. Therefore, the moment in a story when the Note from Heaven breaks through fear's armour will almost always be accompanied by some form of illumination – for example, dark clouds pierced by a healing ray of light causing the sky to become increasingly bright.

Light may also break through as a shaft in a closed room or before a church altar. It may bathe two lovers or a child reunited with its mother and or father, in love, forgiveness etc. As the listener, ask the singer if they can sense or see the light – they usually can.

Sometimes, though, the singer has so little sense of self-worth that they can't experience how beautiful their sound is. In such cases, the singer may just shrug their shoulders at the story, even though it's obvious to everyone else from the singer's vocal expression that the Note from Heaven is shining through. The singer doesn't dare break free from the pain body. It's nice and safe to be a nobody, who is no threat to anyone and will be left alone, and may even find consolation in the bittersweet taste of feeling like a martyr. This means the self-unaware singer can't see, hear or feel the light in their sound, even though we all are overwhelmed, and perhaps even moved to tears, by their singing.

'Well, no, it's nothing special.'

In such cases, I often ask whether any of the other participants would like to be sound-healed by the singer. With everyone having been so affected by the light in the singer's voice, there's usually no shortage of volunteers. Otherwise I put myself forward.

The singer will now experience their light and sound reflected in another person in the sound-healing situation. They will forget themselves, because the one receiving the healing becomes more important, which fits perfectly with their pain-body pattern. Through the exchange of energy, the singer will be forced to listen to him or herself, because it's necessary to listen for resonance from the Note from Heaven during sound-healing.

Afterwards I ask them to sing the light down to themselves again. 'Do you feel the light now? Do you hear your beautiful overtones?' Usually the singer's face is now totally radiant and the answer is a resounding 'Yes!'

Dealing with melodramatic performance

When a singer performs melodramatically, it is because he or she is trapped in their pain body. Their vocal expression has become stuck in a groove.

When they scream, yell or cry for more than one or two minutes, their emotional expression has become indirect. Instead of being energizing, the sound will be empty and draining for those listening. A melodramatic performance is exhausting to listen to and will awaken only negative feelings. The singer may be crying, but there are few tears, or even none at all, and the crying doesn't arouse any genuine feelings in the listener's heart.

The same is true for a singing expression that feels stuck and empty of feeling. The singer can sing for hours and whether they recognize it or not, they need help in order to move on.

From experience I have found that in all cases of melodramatic performance it's best to interrupt the singer as soon as possible. Be sensitive and wait until the singer pauses in their breathing. Give tactful, but honest feedback: 'It seems to me that your contact with the primary feeling is not deep enough. We need to try another way.' Or 'I do not feel your expression in my heart.' Or 'I experience that you are caught in a childhood pattern, am I right?' 'Do you need to be held?' 'Would you like us to see you? Hear you?' 'Who or what do you miss?' 'Whatever you want.'

Of course, you should only say things like that if you can identify with the mother/father role in a natural way without ridiculing the singer. They are often in a state where they will react like a child. The child is happy to get a response wherever they are at that moment. In any situation, a good laugh can activate the *hara* and set authentic expression in motion.

If the singer is showing signs of hysteria, ask him or her to sing high notes. The high notes are narrow, and represent the pure child in us all. Keep calm as a listener, and express yourself with authority. It's a power game. Do not fear, listener.

The aim is to identify and satisfy 'the child's' needs, so they will dare to open up to their true feelings. In this way, an authentic expression can be reached.

In rare cases you may come up against heavy resistance, even be verbally attacked when you try to guide a singer away from their melodramatic performance: 'I'm just about to be released.' 'You've got it all wrong.' 'You're destroying my process.' 'You aren't being therapeutic.' 'I need more time.'

You have to be prepared for aggression from a person whose ego is fighting tooth and nail to avoid acknowledging dangerous feelings. Remember, the longer the singer is allowed free rein, the greater will be their embarrassment – and annoyance – when they are interrupted.

When the listener's navigation sign shows red, he or she must act quickly and aim without flinching. I have experienced melodramatic performers who, unconsciously, crave the limelight. Here the 'performer' has an opportunity to milk energy from their audience. 'Energy addicts' have an overriding need to draw attention to themselves. A child who yearns for his or her parents' attention, and only gets it in a negative form, through misbehaviour, may bring this pattern with them into adulthood.

If the listener allows it, a melodramatic performer can cause the session to go round in circles. For example, they may endlessly argue over some trivial matter. The therapist also needs to be aware that the singer's pattern of self-protection may consist of projection. For example, the energy addict may use criticism to try to knock the listener off course and force them to defend or justify themselves. Never bring yourself down to the personal level. The question of whether the listener is good enough is non-negotiable. Anyone can make a mistake, but do not evaluate these with the participant. As soon as the listener's authority is undermined, the stardust will instantly vanish from all the miracles of that day.

The best way to avoid that kind of manipulation is to recognize the melodramatic singer's behavioural pattern in advance. We're dealing with compensation for genuine love. It's a learned pattern from childhood. It doesn't benefit anyone if a whole group is sucked dry of energy.

In a worst-case scenario, the listener should be prepared to erect a wall (see page 181–182) and allow the participant to wear him or herself out, rather than provoke them further by interrupting their need to exploit the situation.

Don't forget that a genuine outburst of anger can contain an opening to the Note from Heaven, so the listener must at the same time try to concentrate on listening to the sound within the rage and cheer the singer on when a strong sound is expressed. Do not stoop to the personal level. Keep yourself floating above the situation by listening intently to the quality of the sound. Praise the person for the real power that is finally breaking through and releasing the pressure in the room. The aggression that the singer had previously expressed will be dispelled by the appearance of the Note from Heaven. All genuine expressions of emotion are a welcome part of the process. They only become harmful if the listener takes them personally and judges the participant.

The state of consciousness behind listening for and noticing the sound in another person's voice lifts the listener like a balloon above and beyond the range of any artillery.

To be able to keep one's consciousness in a state of love elevated above the personal level is the overriding goal for a listener.

Care and physical contact

One purely physical way that a listener can help a singer to surrender to the Note from Heaven is to lay one hand lightly on the singer's forehead and use the other to support the neck, so that the singer can safely lean their head backwards (a bared throat facilitates surrender).

When a singer delves into experiences from early childhood, he or she will invariably respond well to being held or touched. If it feels natural, the listener can play the role of father or mother expressing unconditional love and care, but remember the golden rule: always ask the singer for permission to touch them.

In some cases, caring behaviour like this can hinder the process, because it implies that the listener does not trust the singer to manage for themselves. When it is time for the participant to stand up to something, they will need to do this on their own. Just as, when the singer is confronted with their ego or their fear, it is he or she who must take the step to embrace the beast, forgive, agree to change their story, etc.

If the singer hesitates for a long time, the listener and the rest of the group can offer support with singing. The choir can build up an almost ceremonial atmosphere, which supports the singer without taking over their process.

Then the listener recites the code words that, at the beginning of the session, triggered strong feelings. If they still cause tension in the body, then there is more to be sung out. Before ending the session, the 'baby' is led back to their real age, which means being able to stand on their own feet when surrendering to the Note from Heaven.

One other thing. You risk disturbing a good transformational process by being too caring – for example, the listener must refrain from wiping away a singer's tears as they sing themselves free. Put a tissue in their hand so they can do it themselves.

Don't ever feel pity for a course participant. To have pity arouses pain. To have compassion awakens light.

Tears are a sign that release is occurring or just about to. Tearless crying is a sign that the singer is not yet in touch with genuine feelings.

Holding one hand gently on the singer's forehead and the other behind their neck has a calming effect, because this physical stimulation connects the consciousness with the reptilian brain and can, therefore, support them in completely letting their voice go.

When the listener touches the singer, they must use their sensitivity and only do what feels natural. If the listener's heart is not awakened by love for the 'child', it is because there is no need for those feelings at that moment. If the listener pretends, then a real release will not occur. The child that is calling for care needs the real thing and, interestingly enough, most course participants working with the Note from Heaven are able to respond quite naturally in a caring manner.

Don't just put your hand on someone's forehead or neck because I've told you that it works. It should be something that you do naturally through a process. Please be aware that every thought, every fear you have is registered by the other person.

Sit under the tree and listen patiently. The fruit will fall into your lap when it is ripe.

Encouraging openness about sexuality

Unfulfilled sexuality is often the underlying cause of physical imbalance and, therefore, disease. Surrendering to the Note from Heaven releases bound-up energy in a manner that has orgasmic characteristics and which compensates for releases that could have happened in another way. When there is resonance and unconditional love between the partners, sexual union provides undreamt-of opportunities for spiritual development. Working with the Note from Heaven opens up the way to this kind of spiritual elevation through erotic union.

In my experience, when I put my cards on the table and find a free, natural and light-hearted way to discuss a taboo subject like sexuality, the course participants breathe a sigh of relief. Sometimes two of them will look at each other in amazement: 'What? You haven't had sex for ten years either?'

Today's sexual freedom, and the breaking down of traditional gender roles, has, to a great extent, resulted in apathy between the two sexes. Just as the positive and negative poles of the earth are getting weaker over time, the differences between men and women are gradually becoming equalized. The subject is so extensive and important that it deserves a separate book.

The listener has to rise above his or her own sexuality, so that the client feels comfortable sharing embarrassing details they have kept to themselves for a long time. I might share my own general sexual experiences with the client if I judge that this will help to liberate them from feeling wrong, ashamed or guilty.

A wound has to be uncovered to be cleansed, tended and healed. By removing the boundaries of conventional 'decency', we also remove the fear of being punished for discussing sex and sexual fantasies. We all have fantasies, since we are all in contact with the astral plane.

When eroticism is elevated to full-blown love, it is raised up to the higher level of the astral plane, where fantasies are unnecessary because dream-like images appear on their own and often cause deep emotional reactions, especially in women. It is very important that a man sees a woman's crying as a great honour, akin to the transformative reactions generated by singing on the Note from Heaven.

'If you bring beauty, truth, health, light or joy into the world, you are doing the right thing.'
Shaman Olga Kharitidi

Shared themes

I often find that many different participants in the same group have issues in common. On one course, four out of five participants had difficulty standing up for themselves and all of them were dealing with a similar problem with their mothers; another time, nine women out of twelve had hip problems and had had, or were about to have, an operation for cysts in their abdomen; and yet another time every participant had been subject to sexual abuse, although only one had mentioned it in advance.

There are also mixed-theme days, but it is striking how often there are coincidences, even though I do not screen participants beforehand. Usually, no one knows each other in advance, as it can be problematic for close friends or family members to participate in the same group. A clean slate, where you can be yourself without anyone reflecting habitual roles back at you, is an advantage in the surrendering process.

Getting locked into tonal patterns

In regressive cell-singing some singers unconsciously repeat certain tonal intervals again and again like mice constantly running the same route up and down the stairs inside a cage. They can't break free from the pattern. It's as if the phrase is programmed into their brain.

These repeated vocal patterns usually come from a singer's 'training', by which I mean that they have learned an identity that is 'nice', amenable, well-behaved. Sensitive souls fearfully fulfil all required conditions in order to secure love.

It can be difficult to let go of a tonal pattern because it may represent a lifeline to those we hold dear. 'If I don't do what is expected of me, then I won't be loved.' Conformity can be a protective armour, and it must gradually be dissolved. In some cases, the armour is so strong that the singer, try as they might, cannot get in touch with any kind of feeling. Like in a mollusc, the emotion lies well protected under decades of deposits that have become flinty shells. Here we must rely on patience. If we are lucky, storytelling, with just the right code words (see page 147), can winkle the emotions out.

Sometimes the emotional awakening just happens spontaneously when the singer's defences are down, as it does in Resonance with Domino Effect (see page 233).

When a question is practical

Many people are cautious about opening themselves up emotionally. Consequently, they come with a simple wish or a practical question.

For example, one woman asked, 'What should I do to get rid of the fungal infection in my lungs?' She thought her asthmatic bronchitis was caused by fungus.

She got a clear answer when she began to sing with a weakened voice (note that the story has been reduced to its essence – it took almost 25 minutes to draw her voice out): 'A sick man is lying down in a little cabin on a ship, which is sailing without a steersman. The journey starts on an icy sea and ends in Hawaii. The ship lands there and the sick man is served by attractive, half-naked women richly decorated with flower wreaths around their necks. They carry him down to the beach on a stretcher. He relaxes here while the women are at his beck and call.'

The answer was very simple: take a vacation in a warm country, relax and let yourself be spoiled.

Another example. A woman asked to be able to sing high notes. She gradually sang herself higher up via a story and, much to her surprise, experienced being able to sing high, melodious notes. We didn't get an explanation. Straightforward wishes often lead to straightforward outcomes.

WHEN THE LISTENER HAS TO BUILD A WALL

'If you say, "I cannot," you don't want to. If you want to, you can.'
Hazrat Inayat Khan

Out of several hundred regressive cell-singing sessions, I have experienced only a few cases where I needed to build a wall, which I describe in the two case studies below. Despite its rarity, this phenomenon is an extremely relevant subject. Building a wall is an important defence mechanism for the listener. If they don't know when to do it, they can end up fundamentally damaging their confidence and losing their power.

To build a wall is needed if a singer attacks the listener with
aggression, criticism and/or drains the listener and group of energy. It is
built solely of conscious thought: I build a white wall, which the singer can
attack without hitting me personally.

Example 1: Nooo, I don't want to sing!

When a young woman who had been subject to extremely damaging
incest in her childhood registered for a course in regressive cell-singing,
she deliberately hid her major social problems. She lived an isolated
private life, had no boyfriend and, in general, felt no desire to live life
here on earth.

In this case, it was quite an advantage for me as the listener to know a
little about her background. None of the course participants received any
information about the young woman.

During the warm-up the girl refused to sing or make any sound.
I accepted her reaction as healthy and dignified. She needed all of her
strength and this strength was bound up in being able to say no.

That had to be the point: to get her to say no. And to whom else
could she say no to other than me? I gave her some time. I approached
her carefully for a couple of rounds, accepting her increasingly obstinate
refusal. The point at which her anger would be influenced by the others'
reactions came nearer. The great balancing act for me here was to judge
the right moment for a final confrontation with the girl. The stronger
her anger, the greater the discharge; but, on the other hand, if she were
pushed too far she might decide to leave the course, and there would be
no way back for any of us. The young woman would feel defeated and
the atmosphere in the group would plummet so far down that it would be
difficult to lift it up again.

I took a chance and asked her to express her 'No' more forcefully:
'NNNNoooo!' That is when the image of building a wall appeared, so she
could fire away at me without doing me any harm.

'More "Nooo", I want to hear more!' The girl let out a deafening
scream! She screamed and screamed. The other participants put their
fingers in their ears and I did as well. (You are fully within your rights to

protect your ears if the sound from a participant is painful to your ears or heart.) The power was indescribably strong. 'More, more, we want to hear all of it, out with it!' I had to yell through her screaming.

To give promptings when a singer takes a short pause during a catharsis is not a good idea as it can bring the process to a halt. For example, saying 'Yes, come on' while a singer is inhaling can make a listener sound impatient. It might suggest he or she does not think the singer is doing well on their own. However, when the singer is in the throes of an outpouring the same phrase can seem completely different. Then, it is like adding fuel to the fire. It always feels good to get a pat on the shoulder, to be accepted and cheered on when you are fully engaged in action.

The best thing is to glide tonally with the singer, so the person feels 'we are together' and the others in the group accept, hear, feel, enjoy and get inspired and healed by the emotionally charged expression. Enthusiastic shouts of encouragement are important during the singing, otherwise the thought 'I wonder what the others are thinking?' might just creep in and stop the process. 'Am I being embarrassing?' 'No – we are with you and are truly enjoying your release.'

The girl screamed and screamed while flinging her slender body about. An empathetic participant handed the girl a tissue for the tears that followed after the screams. The tissue was angrily crumpled up, hurled to the ground and trampled on in an almost euphoric dance. The girl began to smile, and so did the rest of us. This was a body beginning to discover the woman within – a body that had been frozen in a state of 'I don't want to be here.'

After two minutes of screaming, the woman's true voice broke through, as if coming directly from heaven.

In the pauses between the singer's breathing, I did what I normally do – repeat the images that appeared during her expression of the Note from Heaven.

A fishing boat on a rough sea with a pink, ragged sky. The fishermen have caught a beautiful dolphin in their net. The dolphin fights its way loose from the Filipino fishermen and slides back into the sea. Shaking with fear, it dives down and meets a male dolphin. They briefly rub each other's noses, before the female dolphin swims up to the surface of the sea again. The dolphin moves so violently in the water that the fishing boat is washed away by the tidal wave caused by the anger. The dolphin stands up on its tail fin still singing powerfully. The male dolphin waits in the distance.

In the end, the singer burned the tissue that she had trampled on. This was done ceremonially in my teacup. After some follow-up three day-courses, this woman was finally able to get on with her life. The last I heard she had begun painting and was planning an exhibition, and she had also enrolled for a university course.

There are no rules or recommendations regarding the number of sessions. This particular woman felt she needed additional courses – each time with an interval of approximately one or two months to digest the cellular changes from the previous course. It is up to the individual to decide how many courses they need and how long the time period between them should be. There have been cases where participants have come again, but could clearly sense that they had already outlived their trauma. Such a realization is a golden full stop. It's over and they are moving on in life.

Example 2: Wishing for more than you can handle

Another time I had to create a wall was when treating a journalist, whose interest in regressive cell-singing appeared to be more professional than personal. The episode added much to my experience, which is why I mention it here.

The session showed that when a singer intellectually works out their ultimate wish it will be met head on. If the person is not able to handle the ultimate, a mirror image is created that can be extremely provocative when the singer is confronted by it.

When I asked for the first volunteer at the start of the session, the journalist put herself forward without hesitation.

Her wish was for unconditional love – both to receive it and to be able to give it – and her primary feeling was that she was not good enough.

Very unusually, she did not have any code words. The images started to come and at first nothing seemed amiss.

Steep, dark cliffs surrounding water. Dark sky, grey clouds. The singer started to grunt and hiss demonically. A black, oblong, narrow wooden boat. A woman dressed in black with a little child, a man dressed in a dark cowl propels the boat with a long pole. Hopeless feeling. Is it death? The singer did not answer, but continued with the deep hissing tones. There was no ground in the tones, they went in circles and felt unpleasant, in that they seem to affirm themselves in the darkness. After a while, the atmosphere became really heavy. 'Sing the child up into the light; we need an opening up to heaven.' The boat glides drearily on. The singer's sound expression was the same.

Now the child is up on the cliff and the boat has gone. No change in the singer's vocal expression. The little, naked child is lying on the cold, hard cliff. It will die if no one takes care of it. The singer continued grunting and by now the energy in the group had completely dropped. I felt heavy and noticed that I was being drained of energy. It was as if the singer was opposing every opportunity for release out of an inconsolable self-loathing. Now a stork is coming. It stands waiting beside the child with a nappy in its beak.

The singing continued in the same dark, demonic groove. 'The stork says that it will fly off again if you don't help it get the child up into the light.' With that, the singer cracked: 'I need more time, and by the way, the child is not going up into the light at all. It's going to stay on the cliff!'

'Then the child will die.'

'Yeah, well let it die!' she yelled. 'Therapists don't do that. You are not a good therapist!'

I let her know that I needed to be loyal to the energy I channel.

'You're no channel. Do you think you're so pure that you can be a channel?'

At that moment, I created an imaginary wall and invited the singer to shout at me. The journalist did not let herself be drawn in. All of my urgings for her to shout out her anger at me were demolished by her own self-view: 'Don't you dare think you're somebody special!' (In other words: I don't want any help, I am not worth anything, I don't deserve it.) Obstinately, she continued with her grumbling. I closed my eyes and prayed for a way out.

'The stork suggests flying you and the baby over to a strong, warm-hearted peasant woman, who is sitting on a newly harvested field on a pile of hay. Will you go along with that?' The singer nodded slowly and began to sing. The voice was softer now, but still without the slightest contact to the Note from Heaven.

'The peasant woman is bringing you up to her breast and rocking you. You grow warm and feel safe and good.'

The singer obviously wanted to call the shots. It was difficult to guide her through breathing. She strongly resisted every bit of advice, as if I were the enemy.

'A huge, golden sunflower appears in the distance. You are being offered the chance of being lifted up into the sunflower's golden centre by the peasant woman. Here you can receive the light of heaven. Do you want that?'

'No.' The reply came without a moment's hesitation. 'But I would like to pick it and take it with me.' The singer now sang with a self-conscious softness and I got the impression that her attention was focused on the others' opinion of her. As she had now been singing twice as long as her allotted time, I rounded off.

The rest of the day she smiled politely and kept her distance. In the following days, I received quite a number of aggressive e-mails from her; however, they did become softer towards the end of the week: 'I sing now with the cows out in the field and that feels good.'

Wishes can be so contrived that they miss the target. You can have your greatest wish granted and yet be unable to accept it ...

GENERAL PROBLEMS

When a singer does not hear the story

In some cases, the singer can get so caught up in the Note from Heaven that they 'disappear' into their own world. When this happens, I choose to tell the story anyway, as it influences the subconscious mind. I follow the same principle when a singer sings so powerfully that they can't hear what I am saying.

After a long and colourful story, where the voice seems to have sung the story forwards, singers sometimes complain that they didn't catch what I said. I point out that the story is secondary to the release that has occurred. If they have been so 'gone' that they didn't hear the story, this is usually an excellent sign – it suggests that they have been on a higher plane and have been released there. It is my impression that the story gets the voice going and gives the singer a private space in which to feel free. While all the rest of us are engaged in the 'plot', the singer can float around in the healing energy. However, I do retell the story if that's what they want, as the echo of the story offers security, a link to the world so that they can easily find their way home again.

When a singer does not recognize a miracle

'Jesus said: "I am the light that is above them all. I am the All. The All comes forth from me and the All reaches towards me. Cleave the wood, I am there; lift up the stone, and you shall find me there."'
Gospel of Thomas, log. 77

A miracle is within reach for everybody, just as the spiritual world is. But we have to recognize the wonder in order to experience it. So, if you ask for a miracle to happen, you must, at the same time, ask to be open enough to receive it.

The stronger a singer's trust in the higher powers, the more miraculous the manifestations, and the greater the gratitude and surrendering.

When a miracle causes healing or the improvement of imbalances, the effect will only manifest itself permanently if the singer simultaneously expands their consciousness.

The healed person will not always accept the physical proof of a healing as a miracle nor will they feel gratitude in their heart. Singers sometimes deny everything immediately after a miraculous healing: 'Well,

I wasn't that sick anyway. It probably would have gone away by itself.'

Alternatively, a client may give the therapist all the credit: 'Thank you, Githa, for having healed me.' Such gratitude is natural, but testifies to their inability to open up to the essence of the miracle.

It is not out of humility that I refuse their gratitude: it's just that it wasn't my doing! I opened myself up so the energy could flow through me. My trust in the higher power gave the energy the opportunity to work. The power of the Note from Heaven is much greater than that of one person.

'The healing is free, but my time is certainly not!'
Lars Muhl, *The 'O' Manuscript*

So, there is no guarantee that a singer will realize that a miracle has occurred, even if the listener and the other course participants have, without any doubt, experienced it to be so.

'The cure' and the process of the disease have a higher meaning that perishes if they are not also bound up with a strengthening of the client's trust in the divine. The miracle turns a minus into a plus, as the vertical line represents fervent trust. Without connection between the shadow and the light, the plus power vanishes.

A person for whom the miraculous stardust gets lost is bound to the material plane and is then also subject to the laws that apply there. If someone has been physically cured through a miracle, but has been unable to embrace the miracle within their consciousness, it is very likely that the disease will soon reappear.

The soul needs plus energy (nourishment). When it is undernourished or grieving from too much minus energy, imbalances followed by disease will ensue.

If the participant does not recognize that a miracle has occurred, it won't be long before the soul is undernourished once more and cries for help using physical pain as its medium.

Our consciousness is kept supple and elastic through daily singing and surrender to the Note from Heaven. When the fruit falls from its branch with a soft thud, we can lay the table for a feast.|

Example

An elderly woman had signed up for regressive cell-singing, because a clairvoyant had recommended she work with her voice.

For seven years she had suffered from a long list of asthma-related illnesses. These had started immediately after her only son had died in a car accident. Since asthma affects breathing, and with that the whole intake of energy, the reason for her illness seemed clear: the death of her son had given her a tremendous shock with ensuing stiffening that weakened her desire to live/breathe.

The woman sang herself into her illness and a miracle happened:

A captain, wearing blue sailor's clothes and a cap, is on his little yacht enjoying the sun and the spray from the sea. He feels free and happy.

At this point, the singer's voice opened and the breathing became deep. After a while the asthma disappeared. The Note from Heaven broke through on long breaths with its infinitely light and beautiful overtones.

Everyone in the room listened in rapt silence. The sailor wanted to help and work together with the singer. The woman was deeply touched and her whole demeanour changed. Her face was radiant.

When the singer had recovered, she told us that her son had been a ship's captain and had worn a cap and the blue uniform described in the story.

The pain in her body had gone and her breathing had become normal. I felt there was probably more that needed releasing, but that had to wait until this release had had time to be integrated into the body's energy system.

The woman had released so much energy that the air in the whole room quivered.

When she contacted me a couple of weeks later, it was to cancel: her new clairvoyant had told her it was not good for her to sing.

TRAUMA DUE TO BEING IGNORED

I have given you various examples of singers releasing past traumas that stemmed from active abuse, but in fact one of the hardest kinds of trauma to release is that which comes from having been ignored. The following story is an illustration of the harm that can be done by suffering prolonged indifference.

Experiment with rice

When my eldest son started school, his vocabulary developed explosively. To put it plainly, swear words and vulgar terms flew through the air without his understanding the meaning and effect of these words on the people around him. These were words whose vibration has been distorted by deformed, suppressed feelings. They affect our bodies negatively, because they carry negative vibrations that can ignite repressed, as yet unlit emotional bonfires.

Innocence isn't affected by these words, which is why children have fun playing around with them until the day they run into someone who takes exception. Then it becomes even more fun. In the end, the child gets into trouble for it. Then the penny drops! Dangerous, forbidden, interesting. Their innocence is gradually degraded.

Around that time I gave presentations on sound-healing at two conferences where the main speaker was Masaru Emoto, a Japanese scientist and author renowned for his research into how the molecular structure of water reacts to a wide range of vibrational influences. His photos of frozen water crystals at minus five degrees centigrade clearly show that water is not only influenced by music, but by specific pieces of music. In fact, all forms of vibration influence the structure of water, and that includes feelings, thoughts and words.

In his book *Messages from Water and the Universe*, Emoto describes an experiment with rice. Péléh and I decided to try the experiment out for ourselves. I must admit, it is one thing to read about something and quite another to experience it for yourself. So, dear reader, by all means give it a go. The following describes a simple exercise that leads to a big transformation.

We took three identical sterilized jam jars with lids and with the same, clean, spoon put 20 grams of freshly cooked brown rice into each glass. After the rice had cooled down, we put the lids on and put a white label on each.

On the label of the first jar, we wrote the worst swear words my son could imagine: 'Fuck you, idiot!' On the next jar, we wrote the most loving words he could imagine: 'Love, gratitude'. We didn't write anything on the last jar.

After that the three jars stood on the same shelf in the refrigerator for four months. For the first two months we spoke to the jars we had written on at least once a day. We ignored the third jar.

Later, we expressed our feelings to the rice more sporadically. Every time Péleh had learned new swear words, he went and said them to the 'Fuck you' rice. He also remembered the 'love' rice and would loudly and solemnly sing to it: 'love and gratitude', 'I love you.'

Soon the rice in the three jars began to look and smell quite differently from each other.

The ignored rice started turning black after about ten days. Its smell was weak and not at all aggressive. It seemed to have given up, as if it were saying: 'There is no need for me. I am withdrawing.'

A little later, the negatively charged 'fuck you' rice turned brown-yellow and greasy. But whereas the ignored rice withdrew and seemed to shrink, the brown-yellow rice expanded, as if it were fighting back and saying: 'Do what you want, I will survive.' Over time, the smell in the jar slowly turned from pungent and sharp to fermented. It was so strong that it made your eyes water. The colour gradually changed from brown-yellow to turquoise.

The love-charged rice was gradually covered with a white, mould-like layer. The smell was sickly sweet with hints of vanilla, not pungent or sharp.

My son was so enthralled by the experiment that he asked if he could take the rice with him to school. There just happened to be a parents' meeting, so I chose to inform the parents about it so there wouldn't be any misunderstandings regarding rotten rice, bacteria, crazy healers and that kind of thing.

The parents showed only moderate interest in the rice, but I was allowed to show the rice to the children in the class and a couple of them dared to lift off the lids and sniff the contents. 'Well that is incredible!' They looked at me with wonder.

The children were so interested that we had to keep bringing the rice back in to show them whenever it showed any further changes in appearance or smell.

Examples of being ignored

The biggest challenge for a therapist is in those unfortunate cases where a child has been isolated, ignored and treated with indifference. Closeness and loving touch are vital for an infant and their absence, at worst, will cause a child's death – withdrawing into itself, just as the ignored rice shrank and turned black.

Of course, the ignored souls who turn up to a course have received enough care to survive. They have survived like molluscs that have their own safe world under their shells where they can hide and, now and then, stick the tips of their antennae out into the world.

There are many different causes and background stories here. A classic example is the mother who has suffered her entire life from guilt and therefore is not able to open her heart to her infant child. The child's experience is coldness from start to finish, although everything on the surface may have seemed perfect. If the father also was absent or unfeeling the traumatization becomes complete. Often the course participant has not realized how 'bad' their situation is. An ignored person punches into thin air. Their trauma comes from an absence rather than the presence of anything actively harmful that they can react to. 'I was given food, clothes, driven to school ... My parents were good to me. They never hit me.' Fortunately, the organism protects itself by accepting the state of things. You can't lament feelings you don't know exist.

As an adult, the ignored person senses they are stunted emotionally when compared to the people around them. They find it difficult to be aware of emotional reactions in their body.

Some children may also be affected by an experience of physical isolation in hospital when diagnosed with a serious infectious disease. For example, before widespread vaccination children with cerebrospinal meningitis were isolated in hospital, treated by nurses wearing masks and received their food through a hatch. It was normal to ask parents to visit only once a week, at most. When a small child receives that sort of treatment, they become seriously traumatized. In several of the examples I have encountered, the isolation lasted for months.

Treating people who have been ignored

The treatment in regressive cell-singing for course participants with symptoms of having been ignored is very individual and, as always, relies on the listener's intuition developed by working with the Note from Heaven. There may be the merest hint of something that, with sensitivity, can be drawn out using the right word, sound or intonation. Or sometimes the image of a cherished childhood toy can awaken long-suppressed feelings.

Let us say that an infant was never stimulated by the feeling 'red'. The colour still exists in adulthood as a possibility, but is imperceptible on the palette of feelings, because the emotional strings in the child that have never been stimulated will atrophy and lose the ability to resonate, just as a leg in plaster loses its muscle tone. So the encounter with 'red' doesn't awaken any resonance, because its tone is not to be found in the ignored person's fundamental existential patterns.

The question is whether you can soften an atrophied emotional string? In my experience you can, but only with the same kind of repeated training you would use to recondition an atrophied muscle. In most cases I would combine sound-scanning with regressive cell-singing. With sound-scanning, the ignored person receives a gentle stimulation of the passive cells (similar to ultrasound therapy, for example); and with regressive cell-singing, the breathing is activated, and gradually unfolded as the ignored person's feelings are brought back to life. In this way the situation is worked on from two angles that are mutually stimulating.

The ignored person's soul is led back to its original essence in the oneness level – that is, to a state where the emotional string that was not stimulated by the feeling 'red' is intact. Singing the Note from Heaven daily would further support this process.

Another supplementary method is vocal regression (see page 208), where the singer goes back to a time, early in their infancy, or in the embryo or in a past life, when they were able to access their whole palette of feelings. When you can contact your emotions, you can sing the feelings free.

Physical touch

When a singer who was ignored as a child regresses to the infant stage, touching him or her can help them open up to resonance.

As a female listener, it can feel natural to take on the mothering role, but only if it happens spontaneously. It is easiest to do this with one's own gender (if you are heterosexual). When communicating with an infant, words become secondary to touch and sounds.

A trained ear can hear in the singer's voice when the little child is whimpering and reaching out for mummy or daddy. In the cases where it feels right I ask, 'Do you have a need to be held?' If the answer is yes, I start by putting my hand gently on the forehead, or wherever it happens to feel best. If the participant leans their head on me, the next step is to find a position, either standing behind or sitting on the floor behind them, so they can be rocked while 'mummy' is close by, and wants to hear *everything* the little one has to say. While the child is singing you can choose, as the listener, to sing along if the sound picture feels more healing that way.

The inner child in the client experiences being heard and understood on a wordless level. A client once explained after a séance that she felt we were as one. The breathing, the sound, everything.

When the 'child' feels safe the body will, in some cases, make involuntary movements, as if it is trying to wind itself into place again (see the Paula technique, below). Here I follow along and support them as well as I can. When the head lifts and turns around, I have a hand ready the whole time to support, so the neck can rest on a 'care cushion' at any time.

At the end of a regressive singing process, the singer is sound-healed. Close contact between the listener's stomach and the singer's back, where the singer is sitting on the floor with the listener embracing from behind, is an especially rewarding sound-healing position for 'babies'.

In that way energy coming directly from the *hara* chakra resonates over a large area and leads to an experience of melting and becoming whole in the energy, which is extraordinarily healing. Before the séance finishes, it is, as always, important to bring the singer back up to the adult level, where they should be able to manage on their own.

In the days following a release, feelings start vibrating in the body and this can be quite overwhelming and frightening for a formerly quiet and ignored mouse. The reaction is a positive sign that life has returned to previously atrophied emotional strings. It is now time to master your inner harp. Embrace the tones instead of running away from them.

PAULA TECHNIQUE – INTERRELATIONSHIP BETWEEN THE SPHINCTER MUSCLES

Paula Garbourg (1907–2004) was a German-Jewish classical ballet dancer and professional opera singer. In Israel I became acquainted with her book *The Secret of the Ring Muscles: Healing Yourself Through Sphincter Exercise* through a student who had been trained in the Paula technique. In brief, the Paula technique is based on the mutual strengths of the body's many sphincter muscles and the fact that they are connected to each other. Sphincters are ring-shaped muscles that control the opening and closing of bodily passages, orifices, feet and hands (in Garbourg's method).

In her youth, Paula lost her voice for a long period of time and discovered, during dance training, that she could activate her voice by stepping up on her toes. She continued the movements and retrained her voice in that way.

This led to a wish to understand the muscular connection and she found out that the activation of a strong sphincter muscle can influence and strengthen a weaker sphincter muscle. A baby trains sphincter muscles the whole day. The hands, the feet, the mouth open and close in reflexive movements and these simultaneously stimulate the voice, the digestion; they get the entire body going. In Paula Garbourg's book there are numerous examples of the healing of autism, intellectual disability, asthma, migraine, rheumatism, impotence, incontinence and more.

During regressive cell-singing, a participant's body can start making involuntary movements. Some participants shyly suppress the impulse, while others attract attention to the phenomenon. In these situations, I encourage them to let the body do what it wants, no matter how awkward or embarrassing it may feel. The soft palate contains a sphincter muscle. The Note from Heaven can only break through when that muscle is stretched like a dome up in the rear part of the oral cavity. The use of the soft palate's sphincter muscle activates and strengthens the sphincter muscles in the entire body. A pulsating network of imperceptible movements is set in motion.

The interrelationship between the sphincter muscles causes the involuntary movements that occur in some singers. So, there is no reason to panic if a client's body begins to make strange movements. Everything is all right. You can safely let the singer continue their process with the strange facial expressions and body movements, which can be stopped at any moment when and if the singer takes over control of him or herself.

The listener's confidence in everything being all right gives the singer room to feel free.

Pulse and rhythm

If a singer is too inhibited to allow the involuntary movements to happen, then rhythm or a simple pulse beat can do wonders. Dancing becomes a natural extension of the voice's expression. The body joins in.

On my CD *Rising* there is a recording of foetus sounds, where you can hear the pulsating sounds of the umbilical cord vibrating and the beating of the mother's heart. We have all heard and felt the rhythm of these sounds 24 hours a day, from when we were a four-month-old embryo in the womb until we were born. So incorporating a pulse-like rhythm into the session can make it easier for some people to let go. Four-part rhythms give grounding, while three-part rhythms are calming and open up contact with the heart.

In the warm-up session of a course, I like to work with low tones, rhythm and the body. Grounding is a prerequisite for complete surrender. With the roots well anchored in the earth, the organism is able to carry its crown, even endure strong storms, without breaking the smallest twig.

On earth as it is in heaven.

Below as it is above.

RELEASE THROUGH CHANGING THE STORY

'Religious effort is not to be free of sin, but to be equal to God.'
Plotinus

'Fear squeezes the life energy out of the nerves to such a degree that
it lowers the level of vitality in the entire body.'
Yogananda

Readiness for release

Fearful, shameful, disempowering, terrible, painful traumas become
attached to the body, not only as bound-up energy in the cells, but also as
rigid existential patterns.

These can be characterized by anger and judgment of 'the sinners'
– those whom the person blames for his or her state. When blame is in
focus, the body is nourished with negatively charged energy, which is a
delicious treat for the pain body. Therefore, guilt and shame function like
a thorn in the flesh.

We can heal and treat through eternity and this may even soothe the
pain, but we must remove the thorn if the infection is to be eradicated.
This can be achieved through forgiveness and/or changing the stories
and the events that a client has attached to their identity. Out with all the
negative-acting stories and in with some new, refreshing pictures and
feelings that build up healthy energy structures.

Everyone can leave negative-acting emotions behind by opening
themselves up to the divine field of the here and now. In the energy field
that opens up when working with the Note from Heaven, everything
is possible. Just by thinking that freedom is possible you start the
healing process. In addition, the Note from Heaven allows you to open
the gate to heaven more easily. Thus the singer can turn the feeling of
disempowerment into a plus power. The question is, are you ready to
leave your pain body? Can you live without complaining?

When the need to backbite and complain comes with its attractive,
bittersweet taste, stop for a moment and think carefully before you
continue. As long as the pain body has power over you, then your

organism will not be able to integrate new, positive energy structures. The human being is surrounded by potential positive energy. If we are open to its possibility, we will be able to receive it. Fear contracts and closes off. Devotion relaxes and opens up.

In the Aramaic language, which was spoken in the time of Jesus, sin is synonymous with making a mistake: 'To miss the target. To not be present in the moment.'

Considerations

'Can you change something that you know has happened?' is one of the questions I am most commonly asked.

Yes, you can change the energy around the event by emptying its content. You will still remember the event, but you will have restructured it into a harmless memory; an old, empty cardboard box in the attic.

You have moved on. The pain body moans. The question is, are you ready to live without your trauma? How will you deal with your new-found freedom if you have been chained for most of your life?

Remember that, even though the world now lies at your feet, you can still choose to remain living in your dog kennel. Before, you didn't have any choice, but now you do. The freedom to take responsibility for your own life is fundamental to a happy body.

Lars Muhl once wrote to me: 'Just be you, wish for everything you want and you will get it. Everything is love.' It sounds so wonderful, and I have experienced the truth of those words myself. But how challenging they are – because if I don't know who I am, how can I then wish for what I want? What if I make the wrong wish and it backfires!

The fear of wishing for what is best for yourself is an aspect of the fear of changing an identity that has been formed by expectations from your surroundings. An adapted 'I' that, like an outer skin, holds a liquid interior together.

What should I choose, consideration of others or consideration of myself?

Can the true self be happy if it considers itself at the expense of others?

A human being with a balanced, positive, surplus energy projects light and joy onto their surroundings.

A human being that is burnt-out and negative drains their surroundings.

The Buddha pursued the middle way, which led him to enlightenment.

The lifeline is the divine plan. There is only one path that is yours. Maybe you are walking it, maybe you have gone astray. Search for the path and when you have found it, serve it.

'Jesus said: "He who seeks shall find, and to him who knocks the door shall be opened."'
Gospel of Thomas, log. 94

By playing with the thought that *all my dreams can come true*, a seed of trust is planted in the universal mind. A heartfelt wish is, in fact, a desire for a miracle. The purpose of the miracle is not the miracle itself, but to strengthen trust in God. 'Knowing' that my true 'I' is a living miracle in this universe will teach me to listen carefully for signs of the divine.

By searching for the higher meaning in all aspects of life, your focus keeps you grounded, but at the same time leaves space for God to be present. In that way you take responsibility for yourself and your self .

Be prepared that the signs from God manifest in many surprising ways and can be quite amusing! When we change a story or event in regressive cell-singing, we invoke the divine. Your wish calls on the divine to lead you. You cannot go wrong in this process, because anything that might be seen as a mistake will actually expand your consciousness.

Energy is extinguished without free space to manoeuvre in, just as a fire is extinguished without oxygen.

Changing the first layer of a multi-layered trauma

A two-year-old boy with cerebrospinal meningitis isolated in hospital. His mother only allowed to visit him once a week. This went on for two months. As an adult, the man suffered from an extreme need for sex.

When his partner was not in the mood – for example, because she was breastfeeding their baby during the night – the man felt unloved and let down. It was her duty to give him sex. For him, sex was love.

Whenever the man felt rejected, he reacted like a forsaken two-year-old calling for his mother. The male sexual urge is located in the root chakra, which is also the source of the survival instinct. This suggested to me that the trauma of this singer was probably connected to a fear of being unwanted and abandoned.

His primary feeling was 'I get abandoned because I am not good enough.' This feeling was triggered by certain code words such as 'You've been let down', 'You feel powerless', 'You're not lovable', and 'Only when you have sex can you be yourself.'

As soon as the singer released the excess emotional pressure, the Note from Heaven broke purifyingly through. In that state, the man came to a psychological and physical realization of the emotional state induced by the two-year-old boy's experience. The story was already starting to change at this point.

The boy experienced being heard and loved unconditionally as he became filled up by the light and energy of the state of consciousness the Note from Heaven led him into.

Experiencing this state once was not enough, because the child's sense of being let down became thoroughly embedded during the two-month period of isolation. The singer and listener had to be prepared to uncover several layers in this trauma. The cleansing could only be completed if the singer sang the Note from Heaven every day to care for his wounded inner child. On a practical level, his energy was diverted from sex to the Note from Heaven, which improved the relationship with his partner.

In tandem with the emotional cleansing, the singer also needed to address his self-image. His whole life pattern and identity were built around the trauma. It was therefore necessary to change the events of the past, and in that way influence his current life patterns.

Changing the story

The listener asks the singer if he or she is willing to change the story. In order to change the story, not only must the singer consent but he or she must establish an emotional contact to the trauma. Normally the singer and the listener change the story together. This is because, as discussed, it is difficult for the singer to keep a clear head when strong emotions are raging. The listener elicits the singer's wishes by suggesting new ways for the story to pan out.

In the case of the man suffering from a trauma induced by being isolated in hospital as a child, I suggested removing the whole experience of his illness. But this was too big a change of identity for him, so we needed to find a compromise. The reworking that emerged was that the boy was taken care of at home by his mother and the illness was a bad case of flu instead of meningitis. The mother was unusually caring towards him: reading him fairy tales, singing to him, serving him his favourite meals (here we can go into great detail, because the food is very important to a small child), washing his face with a cool cloth, stroking and kissing him.

During the reconstruction of their story, singers usually become overwhelmed by strong feelings. They might chuckle happily or weep with joy.

When certain details in the story seem to nourish a singer, it is good to dwell on these parts for a while and always let singers take the story forward themselves when, and if, they get hold of a main thread. They may get in touch with new facets of their unfulfilled needs.

The listener can add to the story and make it even better, although only ever with the singer's consent. Returning to the example: 'Daddy comes home with a present. What would you like? A teddy bear?' – 'No, a red car '... and mummy and daddy sit close together and hold you.'

'Your siblings are on holiday and your mummy has taken time off work, so there is a lot of extra energy and time to be present with you. Daddy is a loyal and kind husband.'

The listener asked how the singer felt inside when mummy and daddy said that they loved him. The singer's reaction here spoke a clear message. Was there something special that he has always wished his parents would do?

'I want my parents to love each other!' Now his voice was, at last, thick with emotion. There was some deeper issue here.

During the whole reformulation process the singer sings. The sound immediately and unfailingly indicates when a release is occurring. The depth of the transformation is dependent on the brain-wave level the singer has reached. If they are in the alpha-stage, i.e. completely relaxed, the information can easily be led further down to the theta and delta brain-wave length, corresponding to the infant's mind and the grown-up's subconscious mind. If the singer's conscious mind is still active, then his brain waves will be at beta 1 or beta 2 and the transformation won't penetrate so deeply into the subconscious mind.

In this particular case, the child was not released from his betrayal trauma during the first session. There were numerous layers to work on. A little corner had been lifted, but cleaning up under the carpet needed to continue if the trauma was to be released. It took several sessions before a release occurred and the singer had the will to take the path of self-development. This man's whole identity was based on his sexuality. He had left a trail of failed relationships, children here and there, infidelity, letting others down. He was troubled by a strong sense of guilt, but this was coupled with a devil-may-care attitude that hid the pain of a two-year-old boy who had lost his grip on life; he alternated between bragging and feeling sorry for himself.

Forgiveness

Storytelling often throws up situations involving forgiveness. When a singer meets another person in the story, the listener can choose to enquire if that person is familiar. If the singer is in doubt about the other person's identity, the listener can focus on the singer's inner awareness and make a suggestion as to who it could be. Another possibility is to describe the person's appearance in more detail. I remember a case where a woman calmly said, 'Yes, that is my mother.'

'She is asking you to forgive her.'

'Well – no, I'm not ready for that.'

I was annoyed by her answer, because I had a feeling that release was just around the corner. But as the listener, I had to accept and respect the singer's attitude as 'right'. If she wasn't ready, then she wasn't ready. You can't flap another person's wings for them. The mother continued to ask for forgiveness throughout the whole story, but the singer was totally closed towards her and was quite irritated in the end. The Note from Heaven did not manifest itself.

Afterwards, the participant told me that she had had therapy for years to get her mother out of her system. That is why it irritated her that she had now turned up again. The singer thought that she had finished with her mother. A couple of weeks later she wrote to me that she regretted not accepting the chance to forgive and was now ready to do so. This shows how regressive cell-singing can set in motion a process of forgiveness even if a singer resists it at first.

If the person (or people) who seeks out the singer in the story is still alive, then the forgiveness and release also occur here on the soul level. It will happen in much the same way as when the story is changed. The energy structure is opened and balanced. When the singer subsequently meets the person they have forgiven, both parties will clearly sense a change, even without the other person having any knowledge of what has happened. The singer's changed consciousness now carries a different energy that opens up new ways of relating to the other person.

In storytelling I have experienced several variations of the forgiveness process. Unlike the woman in the previous example, the singer is usually ready to forgive. However, before forgiveness takes place the person who has shown up may want to explain themselves, and they start a dialogue with the singer. If it is difficult for the singer to forgive, and there are still differences between the two, the listener can invite the singer to ask for a helping tool.

When the forgiveness is complete, the listener might suggest an embrace, if it hasn't already happened naturally. If the singer is unwilling to take this step, this indicates that his or her heart chakra is still closed and the forgiveness process is not yet complete.

Helping tools

Another way to effect change through storytelling is to provide the singer with a virtual helping tool. The singer closes their eyes and asks for a tool to, for example, protect her self with, so that she can feel safe in daily life. If the singer doesn't see any tool, the listener can share what he or she can see and then often the singer suddenly sees something. 'No, it's not a hat; it's a cloak that I can protect myself with.'

Example 1

A Native American (the singer's 'character' in the story) is standing in front of the tribe that has killed his entire beloved family while he was out hunting. He can't forgive them. The listener suggests that the Native American asks for a forgiveness tool.

'Close your eyes. The first thing you see is your tool. Don't reject the tool if it seems strange or out of place. There is always a meaning.'

The Native American gets a drinking straw. He blows into the straw and one by one the members of his family appear in front of him. In their spiritual state, they forgive the enemy tribe, which now bows before them. The family members reach out to the Native American and ask him to join them in forgiving the tribe. It pains them that he is suffering. They assure him that they are fine where they are and that he must walk his path on earth until it is his time.

I ask the singer if the Native American needs singing support from the group. The female singer nods. The singer now finally gets in touch with her grief, which is released through cry-toning.

After the session, the singer could make contact with the Native American and his deceased family at any time by blowing into her imaginary straw. The tool opened the door to past lives, and enabled her to contact the deceased, as well as other states of consciousness.

Example 2

A singer with mental problems was given a beetle, which she saw as a scarab, the sacred Egyptian symbol that was carved in turquoises and used as a protective amulet. The scarab was given as a key to the state of consciousness she had been in during work with the Note from Heaven – a meditative state she normally had difficulty finding on her own. Following the session, the singer would be able to find that state at any time, using the scarab as a starting point.

Example 3

In one of the most convincing releases I have experienced in regressive cell-singing, the tool that was given was not an object but a high-pitched vocal sound. A female executive had become so worn out by stress that she had been close to being admitted to a psychiatric hospital. She had been on sick leave for several months.

When she arrived at the course, it was hard for me to believe that she was ill. 'Appearances are deceptive,' she said. Before the course, she had told me that a number of years ago she had lost one of her twin sons in a cot death. Now, many years later, she had become overwhelmed by a grief that had totally knocked her for six. The woman was not accustomed to using her voice and was anxious about being able to sing in tune.

She was the first in the group to put herself forward as a singer and her voice went right up into the high notes after only a few seconds. The woman's crisp tones were as clear as a bell and rang out of her mouth.

'He's there, isn't he?' I asked. 'Yes.' The tears were running down her cheeks and she smiled blissfully. She sang and sang and sang. At the end I suggested that she ask for a tool to keep in touch with her son, and the answer came promptly: 'I want the high tones.' At the end of the one-day course, we tried the tool out. The clear bell tones were still there.

After the course, the woman was back at work. A few weeks later we exchanged e-mails. 'I can get in touch with my son whenever I want to. The tones are still there and I have regained my strength.'

WHEN THE SINGER SEES IMAGES

Inspiration without grounding leads to apathetic or hyperactive image sequences. When the singer sees images, it requires skill from the listener to sense if these images will lead to release or if they are unconscious diversions that will knock the process off course. The listener's navigation signs usually give the answer. If the sound or images don't arouse any sensations in my heart, I interrupt the singer and set them straight.

Not everyone sees images. Many have access to them, but do not take them seriously, dismissing them as nothing but flights of fancy. In cases where a singer hasn't been able to see anything before, and suddenly receives images, the listener should proceed with caution.
A new dimension has opened up to the singer, and the mere fact of being able to see images is like stepping into exciting and unexplored territory. What people see differs. Some get colours and sense impressions and experience different, subtle light phenomena. Others suddenly cut into the listener's storytelling and say: 'No, it's like this and this.'

Here the listener can rely only on their hearing and intuition. Does the singer seem excited and authentic? Does the voice sound open? In which case, do the means (the images) justify the ends (the Note from Heaven)? It is the listener's responsibility to see through the ego's diversions.

Example 1: A successful distraction manoeuvre
A well-educated woman was in the process of singing herself into contact with the Note from Heaven. She had a hard time getting in touch with her feelings. In the story she was singing, I could see a house with yellow walls. It was in a mountainous area in South America. A volcano was smouldering in the background. The singer got stuck at the yellow walls. Apparently she didn't want to go into the house. Her expression stiffened.

I asked if she could see something. Yes, she could. 'I'm walking by the edge of a lake. There are ducks and reeds, the trees are beautiful...' As the listener I should have stopped her, but unfortunately, I decided to respect her authority.

She continued describing her ramble as if she were actually going for a walk down by the local lake. Her voice was monotonous, both when singing and talking. The description of the walk was really boring me.

'Maybe we should try to find that yellow house.'

'No, it feels right.' The woman was determined to walk round the lake. I didn't have the heart to stop her, and that was my next mistake.

She had been talking continuously ever since I asked if she could see anything, and in that way, had avoided the Note from Heaven. I spotted that too late. It would now be an impossible power game to force her back to the yellow house from her beloved lake.

By the time she had walked all round the lake and was about to go round again, which she swore was absolutely necessary, I was forced to admit to her, the other course participants and myself that her images had deceived me.

I should have kept to the yellow walls and endeavoured to move forward from that point, because I sensed an impending crisis in the story, and that the woman would do anything not to confront it. Before then, I had believed that all images that appear were important and carried a message. They certainly do, but the question is, what purpose do they serve?

In almost all cases, the ego will try to protect the singer from confrontations with any emotions based on fear. This is a natural instinct. If a listener lets a singer's ego have its way, he or she might as well throw in the towel and bring the session to a halt. With some people, the astral images float to and fro as if they were on an LSD trip, so when singers see images during their own singing, the listener must be fully alert.

Absorption in the Note from Heaven connects us to an all-encompassing, intelligent, mythological power that expresses itself through images, among other media. I refer to this power as the Akashic field, or the universal mind.

When a listener listens to a singer's voice, he or she is aiming to surrender to a consciousness that communicates with this universal mind. I rely totally on what I sense when listening. I don't have any choice but to trust the images and impressions that turn up, because I 'am not there', when I step to one side.

Whether the information is true or not is secondary, because there is no judgment in the energy field. The effect depends on the degree to which the singer and listener can open up.

The field between the singer and listener is like a magnet. If either the singer or the listener is held back by their ego, their pole will weaken the information coming in.

Example 2: Images without a main thread

There was one female singer who saw lots of images. They intertwined with my story, and what started as a wrecked ship at the bottom of the ocean now became a large tanker, which the woman boarded. The whole crew had died of the plague, it stank, and suddenly creatures with abscesses and black spots rose up from the ocean, and parrots, and ... I tried to figure out the meaning and felt nauseous from my attempt to gather the threads. Images from the astral plane were pouring out of the woman's subconscious mind. The singer's sound was vague and reflected her inner state.

With a great effort I got the story and the ship back on course. The woman had to walk the plank, jump into the water and receive the grounding from her tonal power that she needed.

Mindful of similar cases I had come across previously, I interrupted her and told her the truth as I experienced it. This, for me, is always the fairest way to treat a delicate subject: 'It feels to me as if your images are leading us astray. Try to sing yourself into your primary feeling and let me see what images turn up.'

This is when it is particularly useful to have the singer's code words, wish(es) and primary feeling ready on a piece of paper. They are invaluable in helping to keep the participant on track. As far as possible, I try to retain the original story and let it develop further with the images that appear.

When a singer suffers from a large inferiority complex, it can, paradoxically, show itself in delusions of grandeur. Talents have to be displayed somehow or other, and they can, for example, burst out in exaggerated images. The listener needs to use his or her ears. If the breakthrough to the Note from Heaven fails to come or the séance feels heavy and tiring, it is the listener's responsibility to change course as quickly as possible by taking over the helm.

REGRESSION
Regression therapy using the voice

In the two-year education that I offer, some of the students use aspects of the classical regression therapy method, in which the singer lies down. As in regressive cell-singing, the listener supports them as they experience body tension induced by the code words linked to the primary feeling. However, instead of singing him or herself free of the tension, the singer mentally penetrates the tension and verbally articulates the images, colours and feelings they experience. The listener directs the evolving story towards the core of the singer's trauma. If it is difficult to get to, the listener sound-scans the relevant physical tensions in order to free up the emotions. If these emotions become overwhelming, they can be sung free as in regressive cell-singing. You would have to complete my education before practising this form of therapy or would need prior experience with regression therapy.

My personal experience with regression

After ten years of work, and deep involvement with surrendering to the Note from Heaven, I noticed that long, coherent, film-like stories full of exciting and dramatic events would pass by my inner eye when I was in a relaxed state.

The first time it happened, I thought my destiny was to become a writer of novels. The inspiration for the stories simply came to me, without demanding any sort of effort on my part. In the days that followed, however, my body began to react and I was emotionally shaken and deeply involved in the stories. These effects wore off after about a week. I went on to experiment with enquiring about past lives and each time I immediately got a new story.

It is difficult to generate an effective release by practising regression on your own. The ego will fight desperately to protect you from fear and stop you from going to the roots of a traumatic experience. This is only truly possible together with a therapist.

As I had singing pupils that might possibly open up to past lives while working with the Note from Heaven, I felt I needed to become trained in regression, so I registered with André Corell in Copenhagen. Among other things, we learned basic techniques on how to lead a client in and out of a regression, how to zoom in on a trauma and then release it.

My experience, derived both from my work with clients and my training, is that it can be very heavy, even burdensome, to keep diving down into the dark areas of the subconscious. The moment of death, the terror – the experience can easily tip over into the kind of sensationalism that you might find in a tabloid news story. The pain body grabs some tasty morsels along the way.

The most far-reaching regressions I have ever experienced involved being healed between two lives. I especially remember one regression where, after only a few minutes of lying down, my body hummed in a weightless state and was warm with a tingling energy. I felt blissful, as if I were in heaven! Soft hands surrounded my body and healed it with the utmost gentleness and love.

My fellow student, who was supposed to be practising on me, tried to get me out of the state. I asked to remain where I was. Fortunately, André came by and said: 'She is being healed on a higher plane. Give her five minutes, before you continue practising.' The experience remained with me, and now new methods in the field of regression therapy focus on precisely this type of approach – going back to heaven for healing, so to speak.

So, if a singer sings him or herself into a story that is obviously from a past life, I no longer worry about trying to help the client relive the traumas and the painful emotions connected to them. It is enough to acknowledge what has happened and then ask to have the trauma healed on a higher level of consciousness.

Some people apparently need to get down into the mud, maybe because they are too 'light' and need grounding.

Clients who are heavily laden with guilt can have a hard time surrendering to the Note from Heaven. We have grown up with guilt and taboos that steer our instincts and urges in the direction of hell rather than heaven. Many of us, therefore, believe we have to suffer before we can be uplifted. But it doesn't have to be like that.

In regressive cell-singing, I experience more and more cases where the stories become transformed into myths full of symbols, and it is these myths that release the course participants. The myths can easily cover over tragic events in past lives.

In traditional regressions, it is the client who tells the story with the support of a listening therapist who asks leading questions. In regressive cell-singing, the listener does the seeing and telling, so that the singer is free to sing him or herself into a state of being that is pure listening. Thus, the chance of the transformation being ushered down to the subconscious mind during the session via alpha, theta and delta brain waves is much greater.

The inner pictures the listener sees are reflections of the singer's sound. If the singing goes round in circles, then the images do as well. The story and sound merge together.

Experience has shown me that the pictures are usually correct. Time and again I have been surprised at their accuracy. For me, it is always a game. I have no idea where the story is heading. When all the pieces of the puzzle finally fall into place, I am amazed at how much humour and wisdom can be channelled through my brain. I present the storytelling as a 'singing game', where the message of the words is secondary to the vocal release through the Note from Heaven.

There is no greater truth than the sound at its moment of creation.

The pictures have no intrinsic value. Without my faith in them, they are worthless. The listener's faith strengthens the singer's courage to take the leap and experience the Note from Heaven – a faith that is reinforced when the story affects the singer in their heart and only God knows what it is all about. Is there anything more beautiful than a message from heaven?

Regression to heaven

Here is an example of a woman who was expecting to undergo a painful regression, but ascended to heaven instead.

In just a few breaths, the singer sang herself directly up to heaven. She described an incredibly beautiful, paradise-like garden, where she was floating around, feeling light and whole. 'I just feel so good, so completely blissful' she said in wonder. The process took just a few minutes, but then her intellect asked: 'Can it really be so very simple? I was convinced that I had to get down into something bad in order to release my problems.'

After that, the woman asked to go and experience a past life related to her problem. The energy became heavy, the air dry. A desert, a Muslim woman dressed in black. Drought, deep sorrow, no water, dying children. The singer looked round, and we agreed, 'no thanks, it's not necessary.'

We could all feel the change in the energy level and returning to the pain in the incarnation seemed superfluous. The singer's voice still carried gilded veils from heaven – why let it gather dust in the baking sun, death and deprivation? The singer could clearly feel that her trauma had already been released.

Women in orgasmic ceremonies

There are many different themes in regressions. One of the most intriguing ones is when ordinary, conventional women experience being courtesans or temple priestesses, serving the gods through their erotic devotion. Beautiful women radiating an uninhibited erotic life force have always presented a huge threat to the efforts of the religions to suppress human sexual urges.

Example

A woman decorated with flowers and precious jewels is sitting on an elephant on a beautifully decorated howdah. Her womanly qualities are scantily covered by a net of golden opals. Her breasts lie sensually under the rose mala, she is plump and voluptuous. There is a heavy layer of black kohl make-up around her eyes. Small diamonds on her nose. Tilaka on her forehead. Long, loose black hair with elaborately woven pearls and flowers.

She can be seen bobbing above the heads of the masses. Women and men raise their hands up in the air and praise her. The way this living goddess writhes with soft rolling movements causes the air to almost stand still. She is a manifestation of innocence combined with liberated erotic instinct.

She enters the temple and proceeds along the central avenue towards the shrine's altar, where she will be united with a chosen priest. The foreplay has begun. The whole crowd is participating.

The woman is true to her gender, her sexuality, without any hint of reservation. She radiates total confidence in her own purity in the holy grail of reproduction and this is passed on as inspiration to the people.

The singer, a woman in her fifties, had as a primary wish: 'I want to completely acknowledge myself as I am.' Although she had reached a stage in her life where her sexuality was on the back burner, she was totally into the story and I was glad there were no men present in this group. The sound was sensual and powerful at the same time. We were all carried away by the singing and the story.

A special regression

At a one-day course in regressive cell-singing with a group of five, two of the women were friends. While one of them was singing into her problem, she shot back into a regression, to Venice in the year 1365, where a wealthy woman was dying in childbirth. The child survived. The mother's sense of guilt and powerlessness at having left her first child to fend for itself was overwhelming. The Note from Heaven came through strongly in the process of release.

During the birth, the singer's friend suddenly started getting intense spasms in her heart. She writhed back and forth, gasping for air and was unable to explain what was happening. When her face went dark red, my first thought was to call an ambulance. Fortunately, one of the course participants was trained in first aid and, before I could get all the way out of the door to the phone, the woman with the heart pain was able to stammer: 'No, don't go, I am the child!'

We changed the story to a happy one in which mother and child were united, and the woman's pain eased. The two women cried and hugged each other repeatedly.

BOUNDARIES
People who lack boundaries

The primary feeling: 'I am not good enough' is one of the most common themes on courses in regressive cell-singing. Therefore it is relevant that listeners explore the core of this feeling, which I see as being based in having an unbalanced relationship with regard to boundaries. In what follows, two variations of the same theme are described.

Those children, who have had to strive particularly hard to meet the conditions of their parents' or close relatives' conditional love have, like rubber bands, had their boundaries stretched to breaking point. Although neglected children are especially prone to this problem, it is also true to varying degrees for those with a 'normal' upbringing.

In an environment without reasonable boundaries, there is no mirror in which to reflect one's self in. This naturally makes it difficult for a child to recognize and love itself.

Some children are raised with the feeling that life consists of an endless list of deeds they need to carry out to earn love. Little pats on the head in passing, a nod, a smile, the giving of sweets and so on come to function as rewards in a power game. It is a sad, but unfortunately quite common pressure cooker in which to preserve our most outstanding fruit and it is often the first-born or children who have taken on great responsibility at too early an age who are most affected. The fear of not being able to do things well enough leads to over-responsibility, which becomes a substitute for setting boundaries for what the self, as a person, agrees to.

'I have done my duty; therefore you are not allowed to hurt me.'
'I have done my duty; therefore I deserve love.'
These sentences sound a lot weaker than:
'I won't put up with you hurting me.'
'I am lovable.'

We increase our self-respect when we stand up for ourselves unconditionally. If we experience ourselves as lovable, we don't need to have arguments. Conditional love trains children to achieve in order to feel good enough, and gives them the understanding that they are not complete in their essence.

In that way, their whole basic foundation is being defined outside the self. They fumble around, caught in the unhealthy pattern, hungry for approval from others, as if that is the only possible peg on which they can hang their identity.

People who have overly controlled boundaries

In contrast, people who do not have many demands or expectations placed on them or who have been overprotected may lose their self-confidence and, to a greater or lesser degree, their natural feeling of responsibility for themselves. Often the people who have this problem are only children or the youngest in a family.

As I see it, the basis of the unemployment problem lies in the amputation of our children's self-confidence. *We don't need you!* An individual can lose their basic sense of self-worth to such a degree that they become handicapped for the rest of their life. Even trying to live up to being good enough and experiencing ourselves as efficient can be such an overwhelming step to take. We can become sick with fear in the soul, causing a self-perpetuating circle of paralysis. 'No one needs me, I am nobody, I can't do anything.' This can lead us towards irresponsibility as we push our all too painful emotions aside and put a protective membrane over an increasingly infected boil – 'I will only do something if I feel like it.'

Instead of feeling satisfaction at rising to a challenge, we are pulled down by fear of risk. What if mum and dad aren't around to lend a hand in case I can't do it? *What if I am not good enough?* Deep down, we're convinced that we aren't good enough. This pattern can lead even highly intelligent adults to throw out their arms and say: 'I don't feel like it.'

'I am helpless, therefore you can't permit yourself to hurt me.'
'I am helpless, therefore I deserve love.'
These sentences sound a lot weaker than:
'I won't put up with you hurting me.'
'I am lovable.'

The overly responsible and the overly irresponsible fit together hand in glove, but this is not a perfect relationship as they enable each other to indulge the extremes of their characters. The self-confidence of the irresponsible one hits rock bottom through overdependence on the responsible one, who becomes exhausted by the excessive demands of his or her mate.

The overly responsible person admires the irresponsible person's ability to set boundaries without the slightest hesitation, even in small, insignificant situations. This false respect – a substitute for the real thing, which they will never deserve – validates the irresponsible person's behaviour and compounds their loss of self-confidence. Boundary setting effectively covers up the hollow echo of the individual's painful secret: I am not good enough. Of course, the overly responsible person doesn't see this.

Conversely, the irresponsible person will be attracted to the overly responsible in the belief that the other person has the self-confidence that they lack. In reality, they both lack self-confidence, but one reacts outwardly and the other inwardly – two variations of the same theme. I come across these themes again and again in regressive cell-singing. They come in countless different guises, but they can all be traced back to the same root. 'I am not good enough. I am not worth anything. I am unlovable.'

When a person's foundation collapses

When a person makes big decisions in their life, their foundation can be shaken to the core. This can be so painful that the person comes into contact with the fundamental essence of their existence. The fear of hurting loved ones, of being mistaken, of being hurt by other people's opinions – we can always come up with plenty of reasons to hold on to the old patterns.

Your body will always tell you if your soul is not happy and well. Through illness or physical pain or psychological imbalances, it rebels in a way that demands a reaction. If you ignore this call it will, in the long term, result in serious illness that is rooted in the soul's wish to stop living here on earth. It is a crime to commit suicide ... even a slow and painful one. So you can forget any idea of victimizing your self.

When facing a major crisis like the impending end of a long-term relationship, people often lose their zest for life. They can wish themselves far away, be deeply depressed and escape into sleep. It can seem easier to die than to take that terrible step. In so many cases the organism speaks its own language in the form of the sudden appearance of a serious disease – the 'step' is taken for the person.

'Do you want to live or die?' 'I want to live, my feelings have the right to exist despite the consequences they will have on my surroundings.' Ought you to say that?

Only your heart can answer that question. When the fruit is ripe, it falls. One can feel lost in disempowerment.

It is possible to liberate your breathing and emotions on your own with regressive cell-singing when in a crisis. Go for a drive and practise cry-toning when everything becomes overwhelming. In that way, you can avoid disturbing anyone else. If you don't have a car available, put your head in a pillow and go all out. Be prepared to do it daily, as the emotions during a crisis will continue to pop up, until the pattern that triggered them has been changed.

I have had course participants who have received the message during storytelling that the structure of their marriage was the cause of their cancer. Such messages are usually given indirectly, so only the singer understands them.

One participant with cancer, who for most of her married life had not been able to communicate, either verbally or sexually, with her husband, decided to stay with him. She was fully aware that she would pay with her life. She had kept herself alive for many years not knowing what to do. Two months after making her decision, she died.

Should a person sacrifice him or herself? Is it a good thing to be silent about your own pain?

A crisis can be the catalyst leading to a quantum leap in life. Just like when you encounter the Note from Heaven, you have to jump without a safety net.

Are you ready? Dare you jump? Do you want it and does it feel right? In my experience, if a person is truly ready to take full responsibility for their life, and, therefore, to accept the consequences of making the leap, they receive wings that carry them through even the most painful feelings. There are no shortcuts to the wisdom of a broken heart. Remember that even if you take the jump, the world still remains. There is the sun, moon, trees and bird song.

'To dare is to lose one's footing momentarily. Not to dare is to lose oneself.'

Søren Kierkegaard

RELEASE OF GUILT

Since guilt gets its nourishment from the repressions lurking in the subconscious mind, the feeling of guilt dies when the root is dug up and brought into the light.

Guilt is one of the most destructive emotions of all. It gnaws away relentlessly within us and it can also be perpetuated by external situations. For example, a mother might feel guilty when she looks at her child. This causes her pain, so she distances herself from her child. The more she distances herself, the guiltier she feels, the greater the pain, and so on.

The mother doesn't know the reason for her sense of guilt. It has possessed her like a chronic disease. The child becomes traumatized and inherits the mother's sense of guilt. Unconsciously, the child knows that it is inflicting pain on the mother, but it does not know why and it certainly feels guilty! The snowball rolls on, growing bigger and bigger from generation to generation.

Fortunately for all those carrying guilt, an acknowledged guilt can be removed, and what a catharsis the release brings about!

The following example shows how it can be done.

On a course, one woman had the courage to be completely honest about her relationship with her young children: 'I have two children. I love my baby girl with all my heart, but there is distance between me and my three-year-old son. I don't know why it is so difficult for me to hold him close. Problems have now started in the kindergarten. When I look at him I feel guilty, because I know he needs me to love him completely. Something is in the way. It makes me feel miserable.'

The woman sang herself back to a past life in the Mongolian steppes:

A woman with Mongolian features was cutting grass with a little circular knife and putting the grass in a big basket. Her six-month-old son was lying sleeping near the edge of the road, bundled in woven fabric.

Suddenly some Tartar horsemen came thundering by. They looked mean and had bloody weapons. In a flurry, one of the warriors speared the woman's baby boy, laughing coarsely all the while. The woman had thrown herself down into the long grass, so they wouldn't see her. The Tartar rode on with the boy on the tip of his lance, before slinging him roughly out over the steppe.

The woman rushed over to her son as soon as the men were out of sight. The baby was dead. She was overcome with guilt at being alive, at having thrown herself down into the grass instead of protecting her son. She reproached herself for having laid him so close to the road. If only she had done this or that. The memory gnawed at the woman for the rest of her life.

We changed the story to a happy one, so the boy and mother remained unharmed (the Tartars rode the other way). The singer practised cry-toning during the whole séance and the Note from Heaven came through powerfully. A few days after the course, the woman sent me a joyous email. The distance and sense of guilt had gone. Now she could hug her son, and love him with all her heart. Things were also going much better with him in kindergarten.

This example is not unique. A sense of guilt towards one of your children is always possible to remove, because a mother's love is one of the strongest instincts that exists. So, dear, guilt-ridden mothers, step forward and throw off your cloaks.

Release through contact with wise light beings

Some people feel particularly connected to a certain prophet, archangel, saint or other sacred figure. I recall one notable case involving a woman who was suffering from a high degree of guilt and over-responsibility.

Because of the deep meaning these archetypes have for people of different religions, their energies can manifest themselves during regressive cell-singing. The effect is especially strong when the listener doesn't know in advance anything about the singer's special connection to the Virgin Mary, for example, and then this figure becomes part of the story. The magic moment creates an opening. An opening for the belief that anything can happen – and then it happens!

Sometimes I see a figure wearing robes of glory, but I am not able to identify them, due to a lack of mythological or religious knowledge. If I have the slightest doubt, I describe the figure's appearance and the singer often then recognizes the figure. In other cases, the singer may explicitly wish to get in touch with a certain high energy form that they trust completely. The wish is formulated and we see what happens.

A third way is for the singer to ask to be released on a higher level where they can meet these wise spirits and receive answers to their questions. The singer may formulate their wish during the process, or it may occur spontaneously.

The singer I referred to at the beginning of this section had difficulty relaxing, felt guilty about the slightest thing, even things she hadn't done. She wanted to make things right for everyone. She was full of self-reproach and her primary feeling was 'I am not good enough.' Her wish was to be released between two lives.

The woman was lifted up through different levels of consciousness. She was heavy to raise up, because she didn't believe she deserved anything good. However, the voice itself seemed to want it – here the soul speaks its own language.

A group of light beings received her. The woman lay in a kind of hammock in their midst. To get her to relax, they rocked her. The atmosphere was light and full of generosity and laughter. The singer was rocked free of her anxious sense of responsibility. It was only when the singer was completely relaxed and had surrendered that the light beings healed her. The woman was able to ask questions and receive answers to whatever the light beings were allowed to answer.

Gratitude ritual

At the end of each day of a course, everyone participates in a ritual of gratitude to round off the release that has taken place. This is not meant as a formal ceremony, but more as a gesture to touch the heart and confirm the healing that has occurred.

When a person gives thanks for a healing that has occurred, they acknowledge the miracle. By acknowledging it, they create space for it.

There is now space for the consciousness to expand into, which gives the miracle a dimension beyond the now. One can say that the course participant takes the miracle home with them in the pocket of their heart.

Healing lies in strengthening our faith. Not necessarily faith in a particular understanding of God, but rather a general faith in the existence of higher energies which our antennae can pick up and communicate with whenever we need to.

Example

Close your eyes and put your hands on your chest. Give thanks for the love and light that you have received today. Let inspiration guide your words instead of learning something by rote.

Many course participants are moved, because the heart chakra opens when the release is affirmed. If a participant has difficulty in being moved, then either the ego has not opened up enough to the soul or the participant has transferred the credit for any release to the listener.

'The nightingale sang so beautifully that it brought tears to the emperor's eyes ... who declared the nightingale should have his golden slipper to wear round its neck, but the nightingale merely thanked him. "I have seen tears in the eyes of the emperor. God knows I have indeed been richly rewarded!"
Hans Christian Andersen, *The Nightingale*

PHYSICAL REACTIONS
During regressive cell-singing

Spittle, slime, coughing, irritation of the throat and spasm-like movements are normal (see page 195). The listener cannot be squeamish. Be ready with a spittoon and be prepared to urge the singer to spit out their slime. If the hoarseness continues, then you need to find a 'hole' in the voice in a higher or lower region – a place where it is 'clear' so the voice can ring through.

If a singer's need to cough and spit comes after contacting the Note from Heaven, it is a healthy, cleansing reaction due to an activation of muscles and feelings that have hitherto been suppressed.

When the singer is united with the Note from Heaven, he or she will experience involuntary eye movements under their closed eyelids like those that occur during REM sleep. Some participants need to get up and use their whole body during singing – arms outstretched, head back, eyes closed.

Stretching out the arms with the palms of the hands open and turned upwards while leaning the head slightly back strengthens the surrender to the Note from Heaven. Many do it quite naturally. For others it feels awkward and embarrassing.

The right side represents the outwardly moving, dynamic, masculine part of the body. The left side is the inwardly moving, spiritual, feminine power.

Some course participants can feel energy only on the one side. If a person has difficulty feeling 'good enough', then they will often feel they have no right to receive anything. This will lead to their left side being more or less closed. A person who has experienced shock will often have a weakened right side. Their ability to actively respond is reduced. In the case of a child having been ignored, the whole body can be closed down. Those who have been ignored or who have experienced shock will typically say 'I can't feel myself/my feelings/my body.'

In such cases it is important to bring the 'dead' part of the body to life. The sounds of singing can resonate and work only in areas of the body that are energetically open and therefore resonant. The sound can go in under the ice through the opening and gradually work on the part of the body that cannot be felt. The body will open only when it is ready. Here the right code word can open the gates of heaven.

The muscles will ache and hurt after the body has been woken from its slumber through regressive cell-singing.

A hand that has fallen asleep always hurts when you begin to move it.

Illness and pain are the body's request for attention.

'I am here! Here! Give me attention now! NOW!' Pain teaches us to listen to our body. Only when it has received what it is calling out for, will we have peace. Regressive cell-singing is about expressing, and thereby understanding, the body's call.

After regressive cell-singing

Many singers feel charged with energy for days after making contact with the Note from Heaven. Sometimes this energetic opening process continues for months afterwards. In such cases there has really been a breakthrough and the participant can apparently cope with remaining open. This means the energy will continue to work in the person, and a gradual development of intuition will occur. The singer will also experience more synchronistic happenings than can be put down to mere coincidence.

Those participants who are able to accommodate the power in this way will always be able to return to the Note from Heaven.

It is normal to feel tired after regressive cell-singing, even totally exhausted in some cases. A woman participating in a one-day course slept for a whole day and night afterwards.

When the body has been strained by illness it is in particular need of peace and quiet to assimilate the new energy structure. The process of releasing cells that were bound usually continues for a week to ten days after the séance.

Symptoms resembling influenza can appear at the start of the purification process. If this does happen, the symptoms will develop immediately after the course and recede within two days. Because of that, I hold my courses on a Friday, if possible, so people can recuperate over the following weekend.

In rare cases where very intense feelings have surfaced, and not all these emotions have been transformed during the singing process, people have experienced vomiting. A woman was feeling fine at the end of the course, but then felt nauseous in the car on the way home and threw up periodically during the journey. The vomiting continued through the night and then passed. She felt very relieved afterwards. Her theme was incest.

In another case, a male Arabic immigrant vomited during the vocal release of an overwhelming fear brought on by the thought of a hearing the next day involving rights of access to his son. The father's emotions had been so effectively released that the next day he managed to stay calm and under control during the hearing. Any violent emotional outbursts could easily have turned the court against him.

Some people react with physical pains or general soreness. This is particularly common in those participants who are unable to sense their feelings – the pains signify that the body is starting to acknowledge these suppressed emotions. This acknowledgment is closely followed by mood swings – a necessary part of every purification process.

Waves oxidize brackish water.

Yawning

It is a good sign if the course participants and the listener start to yawn a lot. Yawning is a natural physical reaction to the body's letting go of tensions and it always happens when the body instinctively takes a deep breath. The mere thought of yawning makes you yawn. I'm sitting here writing and yawning away.

The body yawns when it releases. You can almost picture steam spewing out of a little hole on the top of the head. During one course where we yawned and yawned, a female participant let us in on a memory that had plagued her for years:

'Someone close to me was being buried. The priest was delivering a speech and earth was being thrown down onto the coffin in the grave. I was yawning almost constantly and weeping at the same time. It was impossible for me to hold back my reaction, despite the fact that I must have appeared rather arrogant and I felt so embarrassed about it.'

The soft palate in the oral cavity lifts up every time you express a genuine feeling. The yawning sets a physical reaction in motion from the lower abdomen up to the crown of the head. The jaw – the joint in the body with the highest number of nerve reactions – is extended and a stretching occurs in the oral cavity. It feels almost like a parachute opening out. Try stretching out your arm and bend the wrist coquettishly downwards and stretch out the pinkies. The movement supports the stretching of the soft palate, the domed roof of the oral cavity. A magnificent chandelier hangs from the highest point. The stretch affects pituitary and pineal glands. Yawn – the eyes start watering. Surrender. The hormone system is activated.

The only vowel that completely stretches out the dome is 'Aaar'. This vowel has led me and numerous course participants and readers to the Note from Heaven.

Giving birth supported by the Note from Heaven

During my second pregnancy, I was assigned a community midwife named Annie Brehmer. She presented herself as an odd type who could get women to deliver easily by moaning and singing on 'Aaar'.

We both experienced goose bumps of pleasure at this first meeting. I have never before or since heard of a midwife who asks those giving birth to sing. Nor could she believe she was dealing with a pregnant woman who had written a whole book on singing 'Aaar'. What's more, it turned out that she lived only 200 metres away from me, so we were able to collaborate closely, among other things on a composition called 'Womb' (a recording of foetal sounds in the womb) on my CD *Rising*.

Annie shared her knowledge with me in preparation for the birth. Experience and a wide range of holistic studies had taught her that the mouth corresponds to the vagina, so that when you open the mouth and sing 'Aaar', the vagina also opens – the muscles work in partnership.

Annie offered to assist me in a singing delivery at the hospital. I felt so very lucky, because I realized it meant our first-born child, then almost seven years old, could be present at the birth. He was used to the Note from Heaven and would understand my way of using it much better than if I was screaming in pain.

The time came, but when my waters had broken and the labour pains were strong, it felt much more natural to go into a deep meditation than to sing. The pains brought me into a state of elation as I stood leaning over a beanbag absorbed in my own inner world.

I don't think Annie realized how quickly everything was going. Fortunately, she left me in peace. They filled the bath with water. Once in the bath the second-stage labour pains started and suddenly I felt the urge to sing.

The Note from Heaven became so powerful that at one point there were four curious midwives watching in amazement. When I stopped the singing because Annie wanted to check down between my legs, the pain reappeared with such a shocking intensity that I instinctively kicked out at her. 'My God, the head is just about to come out.'

With two more pushes, a new soul had come to the world. My newborn son immediately clung tightly to my breast. The birth had taken one and a quarter hours from the breaking of the waters. Our elder son, now a big brother, had been present the whole time. My first experience of giving birth had been long, hard and traumatic, so it was enormously releasing to deliver my second child so easily with the Note from Heaven on my lips.

Giving birth is an initiation. So, mothers-to-be, please do not take any unnecessary painkillers. This is such a sacred moment and can expand your whole being. Do not let fear take the lead. Sing your child out with the help of the Note from Heaven.

GENDER AND SEXUALITY
The gateway between life and death

In the moment of surrender to the Note from Heaven, a letting go occurs that is much like the release of an orgasm. You can no longer resist, you have no choice but to let yourself surrender to the flow of the current in the body's river.

When we stifle a yawn, we stop our mouth from opening and thereby protect ourselves physically and psychologically from momentary exposure. I believe that the erotic fantasy of totally exposing oneself, surrendering unreservedly to another being, is identical to the yearning for the spiritual experience of oneness.

What arouses us most is to overstep the bounds of what is permitted and set foot in the forbidden land. This land is actually a holy land, but as long as we keep it in the shadows we cannot experience it in all its light and glory. It takes women forty years to become erotically and vocally mature... the time Moses and his people spent wandering in the desert.

When guilt is linked to our sexuality, it ties us to the astral plane's domain of images and reduces the likelihood of an orgasmic awakening of spirituality.

Envision lovemaking as something sanctified and performed on an altar, a ritual done with gratitude to the divine. Lovemaking as pure 'being'. Lovemaking accompanied by song.

That is how it once was. The act of reproduction was holy, and it still is, if we allow it to be. The moment just before the orgasm's climax is a door opening to the higher layers of consciousness. In that split second, the ego throws off all its armour and bows its head in recognition: 'Please, God, take over.'

In Walter Schubart's fantastic book *Religion and Eroticism* (1941), the words glow under the professor's pen. It gives me a pleasant jolt of surprise that he defines female sexuality as the 'joy of creation':

'In the joy of creation, it is not coarse feelings of lust that are made divine, but eroticism's uninhibited, bubbling source of all life; the origin of the universe, shrouded in mystery. The joy of creation is a religious feeling. Creation's beauty and fertility overwhelm the human being and force it into a state of worship. The joy of creation leads religious thinking towards speculation about the world's creation, not the world's purpose. It raises the question of where from, not where to.'

To a remarkable degree, Schubart's definition of female eroticism reminds me of the power that is generated while singing the Note from Heaven. It is almost identical to the feelings aroused in my chest during surrender. The experience of the bubbling, whirling energy shower which wraps up my organism awakens a deep, overwhelming gratitude for this divine wonder.

I know that there is a close connection between sexual union between two lovers and the individual person's union with the state of consciousness and energy that the Note from Heaven represents. The main difference is that erotic release is dualistic in its basic form whereas oral, song-based release is closely linked to the heart and has an androgynous character.

The oral cavity has aspects of both female and male genitalia. It has a uvula (corresponding to the clitoris), a hard palate in front (the vulva), a throat (the vagina); the soft palate and the oral cavity can extend and stretch upwards like the uterus. The tongue corresponds to the penis. Try in a private moment to open your mouth and stick out your tongue. It stimulates yawning sensations and some shyness in a surrendering:

I open myself; let myself be filled, while simultaneously giving everything I have.

The uniting of the masculine and feminine principle.

As the root chakra corresponds to the sense of smell, the anus must correspond to the nostrils. One nostril each for the *ida* and *pingala*, feminine and masculine energy, whose common point of origin is in the root chakra.

In yoga there is the concept of warm energy (drawn in through the right nostril) and cold energy (drawn in through the left nostril). Do the female and male reproductive organs, the ovaries and the testicles, correspond to the eyes and does the brain correspond to the intestinal system? The Chinese perceive the stomach as our brain for feelings, so it could very well be true.

No matter how way out this may sound, it makes sense to me and it could be part of an explanation why a free vocal expression liberates the entire body.

The tension between man and woman, the tension between matter and spirit: polarity.

In the experience of the Note from Heaven, the Singer is not one or two in that moment.

He is both.

'Jesus saw children who were being suckled. He said to his disciples: "These children who are being suckled are like those who enter the Kingdom." They said to him: "Shall we then, being children, enter the Kingdom?" Jesus said to them: "When you make the two One, and you make the inner even as the outer, and the outer even as the inner, and the above even as the below so that you will make the male and the female into a single One, in order that the male is not made male nor the female made female... then shall you enter the Kingdom."'
Gospel of Thomas, log. 22

The power of the feminine

What will the consequences be for your life if you become your self?

For women in particular, fear of getting in touch with one's own spiritual power is a common problem in regressive cell-singing. This fear is well founded. The conventional male reaction to meeting a woman who is clearly in touch with her spiritual potential is to position himself for a cockfight: can I possess her/outdo her? This instinct is natural. The primeval sexual power is built around a man's ability to possess a woman. He must be strong for her to want him. This ensures the quality of the offspring.

A woman unconsciously tests a man's boundaries, because she needs to be able to float in his vessel. If she senses that she can trust him to carry her in all her completeness, she will be able to surrender; which means totally yielding to the man's penetrating power (equivalent to surrendering to the Note from Heaven, which is also a question of trust).

The very moment one partner in a relationship changes, the other must adjust. Since women are instinctively created to surrender and, for that reason, are emotionally more fluid than men, they are also more likely to surrender to spirituality. The archetypal challenge for the man appears the moment God takes his wife by the hand. Does he see it as a blessing, or does he see God as a rival, threatening his sturdy castle, in which wife and offspring are kept in a safe strongbox?

If he is able to see her spiritual process as a gift, he will not only win her, but strengthen their love relationship as well. The man shows with his openheartedness that he is not afraid to be tried by God. His castle, his strength is unshakable. She can feel completely safe in the knowledge he will go to the ends of the earth for her. But he acts on his own terms, and she on hers.

This is where men should wake up: conservative dominance and rigid family patterns are no longer acceptable to today's women. When a man clearly works against his female partner's aspirations to raise her consciousness, he digs the grave of his marriage. It is as if he turns off the light in the relationship, saying, 'You must not shine, darling. Stay with me in the darkness.'

Men and women can easily raise their consciousness together. Real men are intuitive.

Business leaders recognize the need for intuition to help them make the right decisions in their fast-paced, pressurized working environment. Interest in the Akashic field is growing; scientists talk about the zero point field, a similar all-knowing layer of consciousness.

Man, take care of your vessel, let the feminine energy in.
Woman, surrender safely in the vessel's encircling power.
A vessel without fluid is empty. Fluid without a vessel is wasted.

It wasn't until I was forty that I realized bubbling with energy and inspiration is a positive thing. There is no reason to hold back my buoyant energy. My power is a gift, a gift that rises above the constraints of marriage. Make or break. No one can take this power from you and it is there for both you and your partner, if he is able to resonate with it. The feminine power is just as important for the man as for the woman. Like a yearning for the all, it is now knocking on your door, stronger than ever before. It is a question of life and death, nature's aspiring to re-establish balance here on earth. If you are looking for a partner, you will get one that fits who you are right now. So why not be yourself? Does your most optimal sound resonate within you? I'm telling you, everything is possible. Love is unlimited.

Open your arms so that you can contain as much light as possible. Receive everything that is given to you. The more you shine, the better you can serve the all. Pure energy flows like water, catches like fire, spreads like love. It must be passed on. If you push it away, you lose it. If you hold on to it, it will be taken from you.

Fear is the yoke that switches off all light.

Woman, pluck your emotional strings. The world needs information in the form of sound. The sound behind the words, the unconscious, the mother ocean – all are of feminine lineage. The woman is of the all. She is closely connected to the universe through the process of pregnancy. The world mother, the pregnant stomach. An egg, a globe, a fertile planet with oceans and lands. Mystery is a natural thing for woman, because she feels it within herself and is influenced without asking any questions. She knows. Life and death are intertwined with pregnancy. Facial features change, become softer and more open. You are humankind's oracle. Lead the masculine power to the oneness level and let it fortify its seed there.

Man, speak your mind and lead the woman back to the earth. Plant your seed in the name of unity. Let the woman vibrate under your wings and know that she loves you more each time you pour her flowing essence into your vessel and gently cool it with your patient breath.

If you put a lid on the vessel, you will lose her. Let her ebb and flow freely within her cycle. Like a moon orbiting and reflecting you, the sun. The stable, unwavering power.

PART III

RESONANCE WITH DOMINO EFFECT

WHAT IS 'RESONANCE WITH DOMINO EFFECT' (RDE)?

In Resonance with Domino Effect (RDE), the liberated prince or princess overwhelms the troll and leads their fellow prisoners out into the light of freedom. Not only are the prisoners liberated, they too liberate others with their song of freedom. Some participants will not be ready to leave the troll's fortress, as they may feel as if they are still chained to the pain body. Even when the chains have been cast aside and the troll is dead, a few prefer to imagine he is still alive, so that they can justify staying in the safe and familiar darkness.

In my small-scale regressive cell-singing courses, I always used to follow the principle that each person should take it in turns to sing themselves free. Whoever was singing should be given special attention, supported and not be disturbed by anyone else's spontaneous need for emotional expression – each person had to wait their turn.

However, on one occasion I allowed a course participant with a great need (she had never been able to surrender totally to the Note from Heaven) to interrupt a singer who had awakened something in her. The woman who interrupted was the least pushy person you could imagine. Shy and reserved in her manner, she felt herself to be unimportant and not worthy of other people's attention. So when she burst in like this, I knew that she must be experiencing something exceptional. After the existing singer had agreed to share her time, the woman with the great need for release sang herself into a state that finally opened her up. She now dared to let go. She had made the leap.

This seemed to be a perfect example of Resonance with Domino Effect – one singer's sound inspiring another to open up. However, in the midst of this joy and release one person was unhappy. The interrupted singer felt rejected, despite the fact that she had agreed to the interruption. Her basic theme of 'I am not good enough' had been reinforced. The episode fed her pain body with the complaint that, once again, she had had to step aside for someone else. 'I'm just not allowed to get any attention. I'm always being brushed aside and that is the main reason why I have had a problem with alcohol.' When she had another opportunity to sing herself free, she couldn't do it.

Having initially been enthused by the possibilities that this episode seemed to open up, I was discouraged by its effect on the interrupted singer and began to doubt whether Resonance with Domino Effect could ever work within the parameters of a course. But the phenomenon continued to knock on my door.

Until a certain point in time, people who attended my lectures on the Note from Heaven tended to open up to the power with more or less controlled emotional outbursts. The energy was usually high, but somewhere within myself I must have radiated enough control so that nobody in the hall went off the rails. Many were deeply touched by the energy experiences, but none, or at least very few, let their feelings out in the way they do in small groups practising regressive cell-singing. However, this would soon change.

At the first large Power of Sound event – a one-day seminar arranged by Hearts and Hands featuring several instructors – I was asked to demonstrate both sound-healing and regressive cell-singing on stage. This was in front of 430 people. I told them at the start that this was an experiment and, if necessary for ethical reasons, I might have to complete the regressive cell-singing in private. Since there were only 45 minutes available for the singing of the Note from Heaven with the full audience, the demonstration of sound-healing with a baby and two adults, and the regressive cell-singing, there was no time for discussing back and forth. In order for the regressive cell-singing to develop as spontaneously as possible, I decided to choose a volunteer from the audience who would offer the best chance of a powerful release: 'I need a woman who believes she is tone deaf or can't sing, and who felt moved in her heart when we sang the Note from Heaven.'

A sea of hands rose in the air. The audience had been briefed beforehand that this exercise might take them out of their comfort zone. A young woman came up on to the stage.

I was just about to enquire into her primary feeling when she opened her mouth – and screamed.

She screamed so that it went right through you. The crowded hall shook. 'Fine, good, how good you are at letting go, stretch out your arms, palms up ... ' The important thing with screaming is to listen beyond the expression to the energy. I enjoyed it; she really aired out her innermost chambers. As we have seen, it is the listener's duty to help the singer to reach a beautiful, divine sound that is energizing and uplifting for the cells at the vibrational level.

Here in front of a completely packed hall, this woman had thrown herself into it. By vocally emphasizing the scream's basic note, I could lead her with me. Soon her voice was like a shimmering column in the air, compelling and full of light. The Note from Heaven. After a couple of minutes in this state, the woman had finished. We had hardly exchanged a word. With a quick thank you, she disappeared into the crowd.

The séance had made an impression on everyone. Many were wholeheartedly enthusiastic, but I also got responses from a couple of people who honestly admitted that they had been shaken to their very foundations. The scream had frightened them and the experience had caused stifled sobs, nausea and discomfort. So there it was again: Resonance with Domino Effect. One of them had even had to leave the hall.

When doing an introductory course at a Holistic Festival, I conducted an experiment with a group of 65 people who had just opened up to the Note from Heaven, by offering them the opportunity to experience collective regressive cell-singing. Something new happened there, which developed into RDE. After a woman had sung herself free of an experience from a past life, a large number of the course participants had lumps in their throats and said they felt that the woman's singing had touched something within them. Like a horse that has been given its freedom, she had happily whinnied outside the stable, while her fellow course participants were still tethered inside. Of course, they grew restless: 'We also want to get out and run around!'

I asked those course participants who had been touched at a deep level to sit in the centre of the group. There were eight people. Each person was assigned two or three 'helpers' who were instructed in how to support their release. One by one they purified their emotions, and more people were touched ... it went on and on.

Principles of RDE singing

1. When working on the collective level, the identity of the person being released is of secondary importance.

The goal of RDE is the release of bound-up energy through contact with the Note from Heaven by using regressive cell-singing.

We are all part of the oneness level. Therefore, when one person sings down the light, everyone receives it. The course leader has to see the group as one energy field – one being, metaphorically speaking, where the pores of the skin are open to varying degrees.

2. In RDE singing, participants can spontaneously sing themselves free when an unresolved emotion knocks on their door.

The law of resonance applies to every expression of feeling. Emotions are archetypal, and certain emotions resonate with certain vibrations. Most of us carry the same set of differently tuned tuning forks within us, which pick up these archetypal, universal emotions. This is how we can understand each other's feelings. We are on the same wavelength.

Anyone carrying the same unresolved emotion as the singer will be affected by the sound produced during a release and will clearly feel an emotional reaction starting in their own body. This emotional chain reaction is at the heart of RDE.

When the body resonates with a fellow human being's feelings, it reacts before the intellect has time to intervene.

The feeling of isolation created by a huge taboo of a problem is dissolved in that wonderful moment when we realize that we are not alone. There is sympathy and total understanding from those who carry the same emotional burden. The emotional fire devoted singing can ignite in a group bound together by mutual understanding is overwhelmingly beautiful. During the release of RDE singing, a flame is lit that awakens true compassion.

3. RDE requires a ratio of 1–3 listeners per singer.

It is impossible to know in advance how many people in a group will resonate with the same unresolved archetypal emotion. In a group of 30 participants, a singer will, on average, affect one or two fellow participants in the first round. These will then affect between two and four more, and so on, until the emotion is discharged from the group. When, on occasion, many are being affected at the same time, it is important, as the leader of a RDE-group, to keep your composure and take it as it comes.

Singers who have gone into mutual resonance are assembled in the middle of a circle where the rest of the group is located.

For participants who feel disempowered by passively watching, it can be rewarding to get involved as a helper in the process. The needs of the resonating singers are explored before anyone begins to support them. Although it is normal to feel safer with some helpers than with others, there are seldom major problems because those who have a burning urge to offer care are usually inspired by an emotion they recognize from close relationships in their own lives.

The listeners should be supporting the neck and hold a hand lightly on the "resonating singers" forehead, while listening to the sound. There can easily be several supporters of one singer at the same time. For example, a second listener might do grounding work by healing/holding the singer's legs and feet. A third listener might hold a hand lightly on the singer's stomach, while supporting deep breathing. The Singers get as much attention as they need. By the end of the session, the singer should be able to sing alone. Laughter rolling around in the spaces between the tones is a signal that release has occurred. It can take from two to six minutes. If singing goes on longer than this, this may indicate that the emotion has been discharged, closed down or that the singer has gone into melodramatic performance.

4. Keep an eye out for 'shy resonants'.

Shy resonants are people who resonate with the same emotion as the resonating singers, but are too shy to put themselves forward for release. During RDE, it is important that the leader keeps a watchful eye on the flock, because there may be shy souls sitting near the back wringing their hands, battling with roused emotions. They can be too proud (particularly in the case of men) or too shy to draw attention to themselves.

Shy resonants usually only need to be offered a helping hand, then the release occurs quite naturally: 'Come on, dear, it looks to me as if you have been affected; your voice can fill the whole room if you want to. We want to hear you. It is wonderful to hear your sound, your voice and your power. Let us hear you sing down the light to all of us.' Sentences like this, when expressed honestly, can have an opening and particularly powerful effect on participants who were ignored as children or whose parents didn't have the energy to give them the attention they needed.

RDE is especially good for shy resonants, because they are in a situation where the focus is not just on them and they can wait for others to make the first move before stepping forward. Many hold back because they are tied down by a deep-rooted shame – a shame that has isolated them with an inner primary feeling of fear of being discovered. They have had no choice but to hide themselves and their all too heavy emotion. When this emotion is openly acknowledged in a fellow course participant's sound, it activates a wish to pull free of the mire. This might never have happened if I had been sitting alone with them as a client with an uninterrupted focus on 'No, I can't do it.'

For some participants the prospect is too frightening. To open up they would have to cast off the chains binding them to their identification with the pain body. They aren't ready for that. However, the experience can easily prick a hole in the membrane of a negatively functioning life pattern, and suddenly one day the person is ready to let go. But it hurts, just like birth pains do after the membrane to the amniotic fluid is perforated and the waters break. A negative emotional reaction from a course participant can be a sign that a positive process has been set in motion.

5. Dealing with images.

It can be difficult to listen in to an individual singer's sound in Resonance with Domino Effect. For example, the sound might come from four singers simultaneously and resemble an infernal fire of energy in its bursting-out phase. Here, the main thing is to lead the singers one by one to the Note from Heaven. The principle is the same as for regressive cell-singing. However, if images appear, it can be difficult to use them constructively when the sound is coming from several people at once. You can't distinguish whom the message is for. But, if you sense the message is for the group, then the images can help focus the energies.

On one course, there was a group of resonating singers whose common theme was Native Americans. They acted like a little tribe and the images I received gathered them in a euphoric song and dance that drew in the rest of the course participants. In such a situation there is no question of 'willing' something to happen. It happens and feels quite natural. There are many courses in the world of alternative therapies where one is encouraged to will oneself into being a Native American or something similar and they always make me feel very uncomfortable. When what you are arises spontaneously from within, it is genuine. It vanishes afterwards. You can remember it had something to do with Native Americans, but since it all took place in the moment, the memory only remembers that it was good: a sweaty face, a plant and the sun outside. A feeling has been acted out.

6. Melodramatic performing.

In RDE, anything can happen. The method is attractive to melodramatic performers, who unconsciously see it as their chance to get attention.

It is important that, even in a large group, the listener is able to spot melodramatic performers and neutralize them as quickly as possible, because the others who have just opened up cannot tolerate the presence of such heavy energy for very long.

A melodramatic performer with a stuck expression can be recognized by a competitive edge to their singing. Usually the melodramatic performer will sing or scream so loudly that none of the others can be heard. The expressed sound does not touch the heart.

Melodramatic performance is an archetypal reaction learned in childhood. The person underneath is innocent and calling for help. It is easy to get irritated, because an individual acting in this mode takes centre stage with no regard for anyone else. The whole group atmosphere can become negative if the person is allowed to drain them of energy and that is why the leading listener of RDE singing must be experienced.

7. The element of surprise.

When I, as course leader, sense the slightest trace of melodramatic performance in the air, I immediately hand the release of any remaining resonating singers over to helpers and concentrate fully on activating the true feeling behind the performance. Here an element of surprise is helpful. I say, do or sing something odd or surprising – for example, playing a cheerful, melodious phrase of music on the piano or a guitar – so that they stop for a second to see what is going on. After that it is possible to improvise what I really want to say and what the person couldn't or wouldn't hear: 'You are so precious. You are perfect just as you are. We love you, we so want to hear the genuine you. We want to see you – to feel your light. You are loved, you are so wonderful, how nicely you are letting go. Wow, how beautifully you're singing now … '

Energy-drainers are used to being met with resistance. Their surprise at being valued transforms the energy. The person may be touched and burst into tears, and then the true emotion can be released through cry-toning.

If the listener is able to quickly recognize a stuck expression and be precise in the treatment, very few will even notice the character of the outburst. The harm will be minimized, the energy raised, the singer released and happy, and the séance will continue without interruption.

I have often heard therapists complain about pupils who compete for attention with a resultant drop in energy level in the group. It is the leader's responsibility to maintain the energy level. So, as a listener, be clear: 'Your sound does not touch my heart, I feel that you are hiding a true feeling. A fear of not being good enough, not being lovable ... Try to express that fear.'

Group singing for dissolving melodramatic performance

The group's singing can also be used to dissipate melodramatic performance. The leading listener needs use their intuition here. The melodramatic performer can be surrounded and sung to. Give him or her love. Focus on their expression and mimic it, in order to resonate with and understand the expressed emotion. Soon the melodramatic performance will be drowned out by the echoing of his or her own expression. This leads very naturally to the person stopping short in amazement and listening. In daily life, the same thing can be done with small children.

It is actually fun to copy someone else's expression. The participants can use this mirror as a shield against the heavy, draining energy. Soon all the heavy vibrations are lightened again by the releasing effect of laughter.

8. All for one ...

Make it clear from the start – as soon as people apply for the course – that the strength of RDE is that *anything* can happen and that one person's release is everyone's release. In this way you effectively avoid people resenting each other, because they feel this one or that one received more time or attention than they did.

Without rules there is freedom. No old pictures on the wall to see yourself in.

Practical organization

Although RDE is inherently unpredictable, courses tend to follow a certain structure.

1 Body and voice warm-ups, grounding and breathing exercises.

2 Singing on the Note from Heaven for about half an hour. If anyone begins to react emotionally before that, they are led into regressive cell-singing and if others begin to resonate with them, RDE is allowed to develop naturally. During a course, we have between three and five rounds with different emotional themes, interspersed with relaxation on mattresses and singing with the Note from Heaven.

   If no one becomes overwhelmed by trauma while singing the Note from Heaven, I release a volunteer and then resonating singers start to pop up. Here the Listener needs to keep an eye open and call on people to come up who seem, from their facial expressions or body language, to be resonating and ready to go. Sometimes the other participants help by giving me a sign that someone's emotions are starting to open up.

3 The course is rounded off by sound-healing. I either heal the whole group myself, or we split up and take turns to heal each other with intuitive healing. The healing is like an astringent skin tonic that allows the cleansed pores of our group body to close again.

   Always have tissues, water and a spittoon ready. A stereo, mattresses, pillows and blankets need to be available in the room. Fruit, tea and water are sources of good, easily accessible energy – I am not a fan of coffee and cake in the breaks. They actually reduce the energy in the long run.

   The singers are given the chance to relax on a mattress or snuggle under a blanket after their release. The listener and carers need to be sensitive to people's needs here. For example, it's nice to get support under the knees.

   After a release, it can feel as if you have been born into a whole new, peaceful universe. Most singers like to relax by lying down and watching the group in peace and quiet – like a baby who has settled down happily in a corner of the sitting room, but still feels part of the assembled company.

   For some adults, especially shy resonants, it can be difficult to accept being cared for. Out of sheer politeness they will refuse the offer with an 'Oh no, it's not necessary,' the implication being that there are others with a greater need than theirs. If the listener persists, the shy person will succumb with a sigh of relief. A pattern from childhood has been broken; the listener's action says: 'You deserve care and attention.'

Example of a course in RDE singing

I hope that this brief account of an actual course will give you a flavour of RDE in action.

On this particular day there were 30 participants. At first five resonating 'babies' were lying in a row crying for their mothers, screaming and kicking. More and more joined the group. Lots of mothers for the babies. A helper knelt behind each singer holding one hand on their forehead and using the other as support for the neck.

The room quickly warmed up, but we couldn't open a window, or else the whole district would think this was a torture chamber. The Note from Heaven flowed through the course participants one by one. There was an infernal noise. Each singer had their own tone, sharp and powerful as a siren. I disappeared into the sound and joy pervaded me. I was whirled into a spiral of energy. The melting together of worlds.

After a few minutes a common note appeared. Everyone in the room sang along with it. Some of the released singers raised their hands in the air, as if in a trance. Nobody cared any longer whether they were sitting in the middle of the room or not. Everything was sound and we were one.

After a short break, a young woman with a crew cut said she wanted to be released in regressive cell-singing. Before we got started, she explained that two months before she had had one breast removed due to cancer. She was a single mother and wanted to live. Her prayer was to find her path here on earth.

As the young woman leaned her head back, spread out her arms, closed her eyes and surrendered in song to the Note from Heaven, an older man broke down in tears. He had participated on other courses and had been able to let go, but there had always been a trace of self-control. He had held his cancer in check for ten years, balancing on the knife-edge of rising and falling prostate numbers. The man's cry-toning was unusually energetic, drawing several from the group into it. Everyone was deeply moved.

He and the young woman formed a sonic symbiosis in a bonfire of prayer. Many participants wished to show caring towards the singers, but in this case care would have suffocated the healing power. The two of them expressed a mature realization: 'I am one with you, my soul. Everything in me vibrates in the presence of oneness. I am vibration, I am light – I am the Note from Heaven.'

is being is sound is life is light is love is joy is happiness is wholeness is the path is devotion is gratitude is

EPILOGUE

Wonderful the earth

Wonderful the earth,
Magnificent God's heaven,
Beautiful the soul's pilgrim song.
Through the fair realms on earth
We go singing to paradise.

Times shall come,
Times shall pass,
Generations shall follow generations;
Never will the note from heaven grow silent
In the soul's joyful pilgrim song.

The angels sang it
First to shepherds in the field,
Beautifully, from soul to soul, it sounded:
'Peace on Earth, O people rejoice,
To us an eternal Saviour is born.'

Traditional Danish Christmas carol, text by B S Ingemann, 1850

ABOUT THE AUTHOR

Biography
Githa Ben-David was born in Juelsminde, Denmark, 23 November 1961, into an atheist family from a Protestant background. From 1985 to 1993 Githa went to India six times to study classical Khyal singing with Mangala Tiwari. She lived in Israel 1994 to 1998, working as a musician, therapist and composer. Today she lives in Denmark with her two sons and her husband, Lars Muhl (author of *The Law of Light* and *The 'O' Manuscript*).

Education
- Trained in classical saxophone at the Royal Danish Music Conservatory
- Studied Indian song in Varanasi, India, sponsored by the Danish Music Council and the Danish Royal Music Conservatory
- Educated as a healer in the Mystical Therapy system by Master José in Israel
- Educated as a regression therapist by André Corell in Copenhagen

Musical career
- Performed with Chægs Bluesband, Atilla Engin Group, Giraf, Conservatory Big Band, Aarhus Symphony Orchestra, Sultan Big Band, Acapulco Salsa band various groups in Israel, as a duo with Omri Ben-David (north Indian song/tabla), Pia Boysen (organ/classical saxophone) and Lars Muhl (vocals/guitar/piano)
- Member of DJBFA (Danish Jazz, Beat, and Folk-Authors)
- Written and performed theatre music for Anatomic Theatre (German instructor), *Bustan Ha Siporim* (approximately 300 performances, Israel), *Notzot ba Ruach* (storytelling, Israel)

Current work
- Runs Gilalai Institute of Energy and Consciousness (including Gilalai Publishing) with Lars Muhl
- Leader of certificated course in Vocal Sound Therapy
- Runs courses in Denmark and elsewhere in Europe
- Runs a Mystery School together with Lars Muhl
- Gives concerts and lectures
- Composer and author

Internet resources
- www.thenotefromheaven.com
- www.gilalai.com
- www.githabendavid.dk (Danish)
- www.larsmuhl.com
- www.cosmoporta.net (film channel for Gilalai: Demonstration of Breathing, the Note from Heaven, Sound Healing etc)
- Facebook: Githa Ben-David

Book publications
Tonen fra Himlen, Borgen, 2002
Syng dig Fri, Universal Gratefulness, 2008
Lyd er Liv , Gilalai Publishing, 2011
Terapeuternes Mysterieskole (with Lars Muhl), Gilalai Publishing, 2012
The Songs of Lars Muhl & Githa Ben-David, Gilalai Publishing; 2015
Liluja (novel), *Gilalai* Publishing, 2015

Books and CDs can be purchased at www. gilalai.com

The practice recordings for this book can be downloaded for free at: www.thenotefromheaven.com (or www.gilalai.com on the English page)

BIBLIOGRAPHY

Andersen, Hans Christian: Fire *udvalgte eventyr* (Egmont Imagination, 2005)

Bailey, Alice A.: *Esoterisk Healing* (Esoterisk Centre Forlag, 1995)

Ben-David, Githa: *Syng dig Fri* (Universal Gratefulness, 2008)

Ben-David, Githa: *Tonen fra Himlen* (Borgen 1.oplag, 2002)

Bertelsen, Jes: *Kvantespring, En bog om kærlighed* (Borgen, 1986)

Bontenbal, Rob: *Your Past Can Sure Get in Your Way!* (SVR, 1995)

Brofman, Martin: Alt kan heales – *The Body Mirror System* (Forlaget Ribergaard, 1998)

Campbell, Don: Mozart *effekten* (Aschehoug, 1998)

Chang, Dr Stephen T: *Bogen om de Indre øvelser* (NSO-Omre Forlag, 1986)

Chopra, Deepak: *De syv spirituelle love for succes* (Borgen, 1995)

Cohen, Andrew: *Embracing Heaven and Earth* (Moksha Press, 2000)

Cohen, Andrew: *Frihed har ingen historie* (Borgen, 2000)

Daniélou, Alain: *The Ragas of Northern Indian Music* (Munshiram Manoharlal Publishers, 1980)

Emoto, Masaru: *De Skjulte Budskaber i Vand* (Sphinx, 2005)

Emoto, Masaru: *Messages from Water* (Volumes I and II) (Hado, 1999)

Garbourg, Paula: *The Secret of the Ring Muscles: Healing Yourself Through Sphincter Exercise (Peleg Balahan, 1994)*

Giri, Swami Sri Yukteswar: *The Holy Science* (Yogoda Satsanga Society, 1990)
Giri, Swami Shankarananda: *Kriya Yoga Filosofien* (Strubes Forlag, 1994)

Giversen, Søren: *Thomasevangeliet* (Gyldendal, 1990)

Grün, Anselm: *At udvikle selvværd og mestre sin afmagt* (Katolsk Forlag, 2006)

Inayat Khan, Hazrat: *Gayan Vadan Nirtan* (Borgen, 1964)

Inayat Khan, Hazrat: *The Mysticism of Music, Sound and Word* (Shambhala, 1996)

Kharitidi, Olga: *Den Første Cirkel* (Viva, 1996)

Larsen, Ole: *Slut med hovedpine, rygsmerter o.a. plager* (Sphinx, 1998)

Laszlo, Ervin: *Science and the Akashic Field* (Inner Traditions, 2004)

Leloup, Jean-Yves: *The Gospel of Mary Magdalene* (Éditions Albin Michel, 1997)

Levine, Peter A.: *Væk Tigeren* (Borgen, 1998)

Lidell, Lucy M., Narayani Rabinovitch and Giris Rabinovitch: *The Book of Yoga* (Ebury Press, 1983, 1990)

Maharshi, Ramana: *Hvem er jeg?* (Sankt Ansgar, 1996)

Muhl, Lars: *The 'O' Manuscript* (Watkins, 2013)

Muhl, Lars: *Den himmelske vej* (Borgen, 2000)

Muhl, Lars: *Det knuste Hjertes Visdom* (Lemuel Books, 2007)

Münster, Erik: *Seksualitet og Samliv* (Peter Asschenfeldts nye Forlag, 1997)

Myskja, Audun: *Musik som Medicin* (Borgen, 2004)

Osho: *The New Child* (Sterling Publishers, 1999)

Pagels, Elaine: *Tabernes Evangelier* (Hekla, 1986)

Rosenberg, Marshall B.: *Girafsprog* (Borgen, 2000)

Schubart, Walter: *Religion und Eros* (Haases facetbøger, 1941, 1969)

Shankar, Ravi: *Min musik, mit liv* (Jespersen og Pio, 1971)

Sharamon, Shalila and Bodo J. Baginski: *Chakrahåndbogen* (Sphinx, 1997)

Simpson, Liz: *Chakra Healing* (Bogklubben 12 Bøger, 1999)

Sirkar van Stolk, Daphne Dunlop: *Hazrat Inayat Khan og sufibudskabet* (*Sankt Ansgar, 1975*)

Stubberup, Michael: *Hjertebøn og Østens Mystikere* (Borgen, 2004)

Tolle, Eckhart: *En Ny Jord* (Borgen, 2008)

Yogananda, Paramahansa: *The Divine Romance* (Self-Realization Fellowship, 1986)

Yogananda, Paramahansa: *Man's Eternal Quest* (Self-Realization Fellowship, 1982)

Yogananda, Paramahansa: *En yogis selvbiografi* (Borgen, 1975, 1991)

Wren, Barbara Wren: Cellular Awakening (Hay House, 2009)

WATKINS

Sharing Wisdom Since
1893

The story of Watkins Publishing dates back to March 1893, when John M. Watkins, a scholar of esotericism, overheard his friend and teacher Madame Blavatsky lamenting the fact that there was nowhere in London to buy books on mysticism, occultism or metaphysics. At that moment Watkins was born, soon to become the home of many of the leading lights of spiritual literature, including Carl Jung, Rudolf Steiner, Alice Bailey and Chögyam Trungpa.

Today our passion for vigorous questioning is still resolute. With over 350 titles on our list, Watkins Publishing reflects the development of spiritual thinking and new science over the past 120 years. We remain at the cutting edge, committed to publishing books that change lives.

DISCOVER MORE ...

Read our blog

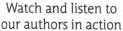

Watch and listen to
our authors in action

Sign up to
our mailing list

JOIN IN THE CONVERSATION

 WatkinsPublishing   @watkinswisdom

 WatkinsPublishingLtd   +watkinspublishing1893

Our books celebrate conscious, passionate, wise and happy living.
Be part of the community by visiting

www.watkinspublishing.com